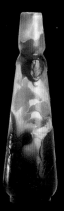

Antique Collector's
Directory of Period Detail

Antique Collector's Directory
of Period Detail

HOW TO IDENTIFY THE KEY CHARACTERISTICS,
SHAPES, AND FORMS OF PERIOD STYLES

Paul Davidson

Deborah Lambert

William Hotopf

Jill Bace

Yvonne Griffiths

Anna Fischel

A Quarto Book
Copyright © 2000 Quarto Inc.

First Edition for the United States, its territories
and dependencies and Canada
Published in 2000 by Barron's Educational Series Inc.

All inquiries should be addressed to:
Barron's Educational Series Inc.
250 Wireless Boulevard
Hauppauge, NY 11788
http://www.barronseduc.com

Library of Congress Cataloging-in-Publication No.:
99-06966

International Standard Book No.:
0-7641-5167-3

QUAR.ACD

Conceived, designed, and produced by
Quarto Publishing
6 Blundell Street
London N7 9BH

Project Editor Judith Samuelson
Senior Art Editor Penny Cobb
Copy Editors Claire Waite, Mary Devine, Tracey Kelly
Designers Karin Skånberg, Johanna Dean
Illustrator Andrew Green
Picture Researchers Laurent Boubounelle,
Neil Hudd / Image Select International
Indexer Dorothy Frame

Art Director Moira Clinch
Publisher Piers Spence

Manufactured by Regent Publishing Services, Ltd, China
Printed by Midas Printing Limited, China

9 8 7 6 5 4 3 2 1

PAGE 1 **Gallé carved,
acid-etched, fire-
polished vase, and Gallé
enameled decanter
and stopper.**

PAGE 2-3 **Venetian
giltwood throne,** *c.* **1800.**

LEFT AND RIGHT
**Three-part Dutch
delft tin-glazed
earthenware vase,**
c. **1690.**

Contents

Introduction

You've volunteered to help clear an attic and you find a tea chest holding some interesting china and knickknacks. Or you are browsing in a secondhand shop full of furniture, china, and collectibles, notice an ancient oak box with a carved decoration on the front, and wonder whether you have made a minor discovery.

There are distinct pointers or clues that will help you form a conclusion about when and where an object was made. These clues may relate to the material or method of manufacture, the object's shape, and most importantly, the style, ornament, and decoration. In many cases, you will discover several elements linking seemingly disparate objects.

Other clues can be deduced from common links between period details and external architectural fashions. For example, the fluted columns on a longcase clock from the mid-eighteenth century may closely resemble the pillars on the front elevation of a grand house of the same period. Or, the lion mask handle on a French porcelain ice pail from 1810 may relate to a similar motif mask on an English chair of the same period. Conversely, differences of detail may emphasize the different periods from which two items originate.

CHOICE OF MATERIALS

We can look at the materials from which an object is made and deduce an underlying historical detail that helps position that object in a particular time and place. If a chair is made of mahogany, it is unlikely to date from earlier than 1730, because it was at about that time that Britain and other major trading nations began to import the wood from Central America. Similarly, a plate made from soft paste porcelain is unlikely to date from later than 1800, by which time European porcelain factories were using hard paste porcelain.

Technical innovation has meant that many new materials and manufacturing techniques have become available, particularly during the last two hundred years. A basic knowledge of these techniques will help you to arrive at a more informed conclusion. Pewter—which was widely used for plates and dishes in the seventeenth and eighteenth centuries—was almost completely superseded in the nineteenth century by ceramics. The same was true for leather, which until then had been widely used for drinking vessels and serving jugs. Being aware of the differences between types of plated wares can also prevent potentially expensive mistakes. Sheffield or fused plate, made from rolled sheets of fused silver on copper, can be confused with newer

LEFT **The opulent form and style of this gilded French commode suggest a date of 1750, but it was actually made over 100 years later.**

electroplated silver on base metal. The ability to distinguish between these two materials, when the style and decoration of two or more objects are quite similar, can play a decisive factor in determining the latter's date of origin and subsequently its value.

A large number of "new" materials have been invented or developed, particularly from the nineteenth century. Many of these, such as bois durci and bakelite, have been superseded by plastics.

STYLE AND FORM

The first, and arguably the most significant, element to consider when placing an object in a particular period is its shape or form. Fashion has always had a significant impact in this regard, along with political, philosophical, and technological factors.

Over the timespan covered by this book, you will see a constant swing between overly ornamental styles and more austere tastes. This is complicated

BELOW **The shape of this ink stand, together with its ornate porcelain flowers, ormolu, and lacquer, place it firmly in the French rococo, *c.* 1745.**

Period Timeline

This chart is intended as an approximate guide to the dates when certain styles were prevalent in three major design regions. In many cases a particular style had less impact in one country than another; at certain times, other countries were more influential in spreading new design ideas than those listed.

The relative wealth and influence of France throughout the periods covered in this book explains its inclusion as a separate entry. Likewise, the economic strength and colonial power of Britain during the eighteenth and nineteenth centuries was deeply influential.

In North America, the melting pot of different influences from Europe, together with the independent development of the applied arts during the late nineteenth and twentieth centuries, explains its inclusion.

At various times, other countries and regions have been as or even more influential than those listed here. The Mannerist and Baroque styles originated in Italy as a final phase of the Renaissance. The auricular interpretation of Mannerism began in the Netherlands: the Dutch influence—partly through trading links with the

Far East—was largely instrumental in disseminating the Oriental influence within the rest of Europe in the seventeenth and eighteenth centuries. During the nineteenth and early twentieth centuries, Vienna was a leading center for the decorative arts, as were certain German cities.

It should be emphasized that identifying a particular style may be only a first step towards verifying the date of a piece. Divisions between different styles are not definitive and tend to overlap by several years.

	1550	1560	1570	1580	1590	1600	1610	1620	
GREAT BRITAIN				First Stirrings of Luxury (Mannerism)					*1680*
FRANCE		First Stirrings of Luxury (Mannerism)							*1660*
NORTH AMERICA									

In 1660, the Restoration of the English monarch, Charles II, led to a refurbishment of palaces and country mansions. This, together with the massive rebuilding campaign following the Fire of London in 1666, led to an explosion of Mannerist design.

by enthusiastic revivals of different styles that were especially popular in the nineteenth century. Neoclassicism and Arts and Crafts were philosophical reactions against the perceived aesthetic decadence of the rococo and mid-nineteenth century fashions, respectively. Neoclassicism was inspired by the architectural restraint and elegance of Ancient Greece and Rome, and by the prediliction of the wealthy dilletante of northern Europe for visiting ancient ruins on the Grand Tour. The Arts and Crafts movement, on the other hand, was inspired by the philosophy of one man: William Morris. Although he is now best remembered for furnishing designs, his writings about society were equally influential and important.

The part played by politics and affairs of state on antique style can be seen during the Baroque period when the French king, Louis XIV, commissioned designers and architects with the express purpose of ensuring his court and country's pre-eminence in the visual arts. The growth of a merchant class, and subsequently, middle class in Europe and North America, however, and the attendant spread of wealth, meant that Louis XIV was the last single patron to have a dramatic influence on object style.

Military success was also influential, most notably in the early nineteenth century. The influence of Napoleon's Egyptian campaign on French designers can be seen in their use of iconography and of materials such as porphyry. In England, Nelson's victory at Trafalgar inspired chair makers to adopt the sabre leg and rope twist splat.

There is often a strong link between prevalent architectural forms and the furnishings of a particular period. The strongest evidence of this can probably be observed in the neoclassical styles of

RIGHT **The mother-of-pearl and gilt metal detail on this miniature secrètaire is typical of work from Palais Royal, Paris,** *c.* **1820.**

	1630	1640	1650	1660	1670	1680	1690
GREAT BRITAIN	*1580*		First Stirrings of Luxury (Mannerism)				
FRANCE		*1550*	First Stirrings of Luxury (Mannerism)		Pomp and Circumstance (Baroque)		
NORTH AMERICA							

With his appetite for exuberant show and thirst for renown, Louis XV, king of France, fostered the excesses of lavish design with his palace at Versailles.

ABOVE **The juxtaposition of different materials can help to identify a piece: this giltwood chair with original needlework covers indicates the reign of the English king, George II.**

LEFT AND ABOVE **Although the shape of this commode from 1770 could easily be French or northern European, the use of satinwood and the lack of ormolu mounts indicate an English origin.**

the late eighteenth and early nineteenth century, and again in the art nouveau and Arts and Crafts movements and onward into the twentieth century.

The range of artifacts produced increased dramatically, spurred on by technical progress and by the demands of an increasingly affluent middle class; in many cases the essential attributes of an item are sufficient to place it within a specific time range. For example, toothpick boxes, which had become an elegant personal accessory toward the late eighteenth century, went out of use with the advent of effective toothbrushes.

Similarly, tea was very expensive during the eighteenth and early nineteenth centuries, and consequently the utensils used to serve it were also highly prized. However, as the price of tea fell when trade with India expanded, tea caddies and other related items became quite modest in style and form.

Many mechanical items, such as cylinder musical boxes and cameras, were not invented until the nineteenth century, and others, such as portable cigarette lighters, did not appear until the twentieth century. With the exception of dolls and some other simple toys and games, the vast range of children's toys did not appear until the twentieth century.

DECORATION AND ORNAMENT

A second way to estimate the date of an item is by examining the style of its decoration or ornament. Different historical styles tend to have their own iconography, so that a prominent scallop shell on a chest of drawers, combined with other factors, may point to the American Chippendale period. Similarly, a single

In France, Baroque styles melded into the rounded and frivolous forms of rococo interiors, architecture, and design.

Classical motifs from archaeological finds inspired a totally new approach to decorative detailing

The simple lines of Queen Anne style reflected the philosophy of pilgrims from Europe attempting to forge a new society in America.

	1700	1710	1720	1730	1740	1750	1760	1770	1780	1790	
Pomp and Circumstance (Baroque) *1730*					Playful Diversity (Rococo) *1770*	Roman Style			*1810*
Augustan Formalism (Queen Anne & Early Georgian) *1735*				The Chippendale Story *1770*	Greek Style			*1810*
Playful Diversity (Rococo) *1765*				Roman Style			*1805*
1725				Greek Style			*1805*
Augustan Formalism (Queen Anne & Early Georgian) *1760*					Roman Style *1815*
The Chippendale Story *1780*				Greek Style *1815*

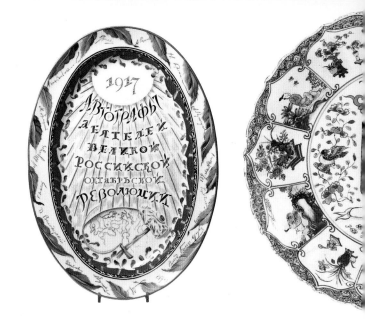

ABOVE **This ebony and ivory inlaid tea chest, with silver mounts and matching silver caddies, reflects the high price of tea in the late eighteenth century when the tea chest was made.**

ABOVE RIGHT **Political factors occasionally affect the decoration of objects. This porcelain propaganda dish, with purple sunburst and hammer and sickle detail, was made in Russia, the year of the Revolution, 1917.**

stylized flower head or bud motif, supported on a slender elongated stem and inlaid on a piece of furniture, is characteristic of the art nouveau period. There is often a close link between the types of ornament used in different artifacts in different media, and this frequently applies to architecture, too. Again this may suggest, rather than definitively claim, a particular period, although other factors should also be taken into account.

During different eras, the iconography of non-Western countries has been highly popular. Dutch, Portuguese, and English links with the Far East had a significant impact on ornamental style during the late seventeenth and eighteenth centuries, both directly, through the import of porcelain and lacquer work, and

indirectly, through the adoption of chinoiserie, notably in the rococo period. Thus, the development of papier-mâché as a popular material in the late eighteenth and nineteenth centuries owed much to its superficial resemblance to Oriental lacquer. In the later part of the nineteenth century, the expansion of trade with Japan was hugely influential, leading to the adoption of imported Japanese styles by many designers and manufacturers.

Factors such as the shape of a chair leg or the stem of a drinking glass can offer the clearest indication about origin and date. By making comparisons, such details become more recognizable as evidence of a style or an era. Baluster forms are often indicative of an eighteenth century date, whereas classical column forms often point to the late eighteenth or early nineteenth centuries. Asymmetry of form or detail is most frequently present in the rococo period and again in the art nouveau period. Many of the

The revival styles of the mid-nineteenth century flourished in North America, and were especially popular with the industrial nouveau riche.

Industrialization resulted in the manufacture of more advanced gas lights. Initially, lighting designs reflected a purely functional aesthetic, but gradually adopted more design-led forms.

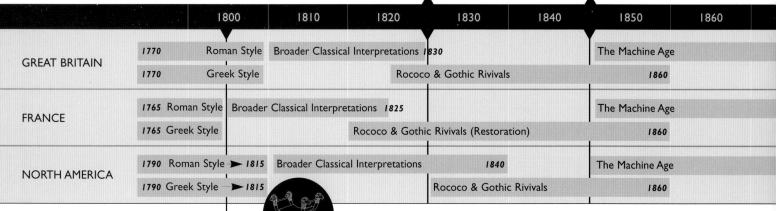

		1800	1810	1820	1830	1840	1850	1860
GREAT BRITAIN	*1770*	Roman Style	Broader Classical Interpretations *1830*				The Machine Age	
	1770	Greek Style		Rococo & Gothic Rivivals			*1860*	
FRANCE	*1765* Roman Style	Broader Classical Interpretations *1825*				The Machine Age		
	1765 Greek Style		Rococo & Gothic Rivivals (Restoration)			*1860*		
NORTH AMERICA	*1790* Roman Style ➤ *1815*	Broader Classical Interpretations			*1840*	The Machine Age		
	1790 Greek Style ➤ *1815*		Rococo & Gothic Rivivals			*1860*		

Napoleon was inspired by his travels to Egypt, and promoted a wealth of new motifs drawn from the aesthetic of the ancient Egyptians.

greatest designers and architects, from Robert Adam to Frank Lloyd Wright, worked in different media, but common traits can be identified in whichever type of material they used.

One word of warning: from the early part of the nineteenth century onward, there was an increasing tendency for makers and craftsmen to revive the styles of earlier periods. Consequently, details of construction techniques, marks, and materials used become increasingly important, and these factors should be considered as being equally significant as stylistic details.

ABOVE LEFT **This pair of famille verte armorial dishes were made in China for the Dutch market,** *c.* **1710–20. Their typically vivid green and pale blue hues contrast with iron reds.**

LEFT **Detail differences can sometimes help to identify the period of an object to within ten years or less, as with these English crystal decanters,** *c.* **1810–1840.**

RIGHT **This leather bombard from England is distinctively seventeenth century in style, but is actually a nineteenth-century replica.**

French and Belgian art nouveau was inspired partly by the fluid forms of the rococo style.

Art deco jewelry combined the minimalist aesthetic of modernism with the luxury tastes of the commercial client base.

1870	1880	1890	1900	1910	1920	1930	1940

1900		Art Noveau		1915	The Emergence of Modernism	1940
	The Arts & Crafts Movement		1910			
		1900			The Emergence of Modernism	1940
		Art Noveau		1915		
		1900	The Arts & Crafts Movement	1920		
		Art Noveau		1915	The Emergence of Modernism	1940

Vernacular styles were a key reference point for the anti-industrial designs of the Arts and Crafts movement.

BELOW AND RIGHT
Nineteenth-cenutry
ormolu table center
pieces with detail.

FAR RIGHT Ivory and silver
walking stick, *c*. 1690.

THOMIRE A PARIS .

The Art of
Dating Antiques

Fine-looking items of furniture, pottery, silver, or other collectibles sometimes turn out to be recently made or of poor quality. Yet there are many ways to check the authenticity of a piece—by seeing how the drawers in a chest are joined, for example, or by studying the shapes and marks of silverware and ceramics. The heritage of a piece is easy to establish once you know what signs to look for.

Furniture

The three key factors to consider for assessing the date of pieces of furniture are style, materials, and construction. Since much of the furniture made from the nineteenth century onward reproduced earlier styles, materials and construction are especially important when dating an item.

DATING BY MATERIALS

Identifying the material in a piece of furniture is a good first step to estimating its date, place of origin, and even maker. In every country the material used for vernacular furniture varied according to what was readily available, and in many cases this applies until the late nineteenth century and beyond.

Before the 1700s furniture was usually made from indigenous woods. This might, for example, be oak in England, walnut in northern Italy, or maple in New England. More exotic woods, such as rosewood, mahogany, and satinwood were largely unavailable in temperate climates before 1700, so they do not appear in European furniture of this period. Ebony was sometimes used as a veneer, but on only the most luxurious and expensive pieces. During the eighteenth century, the cost of importing tropical or near-tropical hardwoods into the main European trading nations, notably Britain and the Netherlands, gradually declined, making these woods, in particular mahogany, widely available and popular in the second half of the century. In North America, mahogany had already been more available, whereas walnut was less frequently used.

Fashion also influenced the choice of wood. For example, the revival of the Queen Anne style in England in the early twentieth century meant that walnut was again widely used, although expensive and therefore applied only in thin veneers. Likewise in Germany, Biedermeier furniture was often veneered in maple or birch because these pale woods were fashionable then, as they were again in the art deco period.

When dating a piece of veneered furniture, always take a good look at the veneer: earlier veneered furniture tends to have thicker-cut veneers than later examples of apparently similar styles.

Other materials were also used periodically in the manufacture of furniture. Cast iron was widely used for garden furniture in the second half of the nineteenth century, but it was also used, particularly in North America, for utilitarian furniture such as stools, desk chairs, and hallstands. By the early twentieth century cast iron had largely been replaced by other materials; chromed or stainless steel was used from the 1920s onward.

CLOCKWISE FROM TOP **Four woods used for furniture making:** ① **African mahogany;** ② **unstained English oak;** ③ **rosewood;** ④ **figured walnut.**

CLUES IN CONSTRUCTION

Many of the designs that were reproduced in the nineteenth century date from the eighteenth century, when the techniques of construction were somewhat different from those one hundred years later. Eighteenth-century manufacturing methods were often cruder than those used later, even though the craftsmanship was of a high standard. An interesting comparison can be made

ABOVE **A seventeenth-century oak buffet.**

ABOVE **A Victorian mahogany display cabinet of eighteenth-century inspiration, with newly defined proportions and a totally new shape.**

RIGHT **This early nineteenth-century ebony veneered cabinet shows the effects of earlier fashions. This type of decoration originated in France in the late seventeenth century, but the exact form is specific to the first half of the nineteenth century.**

between eighteenth-century French or Italian furniture and that made one hundred years later. In the former, the drawer linings and hidden areas, such as the back of a chest of drawers, are crudely finished with bold joints. Eighteenth-century chairs usually have visibly pegged joints, whereas later chairs tend to use glued and dowelled joints that do not have the same visible signs. Reproduction furniture made from the mid-1800s onward tends to be distinguishable because of the mechanized techniques used in its manufacture. Other details to look for when dating furniture include the type of lock: post-1900 examples are often marked with the country of origin and screws are often machine made.

Ceramics and Glass

The style or decoration of any ceramic or glass item is the first indicator of its origin. However, particular styles have recurred from the eighteenth century to the present, so it is necessary to identify other factors to ensure correct dating of the piece.

SHAPE

Both the form of a ceramic piece and its specific use help to identify the date and country of origin. Tea bowls, for example, although always used in the Far East, were not generally made in Europe after the eighteenth century, when they were replaced by tea-cups with handles. Similarly, ceramic candle snuffers were not produced in quantity after the beginning of the twentieth century because of the introduction of other lighting sources. The Royal Worcester factory did, however, produce replicas in recent years for collectors, but these are readily identified by the makers' marks.

Both the shape and type of decoration of ceramic pieces are useful pointers to age.

Many of the shapes of ceramic items have parallels in other materials, particularly silver. One of the early designers for the Chelsea porcelain factory was the silversmith Nicholas Sprimont and some of the Chelsea porcelain closely resembled silver forms being produced in the same era.

DECORATION AND MATERIAL

Printed decoration on porcelain dates back to the 1760s, and until recently was usually monochrome. Therefore printed polychrome decoration is a clear indication of twentieth-century origin and a piece inferior in quality to hand-painted porcelain.

The type of decoration on porcelain may be in the style of a particular period, for example French Empire style, but this does not confirm that the piece is from that period in history. Although the more recent styles of decoration, such as the colors popular in America from the 1930s, have not been reproduced and are therefore straightforward to date, most of the more popular designs of earlier periods have been replicated, albeit quite loosely, so do not be fooled by decoration.

It is important to distinguish between basic forms and materials to identify a particular piece. The main distinction is between

LEFT **Original flaws: a group of Martinware pottery birds showing uneven molding and textures.**

LEFT **A complete set: a collection of Shelley fine bone china teawares.**

BELOW **The decoration and bulbous shape of this Arita apothecary's bottle, and the initials I.C. on the base, indicate a late seventeenth century date.**

porcelain and pottery. Pottery, or earthenware, is completely opaque, whereas porcelain is translucent, although to what extent will depend on the specific type. Pottery includes Delft, stoneware, and salt-glazed wares among the variants. Porcelain can be divided between soft paste and hard paste.

MISLEADING MAKERS' MARKS

Porcelain produced in the eighteenth century sometimes bears a maker's mark; however, the piece may well be a copy. While a mark may be a helpful guide, it is important to consider the "body" of a piece when identifying the factory of origin and consequently its approximate date of origin. In the eighteenth century, porcelain manufacture in Europe was in its infancy; therefore the body of an eighteenth-century piece is likely to be more crudely made than its nineteenth-century equivalent, with mold marks and visible air holes. The French Samson factory and other factories in the late nineteenth century produced an extensive range of copies of English, French, and German porcelain, often reproducing the marks of the originals, so it is only by comparing the body decoration and glazes that the genuine examples can be identified.

UNDERGLAZE AND IMPRESSED MARKS

Marks that have been impressed and underglaze marks are less likely to be spurious than those which have been painted on; that is not always to say, however, that underglaze and impressed marks can be trusted implicitly when it comes to dating. Chinese porcelain often bears the mark of the imperial reign during which

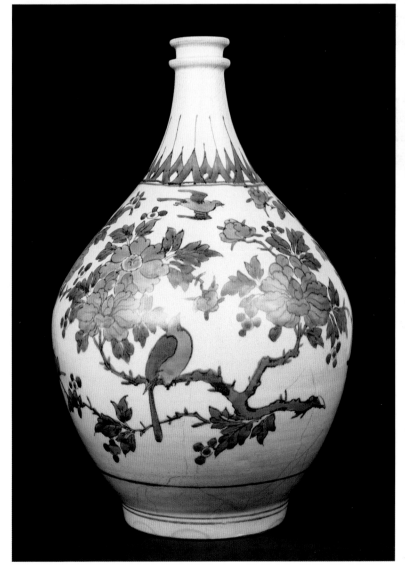

the piece was made, but these same marks are also used to denote pieces made in the style of that reign, sometimes hundreds of years later.

In the nineteenth century, and particularly from the second quarter on, the products of the more significant factories are frequently clearly marked. Collectors should not, however, make the mistake of assuming that a date that appears on a factory mark is necessarily the actual date of origin of a piece. For example, the Worcester factory mark incorporated the date '51 from the mid-nineteenth century onward, and several European factories incorporate the date of the founding of the factory in their mark.

COUNTRY OF ORIGIN

After 1891, because of trading rules, most items made for export had to display their country of origin. Furthermore, English ceramics made in the twentieth century are often marked "Made in England." In general, the more information on a maker's mark the more likely that the piece dates from the twentieth century. The stated country of origin may also help in dating an item, bearing in mind the changes in our geographical history over the years. Borders have moved and countries been renamed, so knowing a country's history can be invaluable.

GLASS

Glassware can generally be dated by its form, but again certain original designs, particularly cut glass, have been later reproduced. The color of the crystal will vary according to its date of origin, with late eighteenth- and early nineteenth-century glass often having a grayish hue, whereas later cut glass is perfectly clear. In the 1820s pressed glass was first produced in the United States, and soon after across the Atlantic. Pressed glass can be distinguished from cut glass by the lack of sharpness in the decoration and often the discernible presence of mold marks.

The range of glass utensils available at different times was partly dependent on fashion and eating and drinking habits. For example, wide bowl champagne glasses, which were popular in the 1920s and 1930s, were subsequently replaced by champagne flutes. Likewise, ale glasses with short stems and tapering bowls went out of fashion in the nineteenth century as strong ale was replaced by other beverages.

Faux Italian Early Venetian glass was widely copied during the nineteenth century, but there is a precision about the copies which contrasts with the slightly uneven character of the originals. Where nineteenth- and early twentieth-century glass such as paperweights and cameo glass have been copied, there is a lack of quality about the copies which can be fairly readily recognized.

Ornamental Innovations Before the nineteenth century, and with the exception of Venetian-type glass and some enameled or gilded glassware–particularly German–most glass produced was principally functional rather than ornamental. This all changed from the middle of the nineteenth century, and ornamental glassware has been popular ever since, from inexpensive carnival glass to highly elaborate hand-carved cased glass by art glass makers such as Gallé, and the extremely expensive cased glass pieces by English makers such as Thomas Webb. Other innovations were the production of paperweights made with glass "canes" by Baccarat, Clichy, and St Louis that stimulated the growth of an

BELOW **Original characteristics: a frosted glass bowl, tumbler, and ewer, England,** *c.* **1675.**

industry in Bohemia, North America, and Britain. At about the same time there was a great expansion in the range of colored glass produced, whereas previously it had been quite rare.

Distinctive Signatures The shapes of glass artifacts have followed the fashions of the various style movements, most noticeable when comparing the sinuous forms of the art nouveau period with the heavier geometric forms of the art deco style. Until the art nouveau period, glass was seldom marked, but at this time the workshops of artists such as Gallé and Tiffany began to sign their products as a matter of course. Thereafter, most of the more expensive glass makers also signed their work.

ABOVE **Various shapes, sizes, and thicknesses: a collection of eighteenth-century drinking glasses and part of a suite of glassware,** *c.* **1900.**

RIGHT **A Clichy flower paperweight, France, mid-nineteenth century.**

Silver

Silverware designs in the nineteenth century were often copies of earlier styles. Therefore a mark is the most reliable guide to dating a piece.

LEFT **Silver decoration: silver was frequently used with other materials in the production of decorative and functional wares. When used in small quantities, silver is often left unhallmarked.**

Most silver is marked and can therefore often be accurately dated. Silver made in most western countries is hallmarked to some extent but only certain countries use date letters, including Britain, the Netherlands, and Sweden. The type of mark made on silver in other countries, however, can often help to date an item to within a few years.

If a piece of silver is not clearly marked it may be possible to ascertain more about its origin by comparing it with similar objects in other materials. For example, the shapes of wooden tea caddies made in England around 1800 almost exactly replicate those in silver from the same period. Likewise the baluster form of mid-eighteenth-century silver candlesticks is similar to drinking glass stems of the same period, and the tapering stems of late eighteenth-century candlesticks are paralleled in other media. However, identifying the style is only one step to identifying the date of origin, since styles are so often reproduced in later years. There are other things to look for in silverware to discover when a piece was actually made.

Silver made in the eighteenth century was usually cast, whereas increasingly in the nineteenth century thinner, gauge sheet metal was often used. However, during the middle part of the nineteenth century more impressive presentation pieces were frequently elaborately cast with a profusion of naturalistic and often classical motifs not normally seen on the purer designs of the eighteenth century.

Much nineteenth century silver is very well made, but in the early twentieth century the average quality began to decline. In several European countries the purity of silver at this time was quite low, 800 or 830 parts per 1000. Sterling silver is an alloy of 925 parts of silver with 75 parts of copper. Often an item is marked with a numeral indicating the alloy proportion, or with the words "sterling silver" or "sterling."

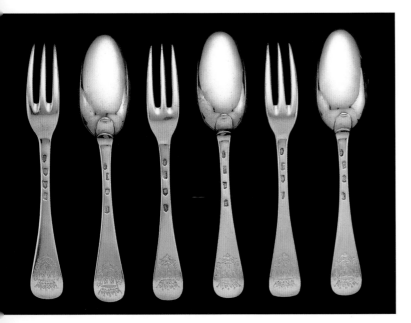

LEFT **The mark of an Englishman: a set of Hanoverian-patterned forks and spoons clearly showing hallmarks of the period, England, 1735.**

RIGHT **Bringing up the shine: pewter plates were polished to resemble silver and remove the metal's natural gray coloring. This English set displays the Walpole family crest.**

During the Arts and Crafts Movement, and throughout the twentieth century, a fashion for hand hammered silver developed. This particular finish was intentionally lumpy and uneven, a style not seen for hundreds of years. This necessitated the use of weighted bases for candlesticks and vases.

If unmarked, plated wares can often be definitely identified only by wear to the surface, revealing a gray, copper, or brass base metal beneath. The technique of electroplating began only in the mid-nineteenth century, so if the metal beneath is gray, the object is unlikely to be earlier than this date. In the preceding one hundred years fused plate (silver on copper rolled sheets) was used. If copper is not actually visible through the silver you can usually see it by looking at the edges of a piece. In eighteenth-century France and England many cast brass items were silvered, but the silver has generally worn away or been cleaned off.

METALWARE

Most eighteenth-century brass artifacts were cast, but from the early nineteenth century sheet brass was more widely used. In general, eighteenth-century brass items were of better quality than those produced later. For example, the undersides of candlesticks made in the eighteenth century would have been turned on a lathe, while the undersides of later brass items were left unfinished.

Pewter was popular for making functional vessels in the eighteenth century, but its use declined in the nineteenth century, to be replaced by inexpensive plated and ceramic wares. Pewter was used again by the Arts and Crafts and art nouveau movements, together with a revived fashion for brass and copper, but, as with much silver of this period, it was generally hand hammered.

LEFT **Gilded bird: bronze was perfect for casting and gilding, as shown by the detail on this Louis XV gilt bronze swan. Silver was rarely cast with this degree of detail.**

Miscellany

Technical developments and innovations are of great significance in dating antiques. At certain points in history new mechanical objects were developed, new power sources tapped, and new materials discovered; this historical information can be used to date some of the more unique items you may discover.

MODERN DAY MECHANISMS

Mechanical and scientific instruments are fascinating examples of technical innovation. Musical boxes were produced from the middle of the nineteenth century, and disc musical boxes from the end of the century. In the field of scientific instruments telescopes and microscopes evolved rapidly in the nineteenth century, and cameras, which did not exist at the beginning of that century, changed continuously for 150 years, and have continued to do so. In the area of horology, longcase clocks (grandfather clocks), bracket clocks, and pocket watches were the main method of timekeeping in 1700 and these clocks were possessed only by the wealthy. By the second half of the nineteenth century domestic wall clocks and carriage clocks had become popular, and pocket watches, which were being mass produced in Switzerland, were relatively inexpensive. During the early twentieth century electric clocks and wristwatches gained widespread acceptance and pocket watches and longcase clocks were soon to become anachronisms.

NEW ENERGIES

Another area that illustrates well how technical changes help to date items is that of interior lighting, which changed particularly from the late eighteenth century, largely because of the availability of new power sources and technical innovation. Prior to this the main light sources were wax candles for the wealthy and tallow candles made from animal fat for the majority. Oil lamps were first used during the 1780s, originally powered by colza oil and then whale oil, both of which were expensive. From about 1850 paraffin oil was used. During the second half of the nineteenth century gas was adopted as a power source for static lighting and by the early twentieth century the use of electricity was becoming widespread and candlepower had virtually disappeared as a primary light source.

BELOW **Essential details: bracket clock by Knibb, England, *c.* 1685. The squat ebony case, brass mounts, and dial are typical of this period.**

RIGHT **Perfect for the home: wall clocks were very fashionable in the early years of the nineteenth century. This Boston-made, Federal-style clock dates from 1815, and the "clean" lines are typical of the period.**

THE MARK OF MATERIALS

The time at which new materials were discovered and became readily available can be helpful in dating an object. Tortoiseshell and ivory were both popular in the late eighteenth century for small items such as snuff boxes and tea caddies, particularly in seafaring nations such as France and Britain that had ready access to the raw material from their colonies. Although ivory was again fashionable in Europe from the mid-nineteenth century because of a new supply from central Africa, tortoiseshell became popular once more only briefly in about 1900 and was imitated by a synthetic version in the 1920s and 1930s. Mother-of-pearl, having been used as an adornment for papier mâché and lacquerwork in the first half of the nineteenth century was subsequently widely used for cutlery handles.

The popularity of papier mâché, particularly from 1800 to 1870, was extremely widespread, chiefly in England, and its uses ranged from snuff and other small boxes to tea trays and large sewing boxes. During the late nineteenth century there was considerable experimentation with synthetic and part-synthetic materials. One of the earliest of these was *bois durci*, a compressed woodlike substance used for small boxes in France. By the early twentieth century a range of plastics had been produced, some more successfully than others, notably Bakelite, which was widely used as a casing for radios and other electrical apparatus.

RIGHT **Austrian ivory figure by Preiss,** *c.* **1925. The combination of bronze and ivory was used almost exclusively in the art nouveau and art deco periods.**

LEFT **A new technique that became the height of fashion: papier mâché box with rich gilded and painted decoration,** *c.* **1850.**

ABOVE **English kingwood cabinet, inlaid with mid-seventeenth century pietra dura plaques.**

RIGHT **Aubusson carpet from France.**

From Baroque to Rococo

This was a period that began with curvaceous opulence in Italy and rapidly took hold in other parts of Continental Europe. There was a formality about the style that was exemplified by the architectural form of much of the furniture and furnishings. The rococo was a more informal showy style based on natural forms but often asymmetrical and with a lightness of form contrasting the solidity of the Baroque.

First Stirrings of Luxury

*Around the middle of the seventeenth century, early settlers in America were building
houses and furnishing them in styles from "home," such as Mannerism from England and
the auricular style of the Low Countries. Originally a sophisticated court style in Italy
and France, Mannerism caught on in the decorative arts of northern Europe. The style
extended the classical language of the Renaissance, while the flowing auricular forms
linked Mannerism and early Baroque.*

In medieval times, tapestries and silver plate had
the status of cars today. But by the 1600s
tapestries and silver took second place to furniture. People left items of furniture in their wills,
especially that quintessential seventeenth-century
piece, the cabinet of curios, ideal to display the
fruits of the passion for collecting.

This love of the bizarre found full expression in
Mannerism in the decorative arts. The style was
loaded with ornament such as strapwork, which
looked like hammered iron or leather thongs,
caryatids (supporting columns in the form of
female figures), and grotesque masks and mythical
creatures depicted on furniture and metalwork.

THE IMPETUS TO MANNERISM

The roots of Mannerism stemmed from Michelangelo and other sixteenth-
century Italian architects and artists who played on the classical Orders and
proportions favored in the Renaissance. The school of Fontainebleau, where
French king François I (Henry VIII's contemporary) had a hunting lodge, was
also influential in spreading Mannerism.

Two artists from Rome, Rosso Fiorentino and Francesco Primaticcio,
brought to the palace at Fontainebleau their innovative combinations of paint
and stucco and totally revamped the interior decoration. They made much use
of the sinuous naked figures so beloved of the style, as well as the grotesque
ornaments that had first found their way into decoration after the discovery of
Roman wall paintings in Nero's Golden House, excavated in 1488. Such
grotesques (from the word "grotto") showed animals, birds, chimeras, griffins,
and sphinxes linked together by leafy scrolls into vertical strips that transposed

ABOVE " **The hall" served
many purposes; it was
used both for dining and
sleeping—in one corner
stands a folding bed—
and before a separate
kitchen was built, it was
also used for cooking.
The fine New England
furnishings date from
the mid-seventeenth to
the late-eighteenth
centuries.**

RIGHT **The Boboli
Gardens in Florence,
Italy, designed by
Bernardo Buontalenti,
spread the sixteenth-
century trend for
grottoes to the rest of
Europe. Grottoes were a
prominent feature of
ancient Roman gardens,
and combined figures
with stonework carved
to imitate stalactites.**

ABOVE **Mid-seventeenth-century Dutch artist Jan Steen's paintings of indoor mayhem, such as *The Dissolute Household,* show interiors where one room serves as a combination bedroom, sitting room, and dining room. The windows are very small and the furniture heavy, such as the linen cupboard used to hang textiles.**

beautifully onto such household items as silver candlesticks or wooden furniture legs, and also wall panels and tapestry.

IN ENGLISH AND DUTCH HANDS

It took time for such styles to cross the Alps to northern Europe. Bombarded with new ideas, northern craftsmen did not always grasp that the improvisations of Mannerism were imposed on purer ideals. Grotesques were tied in with Gothic gargoyles and motifs, and craftsmen mixed Gothic, Renaissance, and Mannerist ranges of ornament.

Some architecture, furniture, and metalwork can look oddly proportioned, with decoration swamping the form. Small wonder that commentator Karel van Mander wrote in 1604 of Flemish adaptations of Michelangelo's Mannerism: " … this rein is so free, and this license so misused by Netherlanders, that in the course of time in Building a great Heresy has arisen among them, with a heap of craziness of decorations and breaking of the pilasters in the middle, and adding on the pedestals, their usual coarse points of diamonds and such lameness, very disgusting to see." However, the story was not all negative.

FINDING THEIR FEET WITH MANNERISM

Printmakers disseminated their schemes, largely via Antwerp, which was a publishing center, so the Low Countries were a hot spot for the transmission of

LEFT **Montacute House in Somerset, England, was built around 1600, when the hallway was much more than a waiting room. With** **friezes, tapestries, ancestral portraits, and richly carved furniture to admire, it doubled as a banqueting hall and music gallery.**

Mannerism. Gradually they established a preference for Mannerism, distinguishing it from the purer Renaissance forms. Metalwork proved one of the best vehicles for expressing the style.

Dutch silversmiths developed the auricular style (also called lobate) by rippling smooth surfaces with creases and ridges. Following the Mannerist love of the bizarre, and scientific curiosity at the time, there was much interest in anatomical dissection. The forms of auricular silver resembled not just ears but also intestines and sinews. Parts of fish and animals punctuated the designs. The van Vianen brothers of Utrecht produced the most dramatic examples of auricular silver in the early seventeenth century.

THE PIONEER SPIRIT

The peculiarities of Mannerism were juxtaposed with the concerns of the pilgrims who set out for the New World. They were as keen to remember their European culture and trappings as they were to forget the social injustices of their homeland. The immigrants found a plentiful supply of timber, especially oak, in the regions that became Massachusetts, Rhode Island, and Connecticut.

They built framed houses around a main hall, with overhanging upper stories. Houses were made of thick oak planks to keep out the cold. Mortise and tenon joinery held together the timbers. The settlers applied the same principles to furniture making. Forms were squared up and solid and usually made of oak and pine. Furniture followed the earlier Elizabethan and Jacobean styles with the emphasis on turned-wood decoration—balusters, balls, and spindles. American objects from these colonial days are sometimes called "Jacobean." Instead of stylized figures and masks, for decoration pilgrims favored Tudor roses, the tulip and leaf, and sunflowers.

As in England itself, sources often included Italy and the Renaissance, France, and the Low Countries. With intermarriages among royalty, most styles were pan-European. Charles II, himself half French, came to the English throne in 1660. His wife, Catherine of Braganza, was Portuguese. She brought with her skilled artisans and new styles of post-mannerist Baroque drama and movement. But such influxes took time to filter through England and out to America.

The more elaborate pieces in Europe were made for royalty and courtiers. The settlers' objects were much plainer. On either side of the Atlantic, for most people, privacy was unknown, and one communal room served as dining room, sitting room, and bedroom. Rooms were furnished just with necessities—there was little space for objects without function. For that luxury, people needed to become more prosperous, as the colonists increasingly did.

ABOVE **The Palazzo del Te was designed by Giulio Romano for the Duke of Mantua. One of the earliest and most sophisticated Mannerist buildings, its prisonlike courtyard was intended as a witty comment on Renaissance architecture—but only** **those in the classical know could get the joke. Pockmarked rustication and dropped triglyphs on the exterior concealed elaborate plasterwork and pretty painted walls inside. Intimidating to many, it sowed the seeds of Mannerism.**

Collector's Gallery

Among both the bourgeoisie and the aristocracy, the first part of the seventeenth century saw a considerable growth in demand for furniture and decorative items. Classical Renaissance architectural forms and decorative vocabulary, along with a sense of geometry, introduced order and symmetry to all designs. Rich layers of color and texture were supplied by imported accessories, from textiles, to exotic timbers, and colored marble.

Cabinets

From the very beginning of the seventeenth century, throughout Europe, cabinets became the most important and the most decorative pieces of display furniture. At first they were small and stood on tables, ① later they became much larger and were designed with their own integral stands. ② Ebony, used as a veneer, was the most favored timber, usually combined with other woods, and was often finished with silver or gilt-metal mounts. ③ Generally of a simple, boxlike form, cabinets began to be constructed with dovetail joints, which produced flush surfaces ideal for laying veneer. ④ In northern Europe, the cabinets usually had doors. ⑤ These were fitted inside with numerous small, symmetrically arranged drawers, ⑥ often surrounding a central, decorative architectural niche.

⑦ Flemish cabinets in particular favored the inclusion of turtleshell, usually referred to as tortoiseshell. This was often colored by pigment in the glue used to lay the shell. Many cabinets from Antwerp replaced tortoiseshell veneers on the face of the drawers with small paintings, usually of religious or mythological subjects.

In Italy, ⑧ cabinets were decorated with *pietra dura*, a technique that used colored marble cleverly cut and arranged to make patterns or pictures; flower sprays and birds were particularly popular. This was to be a direct influence on marquetry in France and the Netherlands later in the seventeenth century. ⑨ Italian cabinets tended to have a much stronger architectural form than those in northern Europe, often looking like miniature palaces or churches.

RIGHT **A seventeenth-century cabinet, ivory- and tortoiseshell-inlaid, ormolu-mounted ebony on a stand, Flanders, *c.* 1640.**

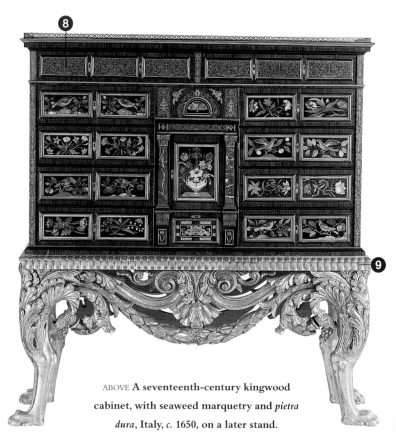

ABOVE **A seventeenth-century kingwood cabinet, with seaweed marquetry and *pietra dura*, Italy, *c.* 1650, on a later stand.**

ABOVE **A seventeenth-century cupboard, in oak, rosewood, and ebony, the Netherlands, *c.* 1650.**

Cupboards and Chests

Up until the seventeenth century, particularly in northern Europe, the chest had been all-important for both display and utilitarian purposes; now it began to develop a greater range of form and function. Growing taller it evolved into the wardrobe or linen press, with interior shelves, ① and gradually drawers began to be fitted. ② Frame and panel construction was used for cupboards and chests, giving them a solid, bulky appearance; oak was commonly used for the carcass and framework. ③ In the early part of the century, feet were formed from the extended ends of the stiles; from the middle of the century it is more common to find ball or bun feet. ④ Decoration was usually based to some degree on architecture, with a frieze and often stylized pilasters or arches. ⑤ Within this framework, further decoration was created using geometric applied moldings, sometimes inlaid with ebony or other exotic woods. ⑥ Carved human faces or animals often formed decorative detail. Wood turned on the lathe began to be exploited, and by the middle of the century turning was a popular form of decoration. Known as split-baluster turning or, in America, split-spindle turning, it could be applied to the framework flanking the panels.

Chairs

Developments in seat furniture continued those already begun in the sixteenth century, in particular in the lightening of forms caused by the removal of solid wooden panels. With the growth of wealthy bourgeois societies in the Netherlands, France, and England in particular, suites of chairs began to appear, usually comprising sets of armchairs and/or side chairs, together with matching stools. ① In the first part of the seventeenth century, using traditional mortise and tenon construction, frames had simple, turned, columnar supports, with stretchers close to the ground. ② By the mid-century, bobbin-turning had become fashionable all over northern Europe. Stretchers began to rise slightly, creating a light, lively effect. ③ The most common form of chair throughout the century was the backed stool, sometimes erroneously referred to as a farthingale chair, which had an upholstered back, often showing no framework, ④ and an upholstered seat. ⑤ The chair could be adapted by the addition of arms, or it could be stretched to create a settee. ⑥ An increasing use of upholstery and textiles was particularly important in seventeenth-century furniture; damasks woven in ornate floral patterns, rich velvets, and silks were all used, often as evidence of the owner's wealth and status.

BELOW **A Charles II beechwood settee, England, *c.* 1660.**

Glass Goblets

In the fifteenth century, glass makers on the Venetian island of Murano developed a type of glass known as *cristallo*, ❶ which is characterized by an almost colorless appearance and shot through with myriad tiny air bubbles. ❷ Typical of this period, Aventurine glass, around the rim of this glass, is colorless glass that has been flecked with particles of copper oxide to simulate gold. ❸ An applied band of *latticino* glass can be seen further down the bowl of the glass. The *latticino* technique involved the incorporation of threads of opaque white glass into a body of colorless glass. ❹ A hollow, molded stem embellished with lions' heads is a typical feature found in late sixteenth-century glassware. ❺ Stem ornamentation is achieved by trailing and pincering decorations, either fused onto an existing stem or to form the stem in its own right. ❻ The foot has a folded edge, a device frequently seen on early glass as a means of strengthening and reinforcing a vulnerable point.

During the seventeenth century, Venetian *cristallo* glassware was much admired and copied throughout Europe, and a truly international style of decoration, based on mannerist

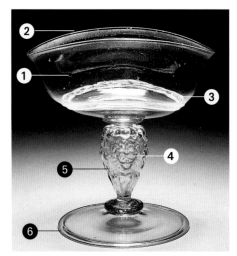

LEFT **A sixteenth-century Venetian *cristallo* goblet with *latticino* and aventurine decoration.**

elements, became fashionable. Such pieces are referred to as façon de Venise, and it is usually impossible to be certain where they originated. ❼ The symbolism of stem formations can be construed as serpents and dragons but the majority are so highly formalized as to defy interpretation. ❽ *Cristallo* glass is blown at high temperatures, resulting in thin-walled vessels that are unsuited for decoration by cutting or wheel-engraving. Therefore, the bowls and feet are plain, ❾ with the exception of the glass second from the left which is an example of *latticino*.

❿ The technique of painting glass with opaque enamels originated in the Middle East. It was taken up by the

ABOVE **A group of early seventeenth-century façon de Venise goblets.**

Venetians, and then passed north of the Alps where it retained its popularity throughout the sixteenth and seventeenth centuries. ⓫ A waisted bucket bowl with a flaring rim is derived from contemporary silver, used in particular for communion chalices. ⓬ Often decorated with a biblical scene—David and Goliath in this case—many pieces were commissioned by the Church. ⓭ Although the date appears very prominent, it has actually been inserted to fill the awkward gap in the design above David's head. ⓮ The highly formalized depiction of foliage, with feathery curling leaves painted in red, yellow, green, blue, and white, is typical of the period, ⓯ as is the depiction of the ground as a simple band of green enamel along the bottom of the goblet's bowl.

RIGHT **An enameled glass goblet, Bohemia, 1575.**

Silver Porringers

In England, two-handled cylindrical cups for holding soup or caudle are known as porringers. The vessels take their name from the French term for soup bowl, or *potager*. Originating in the Netherlands, the auricular style is identified by amorphous, lobate scrolls melting into an illusionistic picture of flowing forms. **1** Decoration

LEFT **A Commonwealth porringer and cover with the maker's mark "HB," London, 1659.**

featuring acanthus leaves and putti can be traced to the influence of craftsmen from France and the Netherlands working in England. **2** The late Commonwealth period saw the domed cover lacking the flanged rim found on earlier examples of porringers. **3** The ancestor of two-handled cups, popular for display in the eighteenth century, was the bellied porringer with a bulbous body and two cast handles in the form of caryatids.

Silver Wine Cups

Silver vessels for drinking wine enjoyed popularity in England from the early seventeenth century until they were largely replaced by glass in the eighteenth century. Wine cups were decorated with embossing, engraving, bright cutting, or chasing, sometimes with matting or punching. **1** The bowls of wine cups are found in a variety of forms, including hemispherical, saucer-shaped, semi-ovoid, beaker-shaped, or bucket-shaped. **2** The interior was often gilded. **3** Most wine cups made at this time have a substantial baluster-shaped stem of varying thickness **4** and a flat, circular foot. The plain, Puritan style is evoked in wine cups like this one, which depend on form rather than decoration, and are frequently left plain **5** or engraved with a simple coat of arms, crest, or inscription, occasionally with chased blooms or strapwork.

RIGHT **A Commonwealth silver wine cup with the maker's mark "M" and a mullet below, London, 1653.**

Silver Spoons

From the Middle Ages until the mid-seventeenth century, spoons were among the most personal items of silver, presented as baptism gifts and carried and used throughout life. The quality of the spoon was dictated by both one's wealth and one's social status. In this period being "born with a silver spoon in your mouth" actually did carry great social significance. Slip-top spoons were popular in England between 1620 and 1650, and were the earliest type of spoon made in the American colonies from around 1670. They are also known as slipped-stalk spoons, slip-end spoons, or slipped-in-the-stalk spoons.
1 The slip-top spoon does not have a finial, deriving its name from the heraldic term "slipt," meaning "cut off."
2 The stem of the slip-top spoon widens slightly away from the fig-shaped bowl, **3** and the owner's initials were frequently engraved on the bowl or on the slipped end.

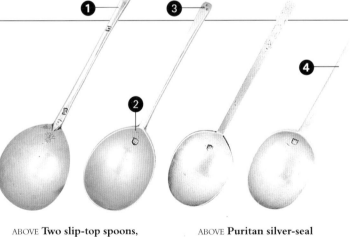

ABOVE **Two slip-top spoons, Jeremy Johnson, 1652.**

ABOVE **Puritan silver-seal top spoons.**

Puritan spoons mark the transition between early English spoons and modern, decorated versions. **4** Like slip-top spoons, the form of the Puritan spoon is relatively plain, but with a stem that is considerably broader.

Drug Jars

From the mid-sixteenth century, Japanese porcelain from Arita was exported to Europe in increasing quantities. Copied from the highly regarded Chinese porcelain of the late Ming dynasty, Arita wares were always blue and white, and shapes were usually based on European metalware and pottery. By the sixteenth century, the production of tin-glazed earthenware had spread throughout Europe. Known as majolica in Italy, faience in France, Germany, and Scandinavia, and delftware in the Netherlands and England, this pottery was admired for its painted decoration, taking its inspiration from the Renaissance.

❶ In the late fifteenth century the albarello—a cylindrical drug jar with a waist— appeared. ❷ At the same time, Italian pottery painters began to adopt the istoriato painting style, illustrating popular narratives of the day.
❸ Monastic pharmacies were important ceramic patrons and their coats of

RIGHT **Urbino armorial albarello, Italy, late sixteenth century.**

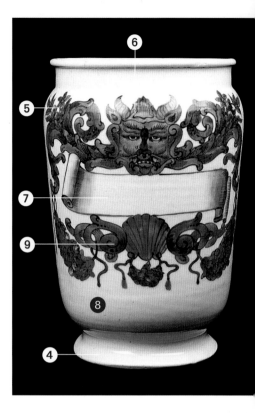

RIGHT **Arita blue and white drug jar, mid-seventeenth century.**

arms would often be incorporated into commissioned wares. ❹ Arita drug jars characteristically had a narrow foot, ❺ with the body rising to a wide rim to allow for easy storage and access. ❻ Designs were both practical and decorative. A devil's head in goat form illustrates the hazards of the jar's contents, ❼ while the scroll gives space for a written label. Often the apothecary's initials would be the only form of adornment, surrounded by a simple classical motif. ❽ Arita coloring differed from its Chinese prototype; whites are a softer gray-blue ❾ and cobalts are usually a darker blue-black.

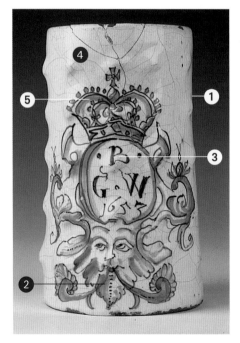

LEFT **A Southwark delft blue and white mug, 1653.**

Domestic Ceramics

Tin-glazed earthenware, copied from Chinese imports, was made throughout the Netherlands during the seventeenth century, most importantly at the town of Delft. Later, these were also made in England and known as delftware. English delft potters made utilitarian goods for well-off country people and the new middle classes. ❶ Mugs often had a simple cylindrical shape, with straight sides, no foot or rim, and no handle. Instead, the body of the mug had indentations for easy handling. ❷ Illustrating the fashions of the period, the male face is painted with a pointed chin and curled mustache. ❸ This is surmounted by a medallion framing the initials B.G.W. and the date. ❹ The base color of the piece is milky white ❺ and the decoration is painted a characteristic pale blue.

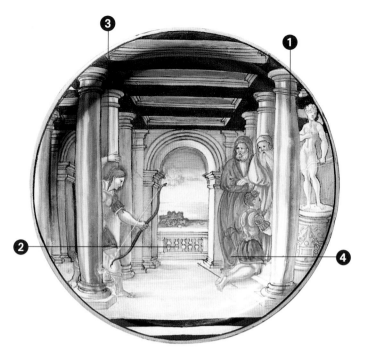

ABOVE **Istoriato dish, by Pellipario Nicola, Urbino, mid-sixteenth century.**

Decorative Ware

Pellipario Nicola was one of Urbino's greatest ceramic painters, particularly associated with the istoriato style. His narrative scenes, painted with a fine palette, were usually copied from, or inspired by, engravings and prints of the contemporary masters. ❶ Italian ceramic decoration often reveals the influence of Renaissance architecture. Here, Corinthian columns line the approach to an archway, ❷ which leads to a balustraded balcony. ❸ As in Renaissance and post-Renaissance fine art, ancient mythology is also a key theme; here, Paris is shown shooting his bow at Achilles. ❹ Typical majolica colors are represented—vivid blue, green, black, yellow, and white.

Tapestries and Needlework

Flemish weavers were celebrated from the fifteenth century for high-quality tapestries featuring flowers, foliage, and biblical and classical subjects. These were frequently drawn from the designs of renowned artists of the day. Both France and England established workshops that were to rival the sumptuous tapestries produced at centers such as Tournai, Bruges, and Brussels. ❶ Scenes from the Old Testament,

ABOVE **Charles II stump work mirror, c. 1670.**

LEFT **Tapestry showing Judith holding the head of Holofernes outside his tent. Woven after an engraving by Christoffel Van Sichem, Bruges, mid-seventeenth century.**

mythological stories, and Flemish and Dutch engravings were popular subjects for needlework and tapestry designs. ❷ During this period, tapestry increasingly came to resemble a woolen or silk copy of a painting, surrounded by a wide, heavily ornamented border.

One of the most popular forms of needlework in the seventeenth century was stump work, or raised work. ❸ This three-dimensional technique was used to embellish caskets, mirrors, and picture frames. ❹ Colorful designs featured royalty, and biblical and mythological themes.

Detail Directory

Mannerism, essentially a court style born in the early sixteenth century as a by-product of the Renaissance, filtered through the decorative arts across Europe. Characterized by elegantly contorted and sinuous forms, bizarre taste, and visual wit, Mannerist ornament decorated furniture, silver, ceramics, tapestries, and sculptures. Attenuated human figures, twisted postures, and strapwork were hallmarks of the style, disseminated throughout Europe via the engraved designs of Giulio Romano, Jacques du Cerceau, and Hans Vredeman de Vries.

Furniture

Mannerism was especially well suited to the decoration of furniture. Bizarre ornament and strapwork motifs copied from influential pattern books were carved onto cupboards, monumental cabinets, and chairbacks, while chests were inlaid with colored woods in a host of whimsical designs. Carved geometric designs also remained popular on English and North American furniture. Architectural details, such as columns, were also incorporated into cabinet designs, particularly in Italy.

Detail of bronze andiron, attributed to Niccolo Roccatagliata, early 1600s.

Draft of table leg, c. 1600.

Detail of walnut side cabinet, France, sixteenth century.

Curved and painted oak and pine chest, America, c. 1670–1710.

Carved table details.

Pietra dura panel of Florentine cabinet, c. 1645.

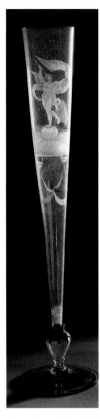

A group of early winged goblets, Venice, mid-sixteenth to early seventeenth century.

Tazza, Venice, late sixteenth to early seventeenth century.

Facon de venise flute, 1662.

Armorial flask, Germany, 1664; enameled glass goblet, 1674.

Glassware

The contours of glassware became more ambitious, with Italian glassmakers producing elaborately colored winged goblets. Surface decoration also became more detailed as engraving tools became more advanced. Dutch and German detailing continued along a more pictorial line and the use of color became more bold.

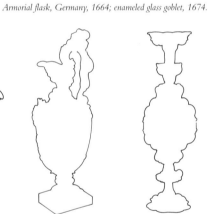

Design for ewer, by Cornelius Floris.

Profile of silver ewer, Genoa, 1621–22.

Profile of parcel-gilt double-cup, Germany, c. 1600.

Tapestry, Brussels, early seventeenth century.

Beadwork mirror frame design, England, c. 1660.

Profile of silver porringer, c. 1660.

Silverware

The Mannerist delight in the bizarre gave rise to exquisitely crafted vessels in silver and gold decorated with an exuberant abundance of fantastic ornament. Favorite motifs, including herms, swags, grotesques, masks, caryatids, cartouches, and especially strapwork, covered the surface of vessels that combined rare metals and precious stones. One of the most exceptional forms of Mannerist silver was the auricular design, based on curving lobate shapes and developed by Dutch silversmiths.

Mannerist decoration on silver urn.

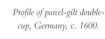

Tapestry

Tapestry workshops used Mannerist motifs, such as herms, strapwork, masks, and grotesques, to decorate the elaborate borders framing table carpets and wall hangings. Traditional designs remained popular and northern European styles were exported to America with the early settlers.

Pomp and Circumstance

Classical buildings of Renaissance Italy inspired the early Baroque period of 1670 to 1720. Italian architects designed with dynamic domes and swooping curves, but King Louis XIV of France rejected such an "emotional" approach. He used the decoration of his palace at Versailles to express his power and opulence, thereby setting the tone for interiors and the decorative arts throughout Europe and, by extension, in America. Louis attached such importance to art that craftsmen grew in status in Europe and America.

Louis XIV—the "Sun King" who reigned from 1638–1715—used Versailles as an instrument of kingship, as had his forbear François I with Fontainebleau. While François I had displayed Italian artistry, Louis XIV used Versailles to promote French art with a classical grandeur.

BLUEPRINT FOR VERSAILLES

The model for the court at Versailles was the chateau Vaux-le-Vicomte, built for Louis' Minister of Finance, Fouquet. At its opening in 1661, Louis was a young man but already autocratic. The chateau was so beautifully furnished and decorated that Fouquet was considered to have upstaged the king. Louis arrested him, seized the chateau, and removed its contents. He then commissioned the three men responsible for Vaux-le-Vicomte—architect Louis Le Vau, garden designer André Le Nôtre, and decorator Charles Le Brun—to create Versailles.

The new Minister of Finance, Jean Baptiste Colbert, promoted the status of native craftsmen by setting up a furniture and tapestry factory at Gobelins, which gave state patronage to those involved in the decorative arts. He also established the *Académie Royale d'Architecture* to encourage study of classical buildings in Rome. Le Brun was head of both, so his restrained, formal classical style united architecture, interior design, and the decorative arts.

Le Brun made designs for every aspect of Versailles: arches, fountains, staircases, tapestries, furniture, architectural decoration, silver, carriages, and doors.

LEFT **Every wall surface at Versailles was richly decorated and gilded with royal crests and sunbursts linking the king to the sun god Apollo. The decorator** **Le Brun created a series of rooms, called the *Grands Appartements*, each named after a planet and culminating in the *Salon d'Apollon*, the throne room.**

Many were engraved by ornamental designer Le Pautre and used as a blueprint for Louis XIV design all over France. Republished in England, the Netherlands, and Germany, Le Brun's work was copied and appeared throughout Europe.

THE GLORY OF THE KING

By 1680 the court of 10,000, the nucleus of France, was installed at Versailles. Its Hall of Mirrors was the wonder of the world: mirrors were rare and expensive. Rare marble was also used extensively, and the furniture was made of silver (subsequently melted down to pay for wars). Similar silver furniture still exists at Knole House in Kent, England.

The palace was decorated throughout with images of Louis as Apollo, Greek god of the sun. The king modeled himself on this classical ideal, and he was portrayed as a god at the very center of the universe. France was at her peak, and the exterior, interior, fixtures, and fittings of Versailles combined to impress visitors with her strength and beauty.

MOVEMENT OF FRENCH CRAFTSMEN

Louis XIV was a man of strong will. In 1685 he revoked the Edict of Nantes, which had allowed freedom of worship to the French. Consequently, Protestants fled the country. Many of them were silversmiths and weavers, and they took their talents far and wide. They rendered the Versailles style in a scaled-down manner, with tall, thin proportions, favoring animals and figures for handles and finials; gadrooning, fluting, and Chinese motifs for decoration.

LEFT **The imposing scale of the Hall of Mirrors at the château of Versailles reflects the importance of Louis XIV, "The Sun King." The shape of the mirrors is repeated in the windows. Glass was much more expensive in the 1670s than it is today, so the effect was even more dazzling at that time.**

BELOW **Castle Howard in Yorkshire, England, was designed by playwright and architect, Sir John Vanbrugh, with a theatrical hint of the Baroque that is rare in Britain. Work on the house, with its central cupola, started in 1699.**

The house was set in a landscape dotted with statuary and pavilions— the effect was an antithesis of French formal planting. The interior contains paintings by Reynolds, Rubens, Gainsborough, and Holbein.

One such craftsman who fled the country was Daniel Marot, a Huguenot (French Protestant) engraver and designer. He took his knowledge of Louis XIV style to the court of William of Orange in Holland. When William married Mary Stuart and they took the English throne in 1689, Marot went with them. He worked on the interior decoration and garden design of their palaces at Het Loo in Holland and Hampton Court in England. Marot developed an individual Baroque style that unified whole schemes—furniture, upholstery, chimney pieces, ceilings, outdoor parterres, and carriages.

DUTCH PROSPERITY FROM TRADE

Holland was a country with a middle-class society with excellent trading links. The Dutch East India Company was set up in 1602, and dominated seventeenth-century trade with the Orient. China exported coromandel lacquer (which was applied to screens), porcelain, wallpaper, silk fabric, and ivory carvings such as chess sets. The West's love affair with all things Chinese was such that by the beginning of the eighteenth century, China was making

BELOW **Paul Revere's timbered house is Boston's oldest building. Constructed around 1680, it is one of the few houses remaining from the** early Colonial period. It is now restored inside, with the heavy beams, large fireplaces, and lack of hallway typical of the late seventeenth century.

porcelain specifically for export. One of Marot's most popular designs in England and America was for cabinets mounted on fireplaces or overmantels to display the fashionable blue and white Chinese porcelain.

The Dutch were beginning to see the potential of art as an investment. Dutch art advisers served in every court in Europe. Antwerp and Amsterdam were art market centers, with dealers and auction houses. People bought porcelain and pictures. It was the age of Dutch genre painting, and still lifes show oriental blue and white porcelain among glassware and curios such as coral. Nearly every household in Holland had a Dutch genre painting on the wall, often portraying a house interior similar to their own—dark and sparsely furnished— or a butcher's shop, inn, or courtyard.

WILLIAM AND MARY STYLE

Around 1700, trade was increasing between London and America, which stimulated interest in the fashions of Europe. The skilled craftsmen who emigrated to America interpreted the styles of their various homelands for the newly prosperous merchants and landowners.

Cities were springing up. Philadelphia (founded 1682) and Charleston (founded 1670) became centers of importance, alongside Boston, Newport, and New York. Networks modeled on the English and Dutch East India Trading Companies developed imports and exports between the West Indies, London, and America. There was a growing awareness that furnishings could reflect social status, and people aspired to own porcelain, textiles, and silver.

As the decorative arts followed the styles and fashions set in England—a few years later—the period 1700–1730 is known in America as William and Mary style, reflecting the English monarchs of 1689–1702. Restrained movement and a greater emphasis on height softened the flat, rectangular, masculine lines of the earlier Pilgrim style.

ABOVE **Built in 1720, Ditchley Park, England, has the grandeur that filtered through from Versailles but lacks the ornate decoration typical of many aristocratic English houses of the early eighteenth century. The doorways and fireplaces borrow from classical architecture, with Corinthian pillars and pediments, resplendent with decorative scrolls and festoons.**

Collector's Gallery

During the late seventeenth and early eighteenth centuries, furniture, ceramics, glass, and silver embraced the theatrical, three-dimensional, and boldly sculptural style of the Baroque. Ornament was underscored by bulbous shapes and elaborate modeling. Architectural symmetry was contrasted with richness of surface decoration or naturalistic ornament. The period also witnessed a development of more practical designs, with simple lines relying on the beauty of raw materials, such as the figure of wood—a characteristic that was to be emulated in the United States.

Case Furniture

Practical, multifunctional furniture, such as the bureau-cabinet, became popular in Europe, and these designs soon found their way to the United States. Bureau-cabinets were originally made in three parts, but gradually the chest and bureau were integrated, with often only a molding remaining. The cabinet was always made separately.

1 Walnut, often burl, was a popular veneer in much of Europe for these pieces. In England, emphasis was on the

LEFT **A walnut bachelor's chest with folding top (bracket feet replaced), England,** *c.* **1710.**

figure or grain of the wood, seeking to simulate tortoiseshell or marble. **2** Japanning, the European imitation of oriental lacquer finishes, remained popular for grand pieces like bureau-cabinets. **3** From 1700, bracket feet began to replace the ubiquitous ball or bun foot and **4** inlay and marquetry became more common. **5** Candlesticks would be placed on the two slides below the cabinet doors, whose panels were often filled with mirror glass.

LEFT **A red-japanned bureau-cabinet, England,** *c.* **1710.**

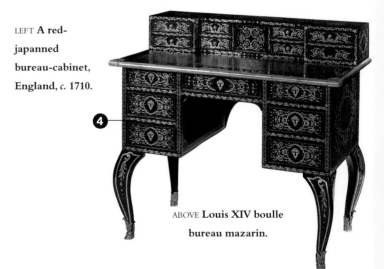

LEFT **A red-japanned bureau-cabinet, England,** *c.* **1710.**

ABOVE **Louis XIV boulle bureau mazarin.**

ABOVE **A walnut cabinet on a stand with inlaid veneers of olive wood, fruitwood, ivory, and ebony, France, *c.* 1690.**

Cabinets

Keeping to the form that evolved earlier in the century, cabinets on stands became even more colorful. Primarily used to store precious curios, they were also used for displaying Chinese blue and white porcelain, which was often piled on top or stood underneath. Italian cabinets continued to be highly architectural, often with sculptural stands. Northern European examples became increasingly simple in form, but an architectural influence remained, evidenced by ❶ a cushion-molded drawer in the frieze and ❷ the legs in the form of classical columns, sometimes spiral-shaped. ❸ Walnut was the most frequently used veneer, but oriental lacquer or japanning, in black or red, remained extremely popular. While *pietra dura*, or stone mosaic work, dominated in Italy, in northern Europe similar designs were translated into marquetry, ❹ sometimes inlaid with ivory or bone, or even pewter and brass. The favorite designs were symmetrical sprays or vases of leaves and flowers, often scattered with birds and insects.

Chairs

Chairs of this period reflect the complex and dynamic decoration also found on tables: bold architectural scrolls or serpentine turning for the supports, often embellished with naturalistic foliate and floral carving. Walnut was widely used for carved chairs, but when they were to be gilded or painted they would be made of beech. ❶ For comfort, the backs were raked instead of vertical. Upholstery continued to be important, but in England it might be replaced by caning on the seat and back. ❷ Many arms had a graceful S-shaped curve, usually terminating in a scroll. ❸ Stretchers were often in an X-shape, and could be shaped like scrolls centering on a finial.

The most overtly Baroque chairs are Italian; in France, ❹ lines were simpler and decoration was on a smaller scale, more formal, and elegant.

RIGHT **Venetian giltwood throne, in the manner of Brustolon,** *c.* 1700.

BELOW **A pair of Louis XIV giltwood fauteuils,** *c.* 1690.

LEFT **Diamond-point engraved serving flask, in the manner of Willem Mooleyser, the Netherlands, *c.* 1680.**

Glass Flutes and Flasks

Venetian-style *cristallo* glass was elaborately decorated with diamond-point engraving. Schwarzlot decoration (meaning black lead in German) was also applied as transparent enamel using a limited palette on both glass and ceramics. ❶ Long necks and squat bulbous body shapes are typical, often referred to as a "shaft-and-globe." ❷ Engraving is very freely drawn, as shown by the tendrils of the vine, contrasting with the roughly shaded grapes and leaves. Other pieces had the entire surface engraved, giving an impression similar to a damask fabric. Schwarzlot decoration was influenced by contemporary prints; ❸ this is particularly evident in the shaded details, such as the bellies of the horses and the foreground foliage. The most popular subjects are landscapes, mythological scenes, ❹ and scenes commemorating battles. ❺ Using insects as decoration was a typical Baroque conceit indicative of the growing interest in nature.

LEFT **Flask with schwarzlot decoration, early eighteenth century.**

Waldglas

Glass makers in northern Europe continued their traditional production of waldglas parallel with the new Venetian *cristallo*. Waldglas, literally "forest glass," is a primitive form of potash glass, thickly blown and characterized by a greenish tinge. ❶ Waldglas roemers were characterized by thick, hollow stems with a high "kick" at the base. ❷ The stem is decorated with applied prunts and raised on a coiled concave foot. ❸ Coats of arms are a patriotic statement. This piece was made for Prince Willem III of the Netherlands (later king William III of England), with the coats of arms of the seventeen provinces of the Netherlands.

RIGHT **Ceremonial roemer with diamond-point engraving, the Netherlands, *c.* 1685.**

Colored Glass Beakers

A deep ruby color was achieved by the addition of finely powdered gold to the glass mix. This technique was revived in the 1670s by the talented German glass maker, Johann Kunckel. This type of glass was highly complicated—the technique involves heating the glass twice to achieve the color—and exorbitant to produce. ❶ Typically, gold ruby glasses are mounted on silver or silver-gilt mounts, engraved to match the decoration on the glass. The shapes of gold-ruby glass tend to be simple; ❷ generally these glasses are blown with thick sides to support the wheel-engraved decoration. ❸ The engraved flowers and foliage show the influence of the designer Daniel Marot, and are similar to designs for floral marquetry and ceramics.

LEFT **Engraved ruby glass beaker, with silver-gilt mount, Potsdam, late seventeenth century.**

Bowls

Schwarzlot decoration was generally applied by hausmaler artists, who were gifted amateurs working from their own homes or studios. Ignaz Preissler was one such artist known to be active at Kronstadt in Bohemia during the 1720s and 1730s. Although none of his work is signed, attributions can be made on the basis of his distinctive style. Preissler is renowned for his use of formalized strapwork to frame his designs. **1** Here, the scrolling foliate strapwork extends on either side of the coat of arms, beautifully balanced but not quite symmetrical. **2** The landscape is rendered naturalistically and rather simply. **3** Note the sheer quality of this work; the bowl has been decorated with great confidence, the design enhancing both its simple shape and the cutting on its lower part.

ABOVE **Schwarzlot bowl in the manner of Ignaz Preissler, early eighteenth century.**

Silver Mirrors

Among the most sumptuous silver items created during the Baroque period was silver furniture, including grand ensembles of mirrors, standing candlesticks, and tables. This extravagant taste spread from the French court to the Netherlands, and to England during the reign of Charles II. The majority of surviving silver furniture was made in Augsburg, Germany. **1** Architectural features such as scrolling acanthus leaves, flower garlands, volutes, friezes, swags, scrolls, putti, and caryatids were essential components of the Baroque style in silver. **2** Motifs from ancient mythology were popular subjects. Heavy, symmetrical forms were layered with an abundance of opulent ornament, creating an overall effect of unmatched grandeur.

RIGHT **The Minerva wall mirror by Albrecht Biller, Augsburg, _c._ 1700.**

RIGHT **Charles II parcel-gilt silver tankard, probably by Jacob Bodendick, _c._ 1670.**

Silver Tankards

Evolving from medieval wooden vessels, the silver ale tankard was primarily intended for private domestic use. Lavishly chased ornament was perfected by German and Dutch makers, whose tankards were chased with flowers, masks, strapwork, and biblical or mythological scenes. **1** Baroque silver is characterized by finely chased scenes of cherubs playing musical instruments, integrated in a swirling design of acanthus, fruit, and foliage. **2** Another essential feature is the depth of the wrought relief, creating a dramatic sense of movement.

Teaware

One of the greatest collectors of oriental porcelain was Augustus the Strong, Elector of Saxony (1670–1733). In 1710 he established a ceramics factory at Meissen, near Dresden, and employed an alchemist, Johann Bottger, to carry out experiments in an attempt to produce true porcelain of the type made in China and Japan. In the course of these experiments Bottger discovered the secret of making red-brown stoneware similar to that used in Chinese wares from Yixing. Known as Bottger stoneware it was produced only until about 1717, and as such, is greatly sought after by

ABOVE **Bottger red stoneware baluster teapot and domed cover, c. 1715.**

collectors. Bottger stoneware is extremely hard with a reddish-brown appearance. Fine-ground and dense, this can be capable of being highly polished on a wheel. ❶ The teapot is a copy of the Chinese teapots from Yixing exported to Europe, together with tea, during the second half of the seventeenth century, when the habit of tea and coffee drinking became popular. ❷ The baluster shape of the teapot (bulbous base rising to narrow neck) reveals its origin as a silver design, its simple shape and highly polished surface being more usually associated with the work of the silversmith than the potter. ❸ The decoration on the handles ❹ and the bottom of the spout is typical of that found on silverware of the period.

ABOVE **A delft, gilt-metal mounted, blue and white oviform ewer, the Netherlands, c. 1700.**

Ewers

Delftware is synonymous with blue and white decorated earthenware. Its greatest period was between 1660 and 1730. Inspired by the arrival in the Netherlands of Chinese blue and white porcelain in the early seventeenth century, delft potters began to incorporate Chinese designs into their wares. ❶ The ewer shows the limitations imposed on the delft painters by the tin glaze that obscured the fine detail commonly found on Chinese wares. ❷ The figures, set within plaques round the bottom of the neck and on the main body of the piece, lack facial features or details of dress and personal ornamentation. Rather, there is emphasis on character in the gestures and posture of the figures, showing how the delft painters developed their own styles within the Chinese tradition. ❸ The ewer shows the skillful use of cobalt blue decoration. The foliage surrounding the figure in the central plaque is accurately drawn and the color evenly spread on a bluish ground to give a superb finish.

ABOVE **A delft, blue and white barber's bowl,
London, inscribed and dated 1716.**

Bowls

Dutch potters came to England and began to produce English delft in the early seventeenth century. The English potteries survived by producing mainly basic tablewares, storage vessels, and other practical items, both for domestic and trade use. Designs and painting were simple and practical. ❶ The barber's bowl is a typical example of the utilitarian wares needed at this time. The attractive polychrome painting and the simple and effective design were both practical and decorative. ❷ The bowl is indented to allow the head or neck of the customer to rest while the barber practiced his skills, ❸ while the decoration in the middle of the bowl illustrates the tools of the barber's trade. ❹ Around the rim of the bowl is inscribed a reference to quarter day, when it was time for gentlemen to pay, presumably an exhortation to customers to remember to pay the barber for services rendered.

Clocks

The growth in trade with the East Indies, China, and Japan meant that a wide variety of exotic woods were imported, thereby stimulating innovations in design and fueling the desire for sumptuous display. The technique of veneering advanced the use of colorful woods, as well as precious materials such as ivory and mother-of-pearl, to great decorative effect. Among the most highly prized decorative objects were clocks, which by the early eighteenth century were furnished with lavishly decorated cases. ❶ By 1675 the bracket clock had become established in England. Great pride was taken in the decoration of the rectangular cases, ❷ with low-domed tops (containing the striking bell), made in a variety of exotic materials, including walnut, lacquer, tortoiseshell, and, as in this example, ebony. ❸ Clock cases made of ebony were usually decorated with

pierced or chased gilt-metal brass mounts, although the grandest examples were garnished with silver in emulation of the lavish taste for splendor promoted at the French court of Louis XIV. ❹ The introduction from the East of the highly specialized art of making lacquerware provided European craftsmen with a new repertoire of fanciful designs. Finishes such as this cream lacquer introduced a lighter touch to the Baroque interior.

LEFT **A cream lacquer bracket clock by Joseph Windmills, England, *c.* 1710.**

RIGHT **A small ebony silver-mounted striking bracket clock by Thomas Tompion.**

Detail Directory

The splendor of Baroque architecture was mirrored in the decorative arts. The court of Louis XIV in France led Europe in the manufacture of luxury goods, with carved furniture, marble panels, paintings, tapestries, and mirrors used to underscore the power of the monarchy. Decoration remained formal and symmetrical, with acanthus, pediments, swags, masks, and lion-paw feet the principal motifs. Rich velvets, brocades, and damasks, and semi-precious stones and ivory were among the opulent materials favored at the time.

Table.

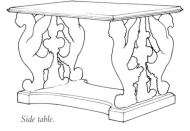

Side table.

Detail of side table.

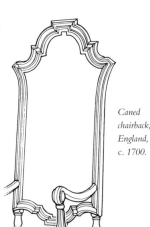

Ornamental leg of cabinet stand.

Leg of table by Pierre Gole, c. 1653–60.

Outline of barley twist leg, c. 1675.

Leg and foot of cabinet, c. 1690.

Ornamental leg from Boulle cabinet, c. 1675.

Furniture

Elaborate cabinets on stands were fashionable pieces of Baroque furniture. Inlaid with marquetry, *pietre dure* panels, or embellished with heavy gilt-bronze mounts, these cabinets were powerful symbols of wealth and prestige, as well as fitting tributes to the glory and supremacy of the French monarchy. Heavy, complex shapes, such as the double-scroll leg and weighty garlands, were typical features of grand Baroque furniture, as was the elaborate carving favored for cabinet stands, chairs, and picture frames. The preference for sumptuous materials reached its zenith at this time. The lavish display of grand ensembles of silver furniture at Versailles started a fashion that spread to other parts of Europe and captured the imagination of all who aspired to imitate the splendor of France.

Marot-style carved dining chairback, c. 1690–1700.

Caned chairback with carving, the Netherlands, c. 1690.

Caned chairback, England, c. 1700.

Surface Decoration

The robust Baroque style fused architectural and sculptural elements, using pediments, heavy scrolls, garlands, and ornate floral marquetry. This style can be found on tapestries, painted and inlaid furniture, silver, glassware, mirrors, and picture frames, where the design is inseparable from its ornamentation. In a lively variant of Classicism, curving lines, sculptural forms, and the effects of textural light and shade are emphasized by bulbous shapes, powerful modeling, and elaborate carving.

Coronet detail from Gobelins tapestry, seventeenth century.

Cherub decorations from Gobelins tapestry, seventeenth century.

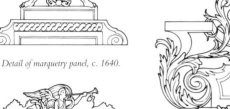

Detail of marquetry panel, c. 1640.

Decorative urn from wall panel, by Charles Le Brun.

Detail of winged cherub, tapestry ornament.

Silver picture frame, 1670s.

Scroll detail from border of savonnerie carpet, c. 1669.

Engraved glass beaker, Germany, c. 1690–1700.

Profile of covered goblet, Bohemia, c. 1700.

William and Mary sugar bowl and cover.

Silver

The taste for opulent materials found expression in the elaborately molded and decorated silver vessels made to supply church treasuries and to adorn the tables and cabinets of the rich and powerful. Theatrical, grand, and boldly sculptural, the Baroque style in silver was disseminated through engravings. Silversmiths throughout Europe enthusiastically took up this fashion, as increasingly sophisticated rituals of etiquette at the French court created a new demand for a variety of silver tableware and furnishings.

Silver altar candlestick, Italy, early eighteenth century.

Glass

The drama and grandeur of the Baroque period influenced glass-makers throughout Europe in the seventeenth century. Important glass-making centers, from Venice to Bohemia, reflected the Baroque taste for ornate designs of unprecedented splendor. Decorative features, such as heavy moldings and deeply carved, faceted, and lobed ornament, typified the Baroque exuberance of German and Bohemian glass, while ornate, fanciful stems and intricate designs created by Venetian glass-makers underscored the spirit of the Baroque.

Augustan Formalism

When Louis XIV died in 1715, his courtiers heaved a sigh of relief. Now that they could move away from the stifling formality of life in the chilly rooms of Versailles. A lightness of touch entered the stiff vocabulary of interiors, in a style known as Régence. Meanwhile, England was moving toward Palladian building, derived from the classical designs of the sixteenth-century Italian architect, Andrea Palladio. America embraced the Palladian ideal, and started to furnish interiors in the style of the English Queen Anne.

After the academic, somber—pompous, even—classicism of Le Brun's interiors, a designer called Jean Bérain lifted the weight. He took over the Gobelins factory from Le Brun in 1683, and his light grotesques, known as arabesques in France, were particularly influential.

LIGHTENING UP IN FRANCE

Within a framework of fantastic architecture and interleaved bandwork, Bérain placed sphinxes, putti, gods and goddesses, monkeys, and Chinese and Moorish figures. These swung on festoons or hung from tasseled lambrequins. Singeries, in which monkey figures mimicked human habits, and chinoiseries were now used in all media.

Such designs appeared on wall panels, silver, faience pottery, and boulle inlay (marquetry decoration using brass and tortoiseshell). Bérain's designs were republished abroad, sending around Europe the style of the Régence (called after the Duc d'Orléans, Regent to Louis XV).

In painting, too, more frivolous subject matter came into fashion. Watteau and his followers painted scenes called fêtes galantes. These fitted in with the Régence furnishings, and became an integral part of the overall design scheme.

PALLADIAN REVIVAL IN BRITAIN

In architecture, England was less under the influence of France. One hundred years before, Inigo Jones had been impressed by Palladian architecture in Italy. In the 1620s and '30s he designed the Queen's House at Greenwich in villa

LEFT **The Palace of Würzburg was designed between 1720 and 1750 by Balthasar Neumann in a powerful Baroque style featuring marble Doric columns. The ceilings were painted by Venetian father and son artists, Giovanni and Giandomenico Tiepolo, and showed allegories of the Prince and the four continents.**

RIGHT **The Giant Order pilasters—as high as two stories of the central section of Clandon House—are typical of English Palladian mansions. They are echoed inside by the** two-story Marble Hall. **The house contains Mortlake tapestries and Meissen commedia dell'arte porcelain figures, which were much in vogue in the 1730s.**

style and the Banqueting House in Whitehall, London in the Italian palatial style.

When Giacomo Leoni reissued the *Quattro Libri* of Palladio, with engravings replacing the woodcuts, the book was snapped up. It coincided with the first volume of Colen Campbell's *Vitruvius Britannicus*, a summary of modern architecture aimed at undermining the Baroque. Although Hawksmoor and Vanbrugh had designed Baroque buildings, the style was considered too papist in Britain where ornament in architecture was frowned upon. Architect Robert Morris wrote at the time: "If you will be lavish in ornament, your structure will look rather more like a fop, with a superfluity of gaudy tinsil, than a real decoration."

Lord Burlington, an amateur architect, took up Palladianism with enthusiasm, building Chiswick House in London in the same classical Palladian villa style as the Queen's House. Symmetry was central to Palladio's work. His villas had an "A: B: A" pattern, where "A" was pavilions flanking a central room "B," fronted with a portico rather like a temple. Such a design slotted into the English hall house idea, with smaller rooms coming off a large central hall.

The English country gentleman liked the idea of a large dining chamber in the middle of the first floor, above the servants in the hall below, literally and symbolically placing him at the center of his home and his own little universe.

In time, the inhabitants of the house appropriated the hall for their own use,

LEFT **The saloon at Houghton Hall, with its huge doorcase and gilded furniture, was designed by William Kent in his favored deep, rich, dark colors. The shell motif picks up the huge shell at the head of the state bed. Houghton was the inspiration for Clandon.**

RIGHT **The tetra-style (four-columned) hall of Marble Hill in Twickenham, England, was intended to resemble an open courtyard. The ceiling was squared off with smaller rooms leading off in Palladian style.**

banishing servants to a smaller hall and the kitchen in the wings. This, together with the introduction of the backstairs, meant that servants could be "invisible." Without their inhibiting presence, life began to lose its formality. Architecture followed suit, with symmetry becoming gradually less important during the second half of the eighteenth century.

KENT'S INTERIORS

Burlington's protégé, William Kent, published *Designs of Inigo Jones* in 1727, and his own work, too, was hugely influential. Close to Palladianism, yet tinged with an austere Baroque acceptable to British tastes, he was the first English architect to design furniture to match his interiors. His designs were rooted in the Baroque style of Italy.

His furniture was sculptural and massive, using eagles, dolphins, cherubs, and sphinxes for legs, and shells and curving foliage as unifying motifs. Pediments and cornices on side tables and pedestals echoed the stucco ornament of huge marble chimneypieces. Richly carved, gilt, and painted, his interiors were as sumptuous as Palladian exteriors were severe, but classical roots united the two.

QUEEN ANNE STYLE

America, like England, was enjoying economic expansion. Trade and travel increased, both between colonies and abroad. With greater prosperity, colonists sought better education with a thorough grounding in architecture, namely, respect for classical Orders and proportion. English Gothic enthusiast Horace Walpole reported having seen one woman wearing "a petticoat decorated with columns of the five Orders."

Classical principles dictated building design. The Georgian plan of Thomas Hancock's Beacon Hill home, built in 1737, was certainly from English architecture manuals. Like William Kent, American designers wanted fixtures to emphasize the classical balance and grand scale of buildings. Broken pediments over windows were picked up in interiors as motifs in furniture. Architectural features such as cornices, quoins, and large figurative sculpture adorned rooms, sometimes toned down in size. The carved scallop shell, so often depicted above the door of terraced Queen Anne houses, became a recurrent motif. Furniture backed up to the wall, except for dining tables and chairs.

Queen Anne reigned from 1702 to 1714, a time when household wares in England were of great simplicity, without ornament. This style in American crafts and furniture ran from about 1720 to 1755. By the late 1720s the heavy C-scrolls and bulbous turnings of William and Mary gave way to more refined and graceful S-curves, ready for the onset of rococo.

ABOVE **Holkham Hall in England was created by the partnership of Lord Burlington as architect and William Kent as interior designer. The Palladian strength of its exterior is repeated** inside in the architectural door frame, with its open pediment and gilded decoration, coffered ceiling, dominant cornice, and heavily patterned wallpaper.

Collector's Gallery

As the eighteenth century progressed there was an increasing reaction against the dramatic theatricality of the Baroque. In France, forms and decoration became lighter, while in England and the United States form became more strictly architectural, with large-scale decorative motifs boldly applied. Everywhere a more organic, curving line began to be introduced.

Tables

Grand display tables continued to be gilded, recalling the style of the previous century, but were often lighter and less complex. Increasingly tables were developed for different purposes such as serving tea, card playing, and eating. ❶ Many tables were constructed with a gateleg; while a more sophisticated construction for card tables was a concertina action. ❷ Cabriole legs echoed those on chairs of the period. ❸ Card tables had fold-over tops fitted with baize, and a deep frieze. ❹ They often had dished corners, to take a candlestick, and small wells for counters. ❺ Pillars on tilt-top tables were often baluster forms ❻ supported by three splayed cabriole legs with pad or claw-and-ball feet.

ABOVE **A carved mahogany tilt-top tea table, attributed to Thomas Affleck, United States, *c.* 1765.**

ABOVE **A walnut concertina-action card table, England, *c.* 1720.**

Chairs

While in France chair evolution was gradual, in England and the Netherlands designs changed radically. Particular changes saw the introduction of smooth, S-shaped curves on the frame, and a solid vase-shaped splat from the crest to the seat rail, a style that would also find favor in the United States. ❶ The broad surface of the shaped splat, as well as the uprights and deep, curved seat rail, were decorated with walnut or mahogany veneers. ❷ A drop-in seat with tapestry upholstery allowed the seat-rail to be seen. ❸ Gradually, carving, usually of acanthus leaves surrounding shells or lion masks, was introduced to the crest and tops of the legs, becoming increasingly elaborate. ❹ The cabriole leg, ❺ frequently ending in a claw-and-ball foot, became standard and, as a rule, was used without stretchers. Similar legs were also used for many contemporary tables.

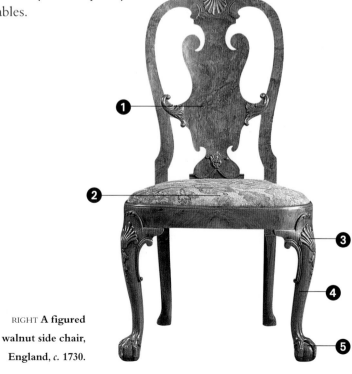

RIGHT **A figured walnut side chair, England, *c.* 1730.**

ABOVE **A block-fronted desk-and-bookcase, Boston, c. 1782.**

Bureaus

Maintaining the form already developed in England earlier in the eighteenth century, bureaus and bureau-cabinets of the century's second quarter are differentiated by stronger architectural references, encouraged by interest in the Renaissance architect, Andrea Palladio. There are close similarities between English and American designs for bureaus and chests, but ① there is a distinct difference in the use of the block front, more reminiscent of Dutch design. Although stylistically associated with this period in Europe, there was a delay before the style reached the United States, where it was still popular up to forty years later. ② Triangular pediments replaced the curved and domed crest familiar in the earlier part of the century. ③ A frieze and pilasters or half-columns flanking the doors also enforced the architectural character. ④ Such architectural pieces were usually made in dark, fairly straight-grained mahogany, initially used because it carved well.

Case Furniture

A number of variations on the chest evolved during this period. In The United States, European types were adapted and acquired a characteristic appearance, most notably the highboy and in the use of the block-front (see Bureaus). ① Instead of a familiar English chest-on-chest form, the upper chest of the American highboy stands on two tiers of drawers on tall, cabriole legs. ② The scrolled bonnet top is characteristic of many American pieces, the bonnet being integral to the structure of the upper chest.

In France, the chest of drawers evolved into the commode, the name coming from *commodious*. ③ By the 1730s, the French commode was beginning to take on a serpentine and bombé form, ④ with three deep drawers, veneered with parquetry and ⑤ decorated with bold, symmetrical gilded metal mounts.

ABOVE **A gilt-bronze-mounted kingwood bombé commode, France, c. 1735.**

LEFT **A walnut highboy, Salem, Massachusetts, c. 1760–1780.**

Glass Goblets

In the early eighteenth century, in central Europe a new type of potash glass of good color and excellent strength was developed. This glass could be thickly blown and proved a fine medium for cutting and engraving. The Zechlin glasshouse in Germany produced some of the most luxurious glass of the period, especially between 1735 and 1740. **1** In Silesia, a part of Europe with a well-established tradition of carving locally mined rock crystal, a distinctive style of engraving in high relief evolved. These glasses emulate rock crystal, with the majority of the engraving left unpolished, giving a frosted, granular appearance. **2** Typical of the style is the faceted base of the bowl of the goblet, raised on a knop or cyst carved in high relief with acanthus decoration. **3** The underside of the foot is cut and engraved to match. **4** Engraved scenes, such as the hunt presided over by flying putti, were realized with high Baroque opulence. **5** Typical of the Baroque treatment, this conical bowl is drawn out a simple shape. The stem has been cut with a stylized petal motif, as has the foot, and heavy gilding is applied to emphasize the cutting. **6** The domed cover is of a shape complementary to the goblet. Note how the finial is cut to match the stem. **7** The bowl has been wheel-engraved, and the engraving has been highlighted by gilding. The design is symmetrical with eagles among foliage above cornucopias. **8** The applied medallion under the crown is decorated with an elaborate princely monogram.

FAR LEFT **An engraved glass goblet and cover, Silesia, *c*. 1710.**

LEFT **A Zechlin engraved and gilded glass goblet and cover, *c*. 1740.**

Amen Glasses

Amen glasses were specially engraved to honor the Jacobite political cause in England and Scotland during the early eighteenth century. Owning such a glass was an act of treason in the eighteenth century, hence it would have been a closely guarded family secret. Individual Amen glasses were named after the supporting families connected to them. **1** Typical of British glass of the 1740s, Amen glasses have a fine, lustrous body of lead glass, requiring minimal decoration and designed with fine proportions. **2** Invariably the word "Amen" is prominently inscribed beneath the cipher of "King James VIII," better known as the "Old Pretender." **3** The body of the glass is diamond-engraved with quotations from Jacobite anthems.

RIGHT **The "Ker" Amen glass, *c*. 1745.**

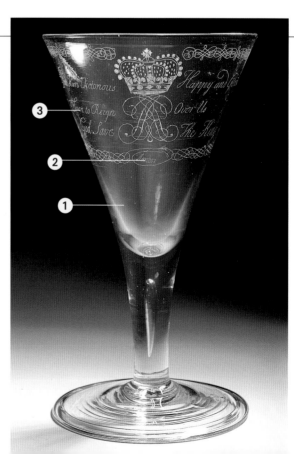

LEFT **A George II silver two-handled cup and cover by John White, 1731.**

Two-Handled Cups

Pride of place in the eighteenth-century dining room was given to the two-handled cup, displayed as a centerpiece on the table or in pairs on the sideboard. Descended from seventeenth-century drinking cups or porringers, they were developed by Huguenot silversmiths into vessels of great dignity and also were used for ceremonial awards. Among the Huguenot contributions to English silver were simple, massive, handsomely proportioned shapes, economically decorated with cast or cut-card designs. ❶ Introduced in the mid-seventeenth century from France, the technique of cut-card work—patterns of relief decoration cut from strips of silver and applied to the body of a vessel—was used to great effect by Huguenot craftsmen during the first half of the eighteenth century. ❷ Sculptural casting, such as the boldly elegant double scroll handles, was also favored. ❸ By the 1720s, decorative engraving or flat chasing, inspired by French Régence pattern books, significantly lightened the austere formality of the early eighteenth-century examples.

ABOVE **Two George II, plain, tapering, cylindrical coffee pots.**

Coffee Pots

Coffee drinking became more widespread in the early eighteenth century, with an increased demand for suitable vessels. The earliest pots emulated Turkish wine jugs, with a spout instead of a lip. These were eventually replaced by teapot forms, with a cover, handle, and spout. A tapering cylindrical form was typical, ❶ with a finial-topped domed cover ❷ and a straight or curving spout. ❸ Decoration was minimal, confined to cut-card work or an engraved armorial between the handle and spout. ❹ Pots were made from a simple sheet of heavy-gauge silver. ❺ The cast foot rim was separately applied.

Sauceboats

Introduced to England from France during the reign of George I, sauceboats for serving gravy or rich sauces became an important addition to the dining service. They were usually made in pairs or, for larger services, in sets of four or six. Throughout the eighteenth century, most examples were relatively plain, ❶ boat-shaped, and sparsely decorated with engraved crests or coats of arms. ❷ Double-lipped sauceboats were a French conceit first introduced to England by Huguenot goldsmiths. Although the form persisted until the 1740s, it had been largely replaced by the more practical single-lipped version. ❸ Decoration on these double-lipped sauceboats was usually minimal, confined to an engraved armorial or a simple gadrooned border around the wavy rim and foot.

BELOW **A pair of George II, double-lipped oval sauceboats.**

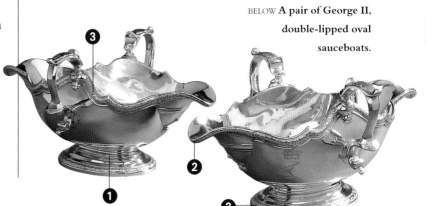

Decorative Tableware

Chinese ornamental vases and tableware were very popular in Europe in the early eighteenth century and were exported in large quantities. Demand in the West for highly decorated and colorful wares led the Chinese to develop *famille verte* (green family) porcelain during the reign of Kangxi (1662–1722). These richly ornamented wares, with their brilliant translucent colors, dominated production until the 1720s when *famille rose* was introduced. ❶ *Famille verte* has an almost pure white china body. This is enameled in iron red, purple, blue, and yellow and finished with a thin, glassy, green enamel overglaze. ❷ Flowers, birds, figures, mythical beasts, or precious objects were the usual subjects of *famille verte* ware. During the Kangxi period, much *famille verte* was decorated with petal- or leaf-shaped reserves enclosing naturalistic themes or narratives. ❸ Highly gilded and ormolu mounts typical of the period were applied to the porcelain by craftsmen in France.

BELOW **A pair of Régence, ormolu-mounted Chinese** *famille verte* **porcelain vases and covers, one cover repaired in the eighteenth century.**

ABOVE **Bottger hausmelerie baluster coffee pot and domed cover painted, probably by Elizabeth Wad, with chinoiserie figures making tea.**

Hausmelerie

Hausmelerie is a term used for porcelains decorated by a group of independent artists. These painters and gilders worked for themselves, decorating in their own workshops items purchased undecorated from factories such as Meissen and Vienna. The trade in hausmelerie flourished in the first half of the eighteenth century, and the quality rivaled and often surpassed that of the factories. ❶ This Bottger baluster coffee pot and domed cover has the characteristic shape of a silver pot, illustrating the debt to metalwork typical of porcelain of the period. The design of the pot closely imitates the popular Japanese Kakiemon style, ❷ featuring lavish gilding on the cover, handle, and spout, ❸ with a large central reserve bounded by a gilded pattern enclosing a chinoiserie decoration. ❹ The cup and saucer are decorated to match the motif on the coffee pot. All three feature figures set in an oriental garden with flowers and stone ornamental furniture, engaged in tea-making activities that reflect a European view of Japanese life. They are painted in colors typical of the Kakiemon style, iron-red, bluish-green, yellow, and light blue.

ABOVE **Bristol blue and white
documentary deep bowl, England, *c.* 1735.**

British Earthenware

British earthenware was admired throughout Europe for its practicality and low cost. Unlike much of the porcelain produced in Europe at this time, it was designed to be used. ❶ This Bristol bowl is in the typical blue and white tradition. Its size and shape, with a deep center, make it versatile and practical. ❷ The potter's inscription on the rim gives his name, place of work, and the date. ❸ In a design that is simple but attractive, the edge is decorated with sprays of leaves interspersed with insects. ❹ The central picture shows a typical country scene with a castle in the background, a humble cottage, and a farmer driving two horses in front of a hand-held plow—a realistic snapshot of life at the time.

The Swan Service

Meissen was renowned for its tableware and dinner services. The Swan Service, comprising two thousand pieces, was the largest porcelain service to be produced in any European factory, and it set the standard for later productions elsewhere. The Swan Service also marks an artistic watershed, since from 1731, with the appointment of Kandler as modeler, designs ceased to be based on metalwork shapes and began to be created specifically for porcelain. ❶ This candlestick is a typical example of the Baroque style of which Kandler was an exponent. The finely molded foot and putti that form the stem are essentially porcelain features. ❷ The molding allows much of the highly prized china body to be left on display while giving space for the decorator to show his skills. ❸ The foot is decorated with gilded leaf work and scrolls. The putti are left undecorated. ❹ The armorial decoration below the putti uses the typical Kandler colors of red, yellow, and black. The overall effect is vivacious.

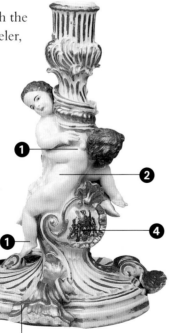

ABOVE **Meissen armorial
candlestick from the Swan
Service, modeled by J.F.
Eberlein and J.J. Kandler
for Count Bruhl.**

Picture and Mirror Frames

The rebirth of the Palladian style in the early eighteenth century, pioneered by William Kent and Lord Burlington, paved the way for a renewed enthusiasm for classicism with dramatic effect in the decorative arts. Filtered through Rome and the Renaissance, the prevailing taste for an architectural structure was occasionally overlaid with ornament reflecting a shift toward the lighter, more organic style of the rococo. ❶ Lavishly ornamented gilded picture and mirror frames occasionally incorporated elements characteristic of the early rococo taste, such as the serpentine apron and scrolling ornament, ❷ within the architectural framework of the Palladian style. ❸ The eagle—especially with outstretched wings—was a favorite Kentian motif based on classical prototypes. Other decorative motifs for pediments and crestings included dolphins, shells, masks, and coronets. ❹ Emphasizing the underlying architectural character of these mirrors is the swan-neck pediment, fashionable for the cornices of bookcases and cabinets at this time.

RIGHT **A George II walnut
and parcel-gilt mirror.**

Detail Directory

After 1700, the strict formality, heaviness, and symmetry that had characterized Baroque taste were gradually supplanted in France by the less ponderous taste of the Régence. During the last years of the reign of Louis XIV, designers such as Jean Bérain had pioneered a manner of decoration that retained much of the classical symmetry of earlier Baroque ornament, but with more delicately rendered arrangements of repeating foliate patterns, scallop shells, and light scrollwork. This lighter, though more restrained, decorative style eventually paved the way for the florid rococo fashion that, by the 1730s, had captured the popular imagination. In England and America, the taste for the plain, uncluttered Queen Anne style surrendered to the Palladian revival championed by William Kent.

Furniture

Restraint, simplicity, and elegance of proportion were the hallmarks of furniture during the early years of the eighteenth century, reflected in the simple, unornamented designs of the Queen Anne period. The architectural Palladian style that followed left its mark in features such as bookcases with pedimented tops, and in marble-topped tables on richly carved supports that incorporated eagles, shells, sphinxes, putti, and masks, reflecting the extravagance of Italian late Baroque.

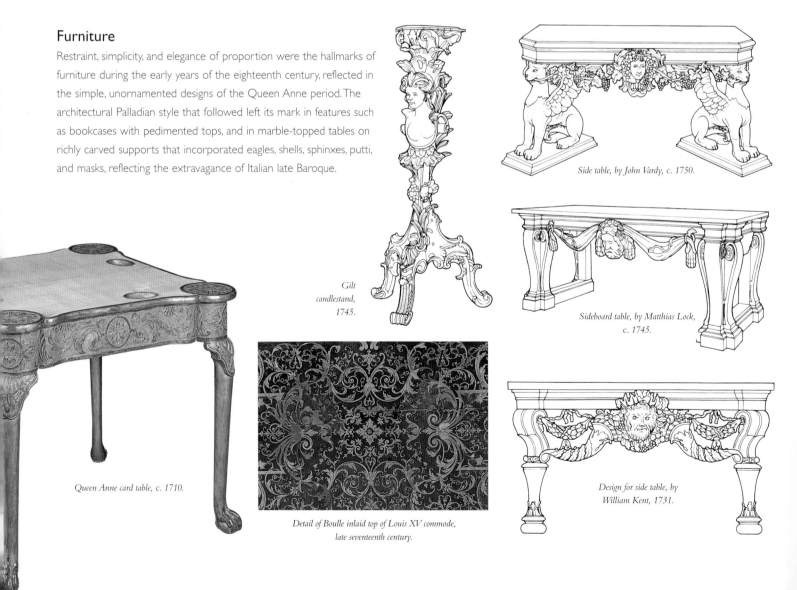

Side table, by John Vardy, c. 1750.

Gilt candlestand, 1745.

Sideboard table, by Matthias Lock, c. 1745.

Queen Anne card table, c. 1710.

Detail of Boulle inlaid top of Louis XV commode, late seventeenth century.

Design for side table, by William Kent, 1731.

Detail of heraldic
tankard decoration.

Outlines of tankards with silver mounts, Germany.

Teapots in the Chinese style, the Netherlands, early eighteenth century.

Domestic Ceramics

Everyday ceramics continued to employ plain, utilitarian shapes and forms.
Tankards kept their simple cylindrical form, occasionally embellished with a
silver hinge or engraved silver cover. German and Dutch teapots fostered
octagonal forms decorated with armorial motifs or floral devices.

Surface Decoration

In the early eighteenth century, the heavy, ponderous ornament
typical of the Baroque style began to lighten. This was due, in part,
to the influential engraved designs of Claude Audran and Jean
Bérain, whose light, elegant, and whimsical style of decoration
hovered on the brink of the rococo. Although remaining in
symmetrical patterns, fanciful scenes were comprised of airy
canopies carried by fantastic term figures, surrounded by bandwork
and acanthus foliage. The designs were adopted for a host of items,
including marquetry on furniture, tapestries, carpets, and mirrors.

Silver dressing table mirror, 1732.   Wall light of silvered bronze,   Gilt bronze dressing mirror,
c. 1710.   c. 1726.

Helmet ewer, c. 1710–20.   Silver cup and cover, 1717–18.   Profile of silver covered cup, c. 1738.

Silver bowl and stand,
by Paul de Lamerie,
1724–26.

Silver

The greatest impact in the decorative arts at this time was made
on silver, largely owing to the impressive influence
of highly skilled Huguenot craftsmen.
Solemn and monumental, their work
was exquisitely modeled, influenced by
the engraved designs of Jean Bérain and
Jean Le Pautre. Although household wares
were designed in simple taste, the influence of
France remained strong. Among the new types of
vessels introduced by Huguenot silversmiths
were helmet-shaped ewers, pilgrim bottles, and soup
tureens. Typically, their austere silver designs were boldly
decorated with cut-card work and cast ornament in the shape
of human or animal figures.

Silver covered cup,
Thomas Farren, 1740.

Playful Diversity

From 1740 to 1770 a new style of interior decoration swept across Europe from France: rococo. In complete contrast to preceding styles, it was organic rather than classical, frivolous instead of austere, pretty, fun, and without deep meaning. Unlike most artistic trends, rococo bypassed the fine arts and pulsated into the decorative, leaving painting and sculpture to fit in as best they could. Though parts of Germany embraced the style, England never quite got the hang of rococo. While rococo flourished in pockets of Europe, Palladianism was adopted with enthusiasm in America.

Visionary Thomas Jefferson (1743–1826) was a great supporter of Palladio, whose architecture came to America via William Kent's book *Designs of Inigo Jones* (the English architect proponent of the Renaissance). Jefferson started building his own house, Monticello, in Virginia, in the Palladian style in 1769.

Although this was classicism at several removes, Palladianism was important in America from the 1740s. Architects could scale the Palladian model up or down according to the means of the owner, and the wings could be extended sideways or folded back into a square plan.

Part of the Palladian style was to rusticate the lower story (using masonry blocks), with multiple smooth-surfaced floors above. The rusticated story was for servants or for informal rooms. In America, builders sometimes cut a wooden facade and sand-painted it to mimic ashlar and quoins. Clapboard did not give the classical feel.

RIGHT **The Schloss Sans Souci at Potsdam, Germany, was a fantasy created for Frederick the Great of Prussia** **around 1750. It has no columns; instead, witty caryatid-type figures hold up the entablature toward "heaven."**

Other popular Palladian motifs included the Venetian window, temple-front porticos, coffering (recessed panels in the ceiling), and giant Orders (columns extending above the height of one story). The main entrance was up the stairs into the hall behind the central portico.

A CAPRICE OF FRANCE

The sturdy, static symmetry of Palladianism was a different story from the elegant poise and asymmetry of contemporary French fashions. One of the protagonists of French rococo was Madame de Pompadour. As mistress to the king, Louis XV, she was one of the most powerful women in France and a major patron of the arts. She symbolized the increasing importance of women in French society, and popularized the growth of more feminine and intimate rooms with informal, spontaneous entertaining and social life. Little tables were placed everywhere, whether for cards, sewing, writing, or to hold teacups. Often painted by François Boucher, Mme. de Pompadour usually sits in a frothy arbor of roses and birds, the epitome of a rococo fantasy.

Rococo dismissed the straight lines of classicism and seriousness of religion and looked to the ephemeral beauty of nature. Popular motifs included rock and shell forms—rocaille—derived from grottoes popular in the sixteenth-century, asymmetrical cartouches (framed panels) of S- and C-scrolls enclosing the singeries and *chinoiseries* of Bérain, and flowers, leaves, icicles, and whirls. The elements, the seasons, and stories from *Aesop's Fables* were popular themes.

ENTIRE INTERIORS IN LOUIS XV STYLE

Like Mme. de Pompadour, rococo—called Louis XV-style at its peak in France—was witty, clever, and appealing to the senses. The dimensions and manageable size of the decorative arts were the best medium to express these organic curves. Architecture and sculpture could be softened to accommodate rococo detail or curves, but in the main needed more solidity and substance.

Rococo was best suited to interior design. Overall schemes included complementary designs for wall panels (boiseries), fireplaces, furniture, and ceilings. Boucher's fashionable pictures were one part of an overall scheme of interior decoration. He often painted his mythological and pastoral scenes of love to fit into the wooden panels of the walls in French drawing rooms. In France, rococo was essentially light, with the play of space another airy dimension, while in Germany and England it usually lost its winsome fragility.

ABOVE **In 1715, Peter the Great went to France and returned to Russia inspired. The Peterhof Palace, Russia, was built in the manner of Versailles, but the interior was decorated in the rococo style. Beautifully light and airy, the restless, sinuous, gilded curves appear to float and dance, a particularly apt setting for the ballroom.**

EUROPEAN TRANSLATIONS

German furniture sometimes had exuberant rococo detail grafted onto solid architectural pieces in a manner that French ébénistes and designers had never intended. In Venice, a bombé commode evolved, with a curious pot-bellied front. Silver and porcelain were more successful vehicles for the style. The development of papier-mâché also made it easier to reproduce gilded frames for mirrors, rather than carving wood.

In England the tendency was to tone rococo down, not up. Huguenot craftsmen from France, often, like silversmith Paul de Lamerie, second or third generation, made vessels in the "modern style," as rococo was known in

England. Sometimes the chased surface decoration recalled the auricular style of the seventeenth century, with its creases and ripples.

As in France, houses and rooms were becoming smaller—the terraced house came into being, supremely elegant in the crescents of Bath conceived by architect John Wood in the 1760s.

The fashion grew for a circuit of reception rooms, each with a different color scheme and style of decoration. Typically, guests came up the stairs, circulated from the music room, through reception rooms to the drawing room, then on through a dressing room and bedroom. The last room was a closet, filled with curios, before guests went back down the stairs.

For the first time the pictures hanging on the walls were not only portraits of ancestors. Light-hearted love scenes and country idylls in the style of Boucher also adorned the walls.

As wealthy people became more literate, they owned more books. The library became a standard room in homes, but this was a male preserve that was rarely, if ever, decorated in the flamboyant rococo style associated with feminine sensibilities.

FROWNING ON FRIVOLITY

The style did not find universal favor. France was in the grip of the Enlightenment, and this Age of Reason did not approve of rococo's whimsy. The levity of rococo had always met disapproval, from respected critics such as Denis Diderot in France and the Whigs in England. By the 1760s rococo designs had become so fanciful that they were unworkable in practice.

Change was inevitable, despite the continued preference of Louis XV and Mme. de Pompadour for rococo. Although the style continued in Germany and Austria, it never caught on in Britain or America.

The rococo plasterwork at Claydon House, Buckinghamshire, was greeted with the reaction: "Mr. Lightfoot's design for finishing the great Eating Room shock'd me so much and is so much the ridicule of all who have seen or heard of it … With regard to the Saloon and the Drawing Room, they are not so bad, and their absurdities might be easily remedied." Anti-French feeling added to the disapproval of rococo designs in England. But by the 1750s, even France herself was reacting against the style.

ABOVE **In 1765, rococo was still in vogue in Britain, although the style had passed its peak in France. This bed, with its domed top and** lavishly gilded cornice, **was designed by Matthias Lock, who played a large role in bringing rococo to England.**

LEFT **Rococo designs for furniture had an overall symmetry of form but asymmetry of decorative detail, as in the rocaille shellwork around the upholstery of this French sofa, 1735. The restless energy extends to the scrollwork of the arms and legs, which leads the eye back and forth from one curve to the next.**

Collector's Gallery

French rococo design evolved out of the grandeur of the Baroque. Leaving classical symmetry behind, it adopted a lively, informal, feminine style. Lines became sinuous, rather than architectural; ornament took its inspiration from twining branches, leaves, and flowers, often combined with the exoticism of the Far East. By the mid-eighteenth century most of Europe had adopted the rococo, often mixing it with existing styles or adapting it to national taste. At their best, French rococo styles showed a balance between form and decoration; elsewhere this balance was replaced by exaggeration.

Small Tables

This period witnessed the beginning of the proliferation of small tables designed for a multitude of purposes. They were often designed and made with as much care as larger, more obvious pieces, and followed the same trends in form and decoration. **1** The marble top of a night table was designed to be safe for the placement of a candlestick, and would not be damaged by spilled liquid. **2** The discreet cupboard below held the chamber pot. **3** Gently curving, long, slender legs supported the table.

For the bedroom or boudoir, the table de coiffeuse was essentially a dressing table. It was fitted with a mirror, **4** drawers for cosmetics and powder, **5** and sometimes with slides for writing and candlesticks.

ABOVE **A kingwood and tulipwood night table, Genoa, Italy,** *c.* **1755.**

LEFT **A tulipwood and floral marquetry table de coiffeuse, France,** *c.* **1755–60.**

Writing Tables and Bureaus

Bureaus and writing tables, matching the prevailing taste for curvilinear forms and ornament, were developed to supply the demand for writing furniture, particularly from women. While the French influence was pervasive in decoration, certain parts of Europe responded to aspects of English furniture, producing forms that were not part of the French repertoire. Bureau bookcase/cabinets were popular in Germany, northern Italy, and Portugal—all areas with strong trading connections with England. **1** Large writing tables, or bureau plat, had a leather inset; tables for ladies were more often decorated with cartouches of floral marquetry. **2** While also having a frieze drawer, small tables would often have a slide (lined with green silk velvet) that pulled out to increase the working surface.

The bureau-cabinet provided more privacy because papers could easily be locked away. **3** This example in walnut is profusely carved with floral swags, foliate scrolls, and cartouches. **4** The upper cabinet or fall-front bureau recalls English forms, **5** but the serpentine of the chest evolved from the French commode.

On this Genoese painted bureau-chest, **6** the decoration of scrolls, leaves, and flowers produces curvilinear frames within the rectangles of the drawers and doors. **7** A mixture of styles, sometimes referred to as "Baroquetto," is often evident on chests such as these, particularly in the cornices of cabinets that recall the plastic architecture of the Baroque.

ABOVE **A walnut bureau-cabinet, Germany, *c.* 1760.**

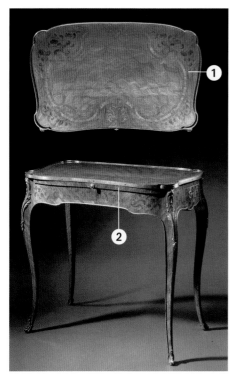

LEFT **A gilt-bronze, mounted, tulipwood, kingwood, parquetry and marquetry table à écrire, attributed to Roger Van Der Cruse, called Lacroix (RVLC), France, *c.* 1755.**

RIGHT **A painted bureau-chest, Genoa, Italy, *c.* 1760.**

Commodes

Commodes were more than merely practical pieces of furniture, taking over the display function of the cabinet on stand in reception rooms. All European countries were influenced by developments in France, where, although the three-drawer version survived, the typical commode had two drawers raised on tall, curved legs.
1 Marble tops, usually color coordinated, were always found on Parisian commodes. **2** The serpentine and bombé form is characteristic of the period, with the legs set at 45 degrees to the body. **3** Construction is often sans travers, without obvious structural division between the two drawers, so that the front surface can be treated as one decorative unit.
4 Gilt-bronze mounts are both practical and decorative; **5** they protect the edges of the veneer and create a framework for the surface decoration of Chinese or Japanese lacquer or floral marquetry.
In South Germany, northern Italy, and Venice, exaggerated outlines still owed something to the Baroque. **6** A top-heavy bombé form was characteristic, with three

BELOW **A figured walnut commode, North Italy, mid-eighteenth century.**

drawers, or two deep ones, and tall, cabriole feet. **7** While marble tops were not uncommon, simulated marble and veneered tops were frequently used. **8** Horizontal cross bands clearly identify the three-drawer structure within the serpentine and bombé form. **9** Despite the drawer structure, the front may be treated as a decorative unit, with matched figured walnut veneers, rather than the floral marquetry usually found in France. Various polychrome painted finishes were also popular. **10** Unlike France, other European countries had less of a tradition for casting gilt-bronze mounts in furniture. **11** Veneered bands may follow the curving outlines of the edges; alternatively carved or painted wood might simulate metal mounts.

LEFT **A gilt-bronze-mounted commode in amaranth, sycamore, and marquetry, François Rüberstück, France, *c.* 1765.**

Seat Furniture

With increasing informality and desire for comfort, seat furniture developed new forms. Usually of walnut or beech if gilded or painted, sets of chairs were made, including open armchairs and side chairs, as well as stools and sofas.

1 The cartouche-shaped backs of open armchairs were made with a gap between the back and seat.

2 Arms, now with upholstered pads, were set back from the front of the seat. **3** As chairs were still intended to be placed against the wall when not in use, the backs were left quite plain.

4 Shells, rockwork, or flowers and leaves were carved into the frame. Sofas were also evolving new shapes, particularly for the boudoir and drawing room. **5** New forms evolved, such as the bergère, where the upholstery filled the space between the arms and seat. Such chairs usually also had a separate squab cushion.

6 Seat furniture sometimes had a dual function.

The canapé à confident was formed of a conventional sofa with the addition of a bergère at either end; these were sometimes made to be detachable.

7 Upholstery, tightly stuffed with horsehair, was nailed to the seat frame. Loose, soft cushions, filled with a mass of feathers, were sometimes added for extra comfort. The chaise longue evolved from the seventeenth century day bed; **8** it had a bergère with "ears" and an extended seat. **9** When the end part of the "bed" was made as a detachable stool, it was called a duchesse brisée.

ABOVE **An open armchair (*fauteuil*), stamped Jean Gourdin, France, *c.* 1750.**

ABOVE **A giltwood bergère, by Claude I Sené, France, *c.* 1750.**

BELOW **A walnut chaise longue, France, *c.* 1750.**

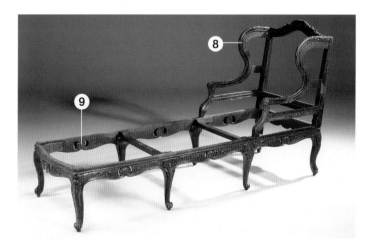

RIGHT **Giltwood canapé à confident, attributed to Nicolas Quininbert Foliot, France, *c.* 1755.**

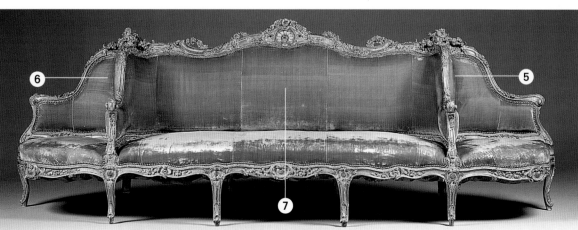

Glasses and Goblets

Three techniques affected glass design. First, Zwischengoldglas, which involved the insertion of engraved gold or silver leaf into a double-walled glass that was then sealed to prevent leaching. Second, stipple-engraving, which used a minimum number of lines filled by single dots. This produced a three-dimensional effect and shading. The third technique was wheel-engraving. ❶ Zwischengoldglas was used in combination with other decoration, such as cutting or painting with opaque enamels. ❷ The join just below the rim of the glass, where the inner wall ends, effectively protects the gold leaf from any liquid in the glass with a flange of glass. ❸ The third glass is later in date, and shows an elaboration of the technique to produce a medallion beaker; the whole glass is double-walled, then an oval has been cut out from the front and a medallion of gold leaf with colored lacquer inserted and carefully sealed.
An indicator that the Netherlands had been a major naval power throughout the seventeenth and eighteenth centuries, ❹ this glass is decorated with a ship. ❺ It carries an inscription around the rim blessing the ship.

ABOVE **A group of Bohemian Zwischengoldglaeser, from left to right: covered goblet, *c.* 1720; beaker enameled with St. Anthony of Padua, *c.* 1730; medallion beaker, *c.* 1790; beaker with silver leaf decoration, *c.* 1720.**

RIGHT **Stipple-engraved glass goblet, the Netherlands, *c.* 1745.**

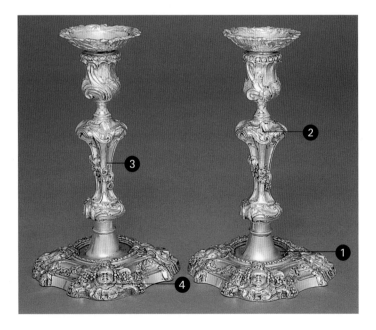

ABOVE **A pair of fine George II candlesticks, England, *c.* 1740.**

Candlesticks

Candlesticks made from the beginning of the eighteenth century tended to be plain, with a square or octagonal base and decorated only with an engraved coat of arms. The more architectural shapes, which had evolved by the 1730s, gave way to the asymmetrical forms, in the rococo style. The technique of casting candlesticks in solid silver was refined by the Huguenot silversmiths. ❶ The base was cast separately from the column that had been cast in two halves. Then all the parts were soldered together. ❷ Although expensive, casting was ideal for creating flamboyant rococo ornament, with asymmetrical, organic forms, intricate rockwork, and florid scrollwork. ❸ The baluster stem remained the popular candlestick form in the rococo period, although its original sleek silhouette grew more complex and the foot more intricately shaped. ❹ The rococo style affected decoration more than the shape of candlesticks, with profuse flowers, cartouches, and putti masks.

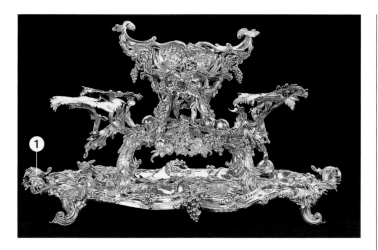

ABOVE **A George II silver gilt epergne and plateau by Edward Wakelin, London, 1755, supplied by George Wickes and Samuel Netherton.**

Epergnes

First used as extravagant centerpieces at the French court in the late seventeenth century, the epergne was both ornamental and practical. It was made up of a single stand with a central basket surrounded by four to six small baskets or pierced bowls. Epergnes became fashionable in England during the reign of George I. By the 1740s they were usually associated with the dessert course. ① The restraint of the early rococo period evolved into an exuberant, organic, asymmetrical style defined by elaborate casting and chasing, with all angles curved or curled.

Throughout the rococo period, the epergne became larger and more complex. ② However, imaginative construction techniques allowed some epergnes to be made smaller by removing the top layer of branches. ③ Rocaille, or rockwork, deriving from rock and shell forms, is one of the period's key decorative shapes.

BELOW **A fine George III epergne by Thomas Pitts, 1771.**

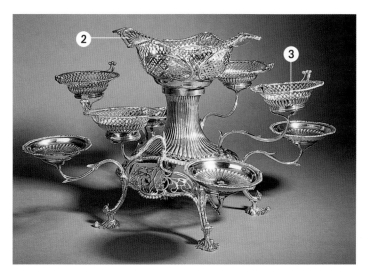

Two-handled Cups

The inventive rococo silversmiths saw form and ornament eventually integrated into a cohesive, sculptural whole. ① The basic symmetrical form of this cup and cover has been enlivened with a dazzling display of movement from the asymmetrical rococo ornament, ② with shells, fruit, foliage, and scrolls. ③ The bold handles are also asymmetric.

RIGHT **A George II two-handled cup by Paul de Lamerie, London, 1742.**

Tea Kettles

The silver tea kettle was made from the 1730s for boiling water at the table. As with teapots at this time, the standard kettle shape was spherical, ① decorated with a swing handle, and accompanied by an ornamented stand and burner. ② Early silver tea kettles tended to be of globular or bullet form with relatively restrained engraved decoration. By the mid-1730s the plain globular shape was being enlivened by chased and cast ornament featuring scrolls, flowers, foliage, and shells. ③ Silver tea kettles typically rest on a stand featuring three scrolling legs ④ with shell feet and a decorative apron cast with motifs. ⑤ The spout, with an S-shaped curve in the form of a swan's neck, dates from the rococo period.

RIGHT **A George II silver tea kettle and stand by William Cripps, London, 1748.**

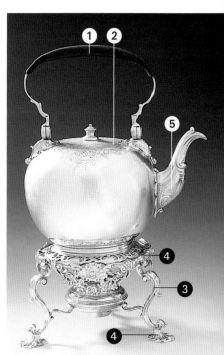

ABOVE **Bow cylindrical mug, England, *c.* 1750.**

Domestic Tableware

Blue and white decorated wares became extremely popular in Europe during the seventeenth and eighteenth centuries. Originating in China, the two-color tradition quickly spread to Europe where important factories sprang up in the Netherlands, closely followed by France and England. This type of china was reasonably cheap to produce, because it needed only one firing. It was therefore particularly suitable for the large-scale production required to meet the demand for everyday domestic wares from the expanding middle classes.

In England, the Bow factory was notable for its blue and white wares aimed at traditional buyers of oriental porcelain. The factory deliberately set out to compete with Chinese imports, styling itself "New Canton" and adapting Chinese designs. ❶ The often delightful and fanciful patterns, known as chinoiserie, came to dominate blue and white china decoration. This mug is unusual in its subject matter: a European lady and an Oriental child play in a fancifully designed gondola. ❷ The simple, cylindrical shape of the mug shows off the fine level of artistry used by the painter, who employed the characteristic bright blue hue found in early productions of the Bow factory.

Decorative Ware

In contrast with Bow, the Chelsea factory aimed to supply sumptuous decorative items to the wealthy. It therefore produced very little blue and white ware, concentrating on the popular rococo styles and the enameling for which Meissen was famous. Goat and bee jugs are among the earliest English porcelains and are believed to have been designed by Nicholas Sprimont, the Huguenot silversmith and an owner of the Chelsea factory. A number of these jugs have "Chelsea" and the date "1745" incised on the base. They are characteristic of the period, displaying to great effect the qualities of both the porcelain and the modeling. ❶ Typical of the early Chelsea porcelains is the fine naturalistic modeling and the delicacy and restraint of the design, which allowed large undecorated areas of the newly developed white porcelain paste to be a prominent feature. ❷ The base of the jug is molded in the shape of two

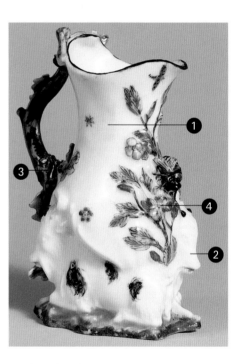

RIGHT **Chelsea goat and bee jug, England, *c.* 1745–1749.**

recumbent goats, one with its head toward the spout, the other facing the handle. They are reclining on a grassy mound separated by a tea plant curving up between them. ❸ Shaped as the branch of an oak, the handle loops out to join the bulbous body of the jug. The oak leaves, goats' tails and horns, and the descending bee were modeled separately and added to the jug before it was fired or glazed. ❹ After firing and glazing, the enamels were applied. The next firing caused them to sink into the glaze, giving an attractive soft appearance. As was typical of early Chelsea painting, the colors are brilliant, but limited to various shades of black, brown, yellow, blue, puce, and green.

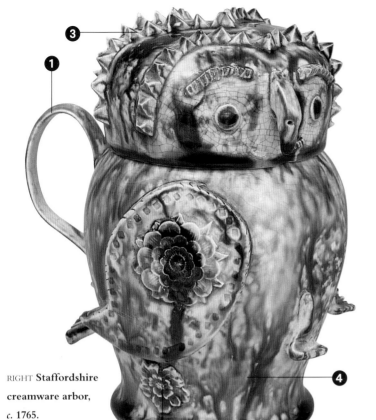

RIGHT **Staffordshire creamware arbor, c. 1765.**

Creamware Jugs

Creamware, a fine lead glazed pottery, was invented in the early eighteenth century and quickly became extremely popular throughout Europe. The economical, butter-colored ware lent itself to mass production. It was easy to decorate with painted or printed decoration, and also took relief molding well. ❶ Animal figures were popular for jars and other vessels. This jar is in the form of an owl with ear-shaped handles and removable lid. ❷ Intricate relief-molding shows leaves, flowers, and animal features. ❸ The owl's head forms the lid with a double row of triangular indentations shaping the face. The eyes and beak protrude, as do the rounded shapes above the eyes, which are indented to match the design of the rim. ❹ Strong colors are typical of Staffordshire creamware. The buttery background shows through the dark brown and green streaky glaze giving a realistic and lifelike appearance.

Ornamental Details

From the late seventeenth century, the influence of the Far East had resonated in the decorative arts of Europe. One of the most enduring decorative themes of the rococo period was chinoiserie. Motifs featuring Chinese figures and mandarins, pagodas, pavilions, birds, and lotus flowers were playfully used to great effect as ornament for many kinds of decorative objects.

RIGHT **An outstanding George II mirror.**

RIGHT **A chinoiserie ormolu clock from the period of Louis XV, by Jean-Joseph de Saint-Germain, 1748.**

❶ The rectangular, architectural form of mirror and picture frames of the seventeenth century gave way in the rococo period to a variety of new shapes, including ovals, cartouches, and scrolled and shaped frames. ❷ The abundance of lavish ornament decorating mirrors and clocks at this time frequently spilled over onto the mirror plate or clock face. Pagodas and ho-ho birds were among the elaborate chinoiserie fantasies popular in the rococo period. ❸ Playful chinoiserie ornament was typically combined with other popular favored motifs, including acanthus, flowers, foliage, rockwork, and C-scrolls.

Detail Directory

From the 1720s, the decorative rococo style grew increasingly more extravagant, exotic, and asymmetrical. With an emphasis on nature, the characteristic motifs of the rococo included imaginative combinations of foliage, abstract rocaille forms of shells and rocks, flowers, and splashing water. Chinoiseries, exotic oriental figures, playful monkeys, grotesques, masks, and pastoral imagery were framed by elaborately curving C- and S-scrolls and asymmetrical cartouches. By the 1740s, this lighthearted style had become fashionable in the decorative arts throughout much of Europe.

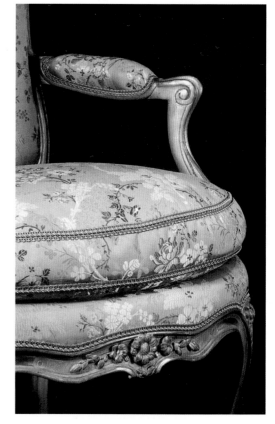

Carved giltwood armchair, England, c. 1750.

Commode decorated with chinoiserie lacquer panels, c. 1750.

Marquetry commode with gilt bronze mounts, France, c. 1745–49.

Furniture

The rococo taste for curvaceous, asymmetrical shapes found expression in the furniture made to accommodate fashionable new schemes of interior decoration. With an emphasis on small, intimate rooms designed for informal entertaining, small-scale furniture shapes featured delicate cabriole legs, serpentine curves for tabletops and chairbacks, and light, elegant ornament, preferably in light woods. The work of pioneering designer Juste-Aurele Meissonier consists entirely of harmoniously flowing scrolls, from which emerge foliage and the occasional cascading water motif.

Perhaps the most enduring success of the French rocaille style is the Louis XV armchair. Light and graceful, with long continuous curves avoiding sharp breaks, it poses a striking contrast to the static strength and architectural massiveness of the Louis XIV period.

Detail of carved and giltwood Louis XV armchair.

Louis XV porce-
lain ewer with gilt
bronze mounts,
c. 1745–49.

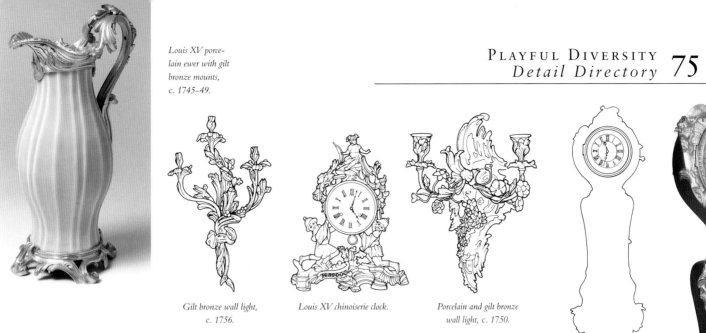

Gilt bronze wall light,
c. 1756.

Louis XV chinoiserie clock.

Porcelain and gilt bronze
wall light, c. 1750.

Gilt Bronze

The rococo movement made good use of gilt bronze. This highly adaptable material was fashioned in an imaginative array of decorative uses, including ornamental mounts for furniture, ceramics, and marble. Other objects, such as clocks and light fixtures, were made entirely of this lustrous material.

Longcase clock with gilt
bronze rococo ornament,
c. 1750.

Meissen porcelain figures from Commedia dell'Arte series, by J. J. Kaendler, c. 1738.

Ceramics

In ceramics, the rococo preference for light, pastel colors was attentively addressed at the celebrated factory at Sèvres, where the fashion for gilt-bronze embellishments was also acknowledged in the lavish gilding that enhanced an extraordinary array of fanciful tablewares and decorative objects. The highly animated sculptural designs of J. J. Kandler at the Meissen factory in Dresden, which embraced the lively, sinuous movement characteristic of the rococo style, were emulated at the numerous porcelain factories cropping up all over Europe at the time.

Detail of Chelsea porcelain plate with
botanical decoration, c. 1750.

Central ornament of porcelain plate.

Silver

Many talented silversmiths imbued their wares with the flamboyant sensibilities of the rococo, creating an unprecedented array of imaginative designs that reflected a highly original vision—a vision that responded to the organic forms found in nature coupled with a feminine, lighthearted spirit.

Outline of rococo tea kettle
and stand, 1736–37.

Draft of coffee pot design.

Outline of silver gilt chocolate pot,
1729.

Silver cake basket,
England, 1741.

Silver tea kettle and
stand, England, 1748.

Profile of soup
tureen and
stand,
mid-eighteenth
century.

The Chippendale Story

By the mid-eighteenth century, English fashion followers were split. The Whigs rooted for Palladianism; the Tories supported rococo. The size and unity of rococo appealed to the growing middle classes, backed by dissident Whigs such as Frederick, Prince of Wales. At the Bohemian center of England lay St. Martin's Lane in London, where painter William Hogarth founded an academy and French painter Gravelot taught students the rudiments of rococo ornament. Out of this melting pot came an English furniture maker who gave his name to a style that dominated America from the 1750s until the Revolution.

Thomas Chippendale (1718–1779) came to London from Yorkshire and by 1748 was established in St. Martin's Lane. By this time the naturalistic shapes of rococo were well known in England. While England had a largely male-dominated society, in France, women had control of aristocratic circles. The feminine, wispy rococo shells and rocks were limited to dressing rooms and bedrooms in England, not seen in every interior as in France. Cabinetmakers toned down sumptuous French design into something practical that suited the British. Mahogany, the favored wood, looked more masculine than the light woods popular in France.

BOOK OF DESIGNS

In 1754, Chippendale published *The Gentleman and Cabinet Maker's Director*, intended to advertise the range of household furniture produced by his firm. It was the first comprehensive book of furniture designs, and he was clever enough to aim it in his title at the patrons and the makers. The 161 plates covered bedposts to tea caddies to pier glasses, as well as chairs and tables.

Chippendale offered designs in what was described as Gothick, Chinese and Modern (rococo) taste. Parallel with rococo ran Gothick (spelled with a "k" at

ABOVE **The matching Chippendale chairs in the drawing room at Harewood House in Yorkshire, England, create an elegant impression. Their rococo arms are set back to leave room for ladies' billowing skirts.**

RIGHT **The Chinese room in the Spanish palace of Aranguez was richly decorated with painted plasterwork walls in the 1760s. Rococo still flourished in parts of Europe, and chinoiserie was popular in Europe and America.**

this time to distinguish it from its pre-Renaissance original form). Gothick had been enjoying a resurgence since the beginning of the century. It was a revival, based on ornament, not form. Designs showed pointed arches, tracery, and crockets adorning display cabinets and shelving. Chippendale occasionally combined Gothick with chinoiserie and rococo curves. The chinoiserie designs for chairs and cabinets gave rise to the term "Chinese Chippendale." Designs used angular forms and square sections with lattice and fretwork. Cabinets were topped with pagodas and bells, the whole japanned black and gold.

Chippendale published a second edition of his book in 1755, and a third, revised edition in 1762. In this, he dropped the Gothick and Chinese for more rococo designs. There is also a hint of classicisim, with the appearance of trophies-of-arms, putti, dolphins, strings of husks, herms, and pedestals. Chippendale did not invent the ornament; he offered designs to copy. Furniture designed in Chippendale style was not always made by his firm, and, since he never stamped furniture, authenticity can only be established by documents.

CHIPPENDALE CATCHES ON IN AMERICA

The continuing flow of immigrants introduced the Chippendale style to America. Freshly arrived craftsmen advertised themselves as "late of London" to appeal to the new colonial rich. Some English furniture was exported, but this was not popular among patriotic colonists. In 1765, a young man was advised how tactless it would be to arrive with a shipload of English furniture: "Household goods may be had here as cheap and as well made from English patterns … In the humor people are in here, a man is in danger of becoming invidiously distinguished, who buys anything in England which our tradesmen can furnish … "

The style was spread through circulating Chippendale's *Director* and other pattern books. By the 1770s, many cabinetmakers were working to Chippendale's designs. The furnishings satisfied the desire for gracious but intimate living among the prosperous inhabitants of America just as much as those of England. The style translated into the dining room as well as the bedroom and boudoir, giving a unity not just to a single interior but to the whole home.

By the late eighteenth century, people tended to scatter chairs and tables around the room for small groups. Guests no longer sat in a formal circle—instead they formed intimate twos and threes. Furniture that was light enough to be easily moved grew in popularity. At home, people relaxed more, no longer feeling they had to sit bolt upright, comfort taking precedence over formality.

BELOW **The pierced and interlaced splats on the chair backs are typical of Chippendale designs, while the drop-leaf table is Queen Anne— then, as now, rooms mixed furniture of different periods.**

To integrate the design of this late eighteenth-century Vermont interior, the dark cornice and skirting board complement the mahogany furniture, setting off the vividly painted walls.

RIGHT **While American interiors were dominated by Chippendale in the second half of the eighteenth century, exteriors were still influenced by Palladianism and classical ideals of proportion. Renaissance-inspired columns, porticoes, and pavilions graced houses in both New England and the southern colonies.**

AMERICAN SLANTS

Cabinetmaking families such as the Goddards and Townsends sometimes added typically American traits to Chippendale designs such as the block-front shape. Chair crests had ears, and vase-shaped splats were pierced and carved. They avoided the extreme elements of Gothick, *chinoiserie*, and rococo.

Philadelphia was the center of colonial wealth and ordered the most copies of the *Director*. Cabinetmakers, such as Randolph Benjamin (1750–1790) and William Savery (1721–1787), evolved their own Chippendale style. Sometimes known as Philadelphia Chippendale, typical details were bonnet or scrolled pediments (where the two sides form inward-pointing S-scrolls), augur flames (finials stylized into a flame-like spiral), cabriole legs, and rich carving.

Mahogany was the ideal wood to take intricate carving and fretwork. Its strength made it more popular in America, and its deep color made the gilding used in France seem unnecessary. As a final bonus, mahogany was impervious to insects—excellent for the warm, humid climate of towns like Charleston.

There were no formal guilds in America, as there were in England and on the Continent. But groups of cabinetmakers stuck to strict guidelines. They began marking and labeling furniture, which showed a growing pride in their work.

RIGHT **Wilton, in Richmond, Virginia was originally built in 1750–1753 for William Randolph III. It was heavily restored in the 1930s by the Colonial Dames, and still features many eighteenth-century elements.**

Collector's Gallery

While the rococo exerted a powerful influence, in England and America classicism would never be relinquished altogether. But engravings of rococo ornament were soon circulating in London, and the vocabulary of rocaille ornament, foliage, and asymmetry began to appear; gradually forms also became more sinuous. By the time Chippendale published the first comprehensive series of furniture designs, The Gentleman and Cabinet Maker's Director *in 1754, the French style had been blended with chinoiserie and a new version of Gothick. It was not long before such designs were being copied and interpreted in America, and applied to other areas of interior design.*

Chests and Commodes

Two forms of chest were popular in this period, one taking its starting point from the established English chest of drawers, the other from the French commode. The French commode table was displayed in the drawing room; the chest of drawers was more usually found in the bedroom as a dressing commode. Noticeably absent was the lavish use of gilt-bronze. **1** The finest dressing commodes were predominantly serpentine, with canted corners carved with rocaille, or Chinese or Gothick fretwork. **2** Commodes were usually fitted with a brushing slide, a sliding shelf below the top. **3** The top drawer might be fitted as a writing or toiletries table. **4** A popular adaptation of French models had two doors enclosing shelves. **5** These were usually decorated with lacquer or, particularly toward the end of the period, marquetry.

RIGHT **A mahogany serpentine dressing commode, England,** *c.* **1760.**

RIGHT **A gilt-bronze-mounted coromandel lacquer and black and gilt-japanned serpentine commode, attributed to Pierre Langlois, England,** *c.* **1765.**

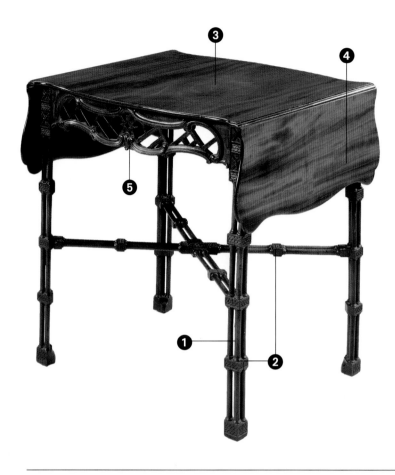

Tables

Tables continued to evolve for different purposes. As for all other furniture, mahogany was the favored wood, with an emphasis on carved decoration in the fashionable styles. Although tilt-top tripod tables continued to be popular, the four-legged table was perhaps the more practical choice. **1** One of the most important new forms of this period was the Pembroke table, for occasional use. It had four slender legs, in this example, **2** bound by pillared blocks and imbricated with dolphin's scales that recall the goddess Venus. **3** From about 1750 to 1770, the tops of Pembroke tables were generally rectangular or serpentine, in this instance, **4** two drop leaves are supported on hinged brackets. **5** The stretcher is a picturesque C-scroll with a lattice-waved frieze.

LEFT **A mahogany Pembroke table, possibly designed by John Hobcroft, England, *c*. 1760.**

Upholstered Furniture

Suites of upholstered furniture were required for reception rooms; such rooms were decorated with a bias towards the feminine, favoring rococo ornament and chinoiserie. In his *Director*, Chippendale stipulated that the proportions of chairs and sofas should be adjusted to the size of the room in which they were to be placed. **1** Although chairs in the French manner with a separately framed back were copied, a more popular form was a completely upholstered back and seat. **2** The broad, deep seat and squarer back are characteristically English, and the overall proportions are larger than most Continental equivalents. **3** Mahogany was the favored wood in England; gilded versions were not uncommon but were made in beech. **4** The upholstery, which has a flatter profile than on French chairs, would have been in tapestry, brocade, or cut velvet, often matching the wall coverings or drapes.

RIGHT **A mahogany open armchair, England, *c*. 1755.**

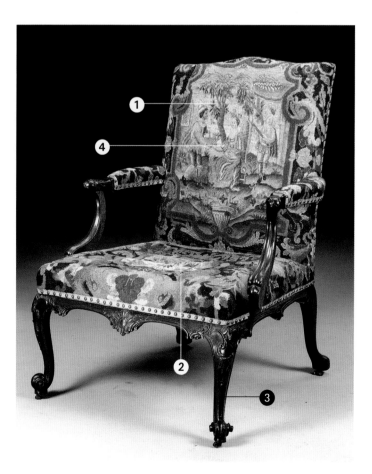

Chairs

The pierced-back chair is perhaps the most original contribution to furniture design in mid-eighteenth century England and America. Large numbers of published designs were then adapted by makers on both sides of the Atlantic. Usually made of mahogany, they reflected all the most popular styles and motifs of the day. **1** The most characteristic design has a pierced-interlaced splat, with sprays of leaves, flowers, and rocaille ornament. **2** While published designs favored scrolled feet, claw-and-ball feet were often used. **3** Bold fretted Chinese rails and pagoda-shaped crest rails are features of the taste for chinoiserie, which was associated with bedrooms and drawing rooms. **4** Gothick style was popular for dining rooms and libraries; it made picturesque use of pointed arches and quatrefoil shapes. **5** As with "Chinese" chairs, these usually had straight legs, sometimes with stretchers.

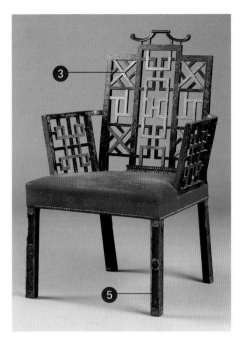

ABOVE **A black and gilt japanned open armchair, by William and John Linnell, England, *c.* 1755.**

LEFT **A mahogany Gothick armchair, by Gillows of Lancaster, England, *c.* 1765.**

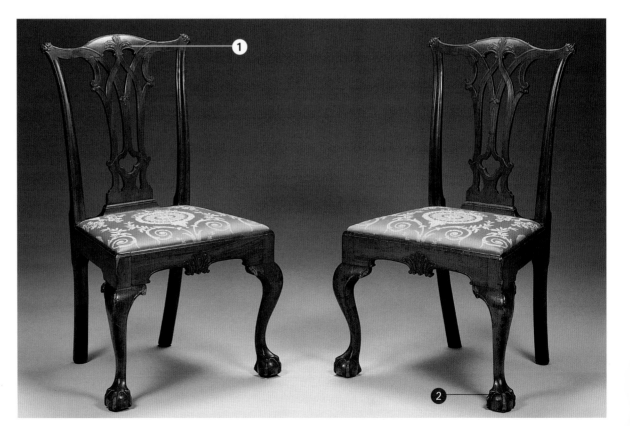

RIGHT **A pair of carved mahogany sidechairs, Philadelphia, *c.* 1770.**

Writing Furniture

After the rapid evolution of writing furniture in the early part of the eighteenth century, there was little radical development during the middle decades. Like bookcases, bureau bookcases and cabinets continued to follow an architectural form, relying for decoration on the application of fashionable ornament and fretwork. Becoming more popular was the library table, used both for writing and for viewing folios of prints and drawings. ❶ Pedestal tables often included a triumphal arch and a classical sense of form. ❷ They were made with solid panels of mahogany, figured veneers, and carved details. ❸ The top was often inset with leather, ❹ and pedestals had drawers or doors which flanked a recess. ❺ Decoration was on a small scale, including classical motifs, rocaille, or Gothick.

ABOVE **A George III mahogany library table, attributed to Thomas Chippendale, England, *c.* 1765.**

Bookcases and Cabinets

Furniture that could be used for displaying books or objects increased during this period. Breakfront bookcases became standard in libraries, which were generally decorated in a classical or Gothick style. Elsewhere, cabinets and hanging shelves were designed to display *objets d'art*. ❶ Rectilinear, pedimented bookcases and cabinets derived from classical architecture, ❷ but the ornamental detail often made reference to the fashionable "modern" styles of the day. ❸ Instead of mirrors, the doors of bookcases and cabinets were now glazed with clear glass, held together by a fine network of glazing bars often relating to Gothick or chinoiserie fretwork.

Very much in the rococo spirit, decorative hanging shelves came into their own. ❹ Chinese rails, ❺ pagodas, and ❻ ho-ho birds were familiar motifs, complementing displays of porcelain.

ABOVE **A mahogany breakfront bookcase, England, *c.* 1760.**

LEFT **A set of mahogany chinoiserie hanging shelves, England, *c.* 1755.**

Beds

Although losing their formal seventeenth-century function as status symbols, beds continued to be designed for display. They retained the four-poster structure with a canopy or tester, but by the middle decades they had taken on a much lighter character. **1** As a rule only the foot posts, and perhaps the bed rail, were exposed; **2** shaped like slender cluster columns springing from balusters carved with delicate acanthus leaves, they were supported on carved plinths, or sometimes paw feet. **3** Characteristic was the shaped, pierced cornice of C- and S-scrolls and stylized shells, often covered with textiles. **4** The underside of the tester was usually elaborately constructed with matching or contrasting textiles and abundant fringing, or braid detailing. **5** Red damask and moreen were the most popular textiles for bed hangings, and would have been coordinated with drapes, wall hangings, and chair coverings.

BELOW **A four-poster bed (new hangings), England,** *c.* **1760.**

ABOVE **A pair of George III giltwood mirrors, by Thomas Chippendale.**

Mirrors

As with furniture, Chippendale mirrors showed a wide vocabulary of motifs plundered from classical antiquity, **1** such as acanthus leaves, anthemion, palmettes, egg-and-dart patterns, and urns on pedestals. Classical ornament was applied over simple geometric forms. **2** Highly valued mirror plates, for example, were fitted with looking-glass frames styled as elegant ovals, **3** overlaid with delicate classical ornament such as festoons of fruit and foliage, laurel branches, ribbon bows, flowers, and scrolls.

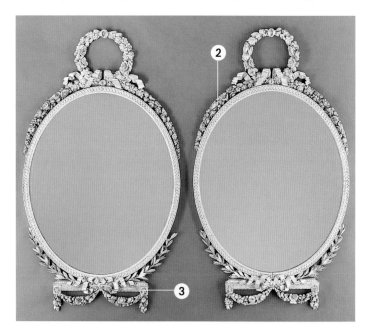

BELOW **A pair of George III silvered mirrors, by Thomas Chippendale.**

Wine Glasses

The art of enamel painting on glass in England reached a pinnacle in the 1760s and 1770s with the work of William and Mary Beilby of Newcastle-upon-Tyne. Much of their work was executed in opaque white enamel that has developed a characteristic bluish tinge over the years. The Beilbys also perfected polychrome enamels painting: much of their early work shows coats of arms for armorial commissions. Although the Jacobite cause was effectively lost by 1746, there also exists during this period glassware carrying engravings of Jacobite significance, although one should be sceptical about the significance of the Jacobite elements in such glasses: the iconography was deciphered in the
twentieth century, by which time the Jacobite cause was seen as a romantic ideal. Support for the Jacobites in the eighteenth century was more contentious, and it may be that glasses were decorated with no intention of this latter day interpretation. ❶ Opaque twist stems support a variety of bowl formations in the set below. ❷ The idiom of the

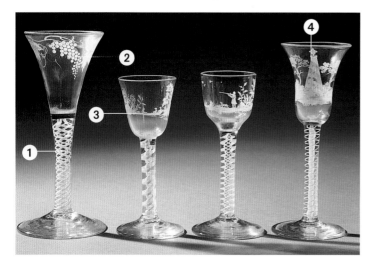

ABOVE **A group of wine glasses with enamel decoration by the Beilbys of Newcastle, England.**

decoration on these glasses is rococo, with asymmetrical bunches of grapes and landscapes featuring "exotic" elements: ❸ note the chinoiserie scene painted on one of them. ❹ The neoclassical obelisk painted on the glass on the far right is redolent of the emerging Adam style of rococo classicism. On this armorial glass, ❺ polychrome enamels were used with the more commonly seen white enamel decoration, giving a pleasing contrast. ❻ Note how the coat of arms has been given a rococo twist and has been placed in an escutcheon, delicately formed out of foliate

RIGHT **Opaque twist wine glass with colored enamel decoration, England,** *c.* **1765.**

C-scrolls. The crisply drawn wheel-engraving is a consistent feature of Jacobite glassware. ❼ The glasses themselves are typical light balusters of the period with drawn trumpet bowls ❽ raised on beaded knops and true baluster stems. ❾ Political symbolism enters the design of these engraved glasses: a daffodil flower on an oak branch attended by a butterfly and a bee; the oak represents Charles II, who had hidden in an oak tree to escape the Roundheads. Although the Pretenders were descended from his brother, the oak remained a symbol of the Stuart dynasty. The butterfly is symbolic of James Edward, the Old Pretender, and the bee of Charles Edward, the Young Pretender. The daffodil represents the hopes of the future

BELOW **A pair of light baluster wine glasses with disguised Jacobite engraving,** *c.* **1760.**

Detail Directory

In England, the Yorkshire designer and furniture maker Thomas Chippendale combined the flamboyant excesses of the French rococo with the more practical and reserved English taste. His designs embraced Gothick, Chinese, and rococo styles, offering ornament that could easily be adapted to suit personal preference. Pointed arches and tracery were combined with fanciful chinoiserie, and the fashionable rococo decoration of the day was reworked to suit the rather more conservative designs favored by the English.

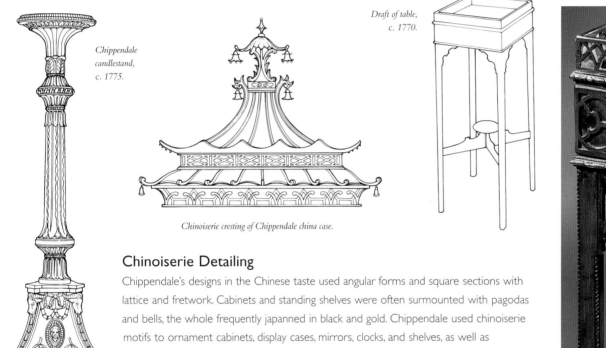

Chippendale candlestand, c. 1775.

Draft of table, c. 1770.

Chinoiserie cresting of Chippendale china case.

Chinoiserie Detailing

Chippendale's designs in the Chinese taste used angular forms and square sections with lattice and fretwork. Cabinets and standing shelves were often surmounted with pagodas and bells, the whole frequently japanned in black and gold. Chippendale used chinoiserie motifs to ornament cabinets, display cases, mirrors, clocks, and shelves, as well as designing furniture in this exotic style. However, authenticity was not always paramount in the adaptation of Chinese motifs, and this style was often mixed with French rococo and even Gothick elements.

Carved chinoiserie detailing.

Back of Chinese chair.

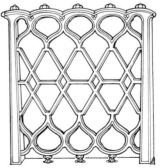

Gothick-style chairback.

Back of Chinese chair.

Designs from Chippendale's The Director.

Ladderback chairback, c. 1760.

Gothick detailing from library bookcase.

Gothick-style mahogany chairback, early nineteenth century.

Detail from canopy of Gothick bed, from Chippendale's The Director.

Chippendale "Gothick"

Chippendale plundered medieval motifs, which were recommended in his *Director* as ornament for display cabinets and bookcases, chairs, mirrors, and tables. Tracery, cusps, crockets, and pointed arcading were frequently combined with elements borrowed from chinoiserie and the rococo. Chippendale applied Gothick ornament to some of his most extravagant designs, including canopied beds, massive library bookcases, cabinets, and organ cases.

Chippendale chairback design.

Pierced splat chairback, c. 1750.

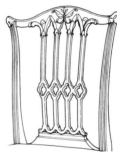

Chairback with lyre-shaped splat, c. 1770.

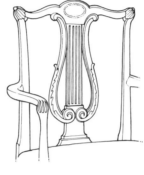

Gothick-style mahogany dining chairback, c. 1765–1775.

Design for chairback from The Director.

Chippendale carved chairback, America, c. 1765–75.

Pierced splat back of mahogany dining chair, c. 1760.

Chippendale "French chair," c. 1750.

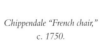

Detail of chimneypiece.

French-style Ornament

Chippendale considered the complex French rococo style to be the "most fashionable taste." Many of his designs, in what is referred to as the Director style, were borrowed freely from English and European pattern books. Extravagant and fanciful ornament was lavished on everything from commodes and candlestands to cabinets, chimney pieces, pier glasses, and chandeliers. Many of the designs verged on the impractical, nonetheless, they were highly influential, prompting countless furniture makers at this period to work in the Chippendale style. When the designs were put into practice, they were invariably simplified and more practical than the designs from which they were taken.

Detail of Chippendale slant front desk, America, c. 1760–80.

ABOVE **Painted side table, *c.* 1770.**

RIGHT **Louis XVI porcelain vase and ewers.**

Neoclassical Directions

During the third quarter of the eighteenth century, architects and designers began to turn to the ancient world as a source of inspiration. The formality and calculated proportions of Greek and Roman architecture were a reaction against the more excessive examples of rococo design. The ornament used was stylized and uncluttered with decoration concentrated on friezes and architectural motifs, such as swags and festoons.

Roman Style

In the second half of the eighteenth century, the Western love affair with the classical world resurfaced, partly as a reaction to rococo and partly because of archaeological digs at Herculaneum in 1738 and Pompeii in 1748. For the first time, tourists and students of classical architecture saw Roman ruins in their own right, not filtered through Renaissance eyes. The grand tour—a tour of continental Europe taken by young aristocrats—became highly fashionable in the eighteenth century, especially among the British well-to-do, although Americans such as Thomas Jefferson went, too.

A typical grand tour took three or four years. The journey led from France, over the Alps into Italy, down to Naples and back via Austria, Germany, and Holland. Greece and Spain were not favored on the itinerary. Travels were both arduous and exciting and gave tourists a taste of superior—as it was perceived—Italian civilization.

The grand tourists were usually aged only about eighteen when they set off, but they knew Latin and Roman history and began to take an interest in archaeological exactitude. English noblemen came back many with "souvenirs"—a portrait by Italian artist Batoni was *de rigueur*, as were a few Canalettos and sculpture busts. Holkham Hall in Norfolk, England, designed by William Kent, is full of tour treasures and Lord Burlington bagged 878 suitcases of trophy.

THE ADAM STYLE
Scottish architect Robert Adam (1728–1792) went on his grand tour in 1755. He studied in Rome, where he met Sir William Chambers, an English architect who was pro-Italian and anti-Greek, and Piranesi, a skilled Italian architect whose engravings became widely known.

LEFT **The chairs in the Etruscan Room at Osterley Park, England, were designed by Robert Adam to complement the walls and ceiling. Typically neoclassical, the furniture is constructed with straight lines and delicate proportions.**

From 1773 Robert Adam and his brother James published *The Works in Architecture*, which integrated building exteriors with interior design and objects. Their motifs—swags and festoons, guilloche, griffins, chimeras, vases and urns, husks and paterae, anthemia and palmettes—made use of what Adam had seen in Rome and Pompeii and, later, in Greek and Etruscan ruins.

Not everyone liked the brothers' work. Horace Walpole referred to it as "ginger bread and snippets of embroidery." But the Adam style breathed new life into the British arts, especially silver and furniture. Archaeological finds provided the forms for vases, coffee urns, and tureens, ornamented with bead molding and swags. In Philadelphia, silver appeared in this style from 1774 and spread.

Adam's neoclassicism had its own roots in Italy. Interiors were lighter, brighter, and more delicate. Colorful carpet design linked with painted and stuccoed ceilings. Pier tables stood below pier glasses, flanked by urns. Rooms and the furniture in them were broken into squares, rectangles, ovals, and circles, unified by the decorative scheme: Adam paid attention to detail, right down to escutcheons and drawer handles.

BACK TO THE DRAWING BOARD IN FRANCE

France had different reasons than England for returning to a classical mode. The rococo style had reached the ultimate in airy asymmetry, and renowned thinkers such as Henri Rousseau believed that the people were degenerate and needed to go back to basics. Devotee of the noble savage and the primitive hut, he believed rococo to be effete and that design should be rid of superfluity.

ABOVE **In the 1760s, Robert Adam transformed Osterley Park from a dilapidated Tudor mansion into a neoclassical villa. The green of the walls and ceiling was a favorite color at the time, particularly for an elegant dining room, lightened with decorative white plasterwork.**

For the first time, America took her lead from France rather than Britain. France sided with America in the Wars of Independence. As both countries neared 1789 and revolution, looking to the past grandeur of the Roman Republic as a model for the future appealed to visionaries such as Jefferson as much as to French neoclassical painters such as David.

The break with rococo was gradual. The so-called "transitional style" in French furniture had elements of rococo and neoclassicism and lasted until about 1780. Legs were still cabriole, but there was less gilding. Despite curves, chairs and tables had a vertical straight axis, each section compartmentalized with a reeded mount. The breakfront form, where the central panel protrudes, came in. The worktable so beloved of rococo continued, now with cubed or trellis marquetry.

THE PROMISE OF AMERICA

In America, neoclassicism coincided with the Federal style, chiming in with the new nation and its central government. Chippendale went out with the Revolution. Federal furnishings, grand in proportion but spare in ornament, became the icons of the new nation, shedding the colonial style that had existed from the 1650s until the end of the Revolution.

ABOVE **The gardens of Stourhead, designed by Henry Hoare II, were laid out between 1741 and 1780 in the best English landscape style. The miniature Pantheon was one of** several classical focal points dotted around the lake. The garden had two circuits of changing vistas, a short one for walking and a longer one for riding and driving.

RIGHT **The Shirley Plantation in Charles City, Virginia, displays the clean lines of the Federal style, a movement based on ideas gleaned from Thomas Sheraton's influential design book.**

American neoclassicism was eclectic, depending on individual architect's own preferences. The French influence was still strong in Philadelphia, while other towns, such as Baltimore, favored the English Adam style. B. H. Latrobe followed the spirit of C. N. Ledoux, a French architect. Thomas Jefferson had Palladian models in mind; he had seen them himself on his visit to Venice. Jefferson also used pattern books. The architect Charles Bulfinch (1763–1844) and the woodcarver Samuel McIntyre followed European models. McIntyre was also an architect: he designed the Pierce-Nichols house in Salem. His distinctive carving often features baskets of fruit.

BELOW **The amorous content of this print shows a love nest decorated in neoclassical style. The fireplace has an entablature based on classical temples, and straight lines replace rococo curves on the chair. X-frame stools, such as the one by the window, were based on ancient Roman designs.**

HEPPLEWHITE'S STYLE

McIntyre drew heavily on George Hepplewhite's *The Cabinet-Maker and Upholsterer's Guide* (1788). Bow-fronted furniture, chairs with oval and shield backs, and plain vertical fluting are typical. Hepplewhite's designs were severely neoclassical, without the delicate ornamentation of early Adam. However, Hepplewhite used certain Adam motifs such as urns and festoons—rosettes and Prince of Wales' feathers also appear.

Thomas Sheraton also published an influential book of designs, *The Cabinet Maker and Upholsterer's Drawing Book*, from 1791 to 1794, making each and every detail perfectly clear to craftsmen. His often rectilinear designs used Adam motifs as well as French-style brass galleries on tables and desks, and lyre shapes.

Sheraton gave general advice, too. For example, suites of furniture, as well as fixtures and fittings, used for the dining room "should be substantial and useful things, avoiding trifling ornaments and unnecessary decoration." Sheraton's book, highly popular in America, formed a basis for the early Federal style that be came so prevalent.

ABOVE **Georgian houses in America were heavily influenced by classical styles of architecture. A portico gave an imposing entrance and separated the central section and two flanks of the building with Palladian symmetry.**

Collector's Gallery

Neoclassical ideas extended beyond architecture to grace eighteenth-century interiors with sleek, elegant lines. From furniture such as Adam tables, dining chairs, and torchères, to tableware such as cut glassware and silver coffee urns, the influence of Roman style was felt.

Commodes

In Britain, in the second half of the eighteenth century, cabinet makers took to using satinwoods and timbers from a variety of exotic hardwoods found in the West Indies, much admired for their pale color and dramatic figuring, and considered ideal for the realization of furniture designs by the Adam brothers. Straightforward rococo elements, **1** such as the serpentine form, **2** the use of diaper pattern panels, **3** and ormolu mounts, remained in fashion throughout the period. **4** The pair of decorative incense burners is typical of ancient Roman domestic furnishings. In pieces such as this demi-lune, or "half-moon" marquetry commode, **5** ancient Roman style grotesqueries, such as the ram's skull and anthemion, stylized swags, flower heads, and ribbons relate to the interior decorations uncovered at Pompeii. **6** Square tapering legs, raised on block feet, are a strong architectural form that gained popularity around this time.

ABOVE **George III satinwood and inlaid serpentine commode.**

LEFT **An Adam period, neoclassical, demi-lune, satinwood and marquetry commode.**

Lacquered Furniture

Despite the fact that oriental lacquerwork was unknown to the ancient Roman world, eighteenth-century Europeans were fond of the art. This superb piece, supplied by Thomas Chippendale to Harewood House in 1773, shows how lacquer was used in conjunction with the latest classical styles.

ABOVE **A George III satinwood and marquetry card table, with giltwood frieze and legs.**

ABOVE **George III lacquer lady's secretary.**

❶ Although japanned furniture had been produced for many years in Europe, the finest quality lacquer was still obtained by the extravagant practice of cutting up imported screens. ❷ Gilt-metal mounts, redolent of the Adam style, were applied; ❸ note the flower heads around the top ❹ and the treatment of the vertical columns with a modified guilloche. ❺ Giltwood was used both for moldings and for feet, which were carved like elongated lotus flowers and raised on square blocks.

Giltwood Tables

The traditional manufacture of luxurious and formal furniture using carved wood finished with gold leaf continued through this period, with designs becoming more highly stylized, almost to the point of abstraction. ❶ The combination of giltwood tables with marble tops had been seen throughout the eighteenth century, but the use of giltwood with veneers and marquetry was a happy innovation of this period. ❷ Ornamentation of the giltwood is rigidly symmetrical: ❸ legs and columns supporting the tables are finely drawn to give these pieces an elegant lightness. ❹ Typical decorative features included square tapering legs ornamented with harebells and united by swags of floral carving, or fluted, turned tapering legs. ❺ Friezes were often composed with simple vertical fluting divided by rosettes and paterae.

BELOW **An Adam giltwood console table, c. 1770.**

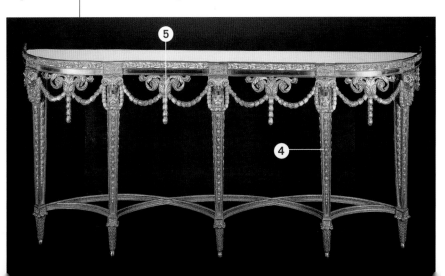

Lighting

Torchères were designed as tall stands on which candelabra could be placed to provide illumination; in effect, they were the precursors of modern electric floor lamps. **1** The coloring of these torchères is very characteristic. Adam-style furniture was generally conceived as part of an entire scheme of interior decoration; cream painted surfaces often formed a background with contrasting decorations in muted greens, terra-cotta, and, of course, gold. **2** The form, with a circular top raised on three elegantly drawn columns centered on a fourth turned and carved column, **3** and raised on a tricorn base, is inspired by ancient Roman models; note the similarity to the pair of incense burners on the doors of the serpentine commode on Page 94. **4** Rams' heads adorning the tops of the outer columns **5** are complemented by hooved feet at their bases.

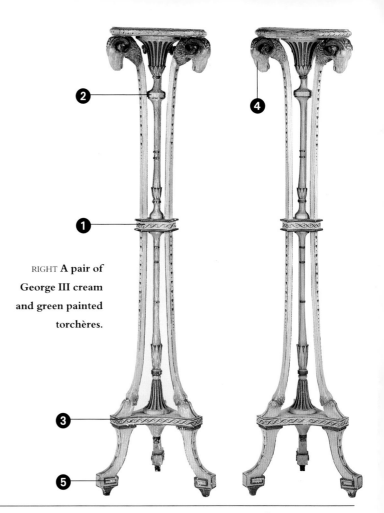

RIGHT **A pair of George III cream and green painted torchères.**

Dining Chairs

Dining chairs of this period remained generously proportioned: seats were wide and deep and backs relatively high. They were usually constructed from mahogany, in keeping with the dining tables they would have surrounded, and decorated with carving and piercing in accordance with the general decorative scheme of the dining room.

RIGHT **A George III mahogany dining chair.**

1 Pierced baluster back splats remained in fashion; note the introduction of classical elements, in particular the rosettes and floral swags and the rather subdued carving of the rest of the splat.
2 Oval-backed chairs made an appearance. Particularly popular in combination with serpentine seat fronts, the treatment of the backs of these chairs resembles the incense burners used as a marquetry device on the serpentine commode illustrated on page 94. **3** Front legs were either of square, tapering form, here seen with applied harebell molding, or a variety of turned tapering forms.

LEFT **A pair of Adam oval-back mahogany dining chairs.**

LEFT **A pair of Adam
period oval-back side
chairs, England.**

BELOW **A Louis XVI
giltwood armchair.**

Upholstered Seat Furniture

The Adam style crossed the English Channel and achieved
high popularity in France during the reign of Louis XVI,
where, much admired for its sumptuous elegance, it
was enthusiastically endorsed by leading cabinet
makers. **1** Both the English chairs and the French
example, with generously large seats and fully upholstered backs, combine luxury with comfort.
2 The seat rails are fully carved with classical
devices such as stylized laurel leaves, anthemia, and
palmettes. **3** The rails are united to other members such as arms, **4** and backs are decorated
with a variety of stylized acanthus leaf moldings.
5 At this period one of the best indications
whether a chair is of English or French origin is
the angle at which the back legs are set; note how
on the English chairs these legs are splayed at an
angle away from the back; **6** on French chairs,
the angle is closer to the vertical.

Wineglasses

In England, from about 1750, handsome glasses were produced with twisted stems. Initially these were formed by drawing out and twisting air bubbles into the base of the bowl. As time progressed these stems became more elaborate with the incorporation of opaque white glass threads, and by repeating the twisting process to enclose one

twist within another. Great care should be exercised when buying color-twist wineglasses. Condition is of primary importance. The golden rule of eighteenth-century English wineglasses is that the diameter of the foot should exceed that of the rim. Contemporary copies were made cheaply out of soda glass; these are easy to distinguish since the colored threads tend to be pale and watery. These glasses also lack the weight and luster of lead glass. Later copies also exist, but frequently these have uneven twists and poorly constructed stems. **1** English eighteenth-century wineglasses had simple bowls and plain conical feet for a distinctive and balanced sense of proportion. **2** Threads of opaque and translucent colored glass were used in combination with opaque white for contrast. Air-twists (as in the glass on the far left) are now a great rarity. **3** Color-twist within a molded bowl is more rare, **4** and the waisted bucket bowls on the glasses to either side are innovative for the time.

Glass-makers experienced great difficulty producing an opaque yellow glass of true color. **5** Of all the color-twist glasses, the rarest and most highly prized are the canary-twists, which sport yellow threads in their stems.

LEFT **Group of color-twist wineglasses, England,** *c.* **1770.**

Table Glass

A wide variety of urns were made for use at the table during the late eighteenth and early nineteenth centuries. They were used for serving preserves, honey, or sweetmeats. Occasionally, large rummers were supplied with covers, giving them a dual purpose. **1** Rummer feet were often molded and cut square; the famous "lemon-squeezer" foot is typical of the period. **2** The covers of the urns and of the large rummer display the current shapes—

concave-sided, domed, or bell-shaped. **3** Each cover is topped by a finial and cut to match the body of the vessel beneath it. **4** The distinctive shallow cutting is complemented by wide, open diamonds and slanting flutes. These features maximize the limpid appearance of the lead glass from which they are made.

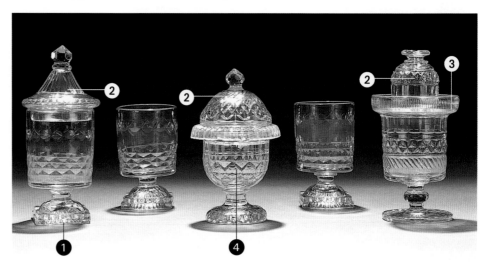

RIGHT **Group of cut table glass,** *c.* **1790–1810.**

Domestic Silver Wares

By the mid-eighteenth century, the classical tradition began to assert itself in silver in a deliberate rejection of the excesses of the rococo style. The influence of Roman antiquity was particularly strong, prompted by recent excavations at Pompeii and Herculaneum. **1** During this period, the architectural form of antique vases and urns was especially favored for a wide range of hollow silver vessels, including coffee pots, wine coolers, tea urns, tureens, and sauceboats. **2** As design motifs from classical antiquity

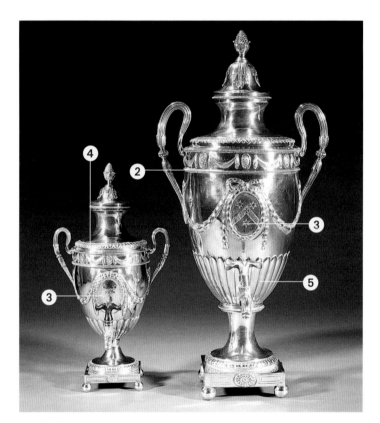

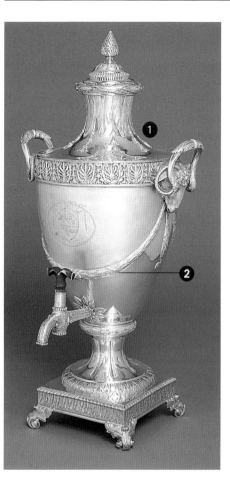

LEFT **A fine George II, two-handled vase-shaped urn by Andrew Fogelberg, England.**

LEFT **A George III silver tea urn and matching coffee urn with the maker's mark, "John Romer, London, 1777."**

became familiar through a growing number of archeological publications, the goldsmith's repertoire of ornament for decorating silver included festoons, palmettes, scrolling friezes, anthemia, acanthus leaves, rams' heads, and guilloche borders. **3** Among the ornaments popular for silver in the neoclassical period was the medallion, based on classical and Renaissance gems and cameos. It was frequently oval-shaped and bound by ribbon bows. **4** Silver tea urns were frequently modeled after the amphora shape from classical antiquity. **5** Fluting, long a popular decorative motif for silver, became more delicate and shallow. **6** At this time, gadrooning was often replaced by bands of silver beading around the rims of silver vessels such as these sauceboats.

LEFT **George III sauceboats by Charles Hougham, England.**

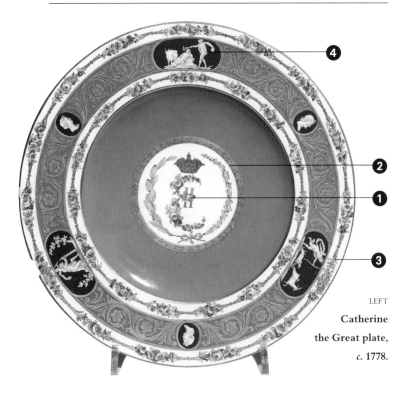

LEFT
**Catherine
the Great plate,**
c. **1778.**

Royal Tableware

The Vincennes factory moved to Sèvres in 1753 and began producing expensive porcelain in rich colors with lavish gilding. The factory was famous for its grand and elaborate dinner services, produced to order for royalty and nobility. The grandest and most expensive dinner service of all was produced for Catherine the Great, Empress of Russia. It consisted of 797 pieces divided into dinner, dessert, and tea and coffee wares for 60 places. ❶ In the center of the plate is a medallion of a crowned floral monogram: "E" for "Ekaterina," enclosed by bunches of laurel and myrtle tied up with ribbons. ❷ The medallion is separated from the rich, turquoise blue ground by gilt bands. ❸ Narrow bands of white reserves with flowers and gilt harebells decorate the rims and turquoise center rounds; ❹ between them is a band of turquoise, richly gilded with foliate scrolls and cameo motifs of mythological scenes on a reddish-brown ground inlaid into the surface of the porcelain.

Tea and Coffee Wares

The Berlin factory responded to a new demand for tea and coffee wares by producing finely painted services. ❶ Berlin ware is notable for its bright white background, center decorations (this one in monochrome red), ❷ and intricate gilding around the rims, spouts, and finials. ❸ Coffee pots are pear-shaped with domed lids; ❹ teapots, dome-shaped with a flower-petal finial. ❺ Cup and saucers are cylindrical with a shallow base and slightly flared rim. ❻ Retaining a touch of the exotic, the tray is hexagonal with protruding solid handles with indented rims.

BELOW **A Berlin ware solitaire,** *c.* **1775.**

ABOVE **Two Vienna plates, after Roman frescoes at Herculaneum,
late eighteenth century.**

Decorative Ware

After 1784, the Vienna factory produced mostly in the neoclassical style that had become popular in the wake of discoveries of Roman frescoes at Herculaneum in Italy in the 1780s. ❶ Typical of this factory is the lavish gilding surrounding the central picture. ❷ Delicate patterns alternate with a concentric band of gilding to frame the painting. ❸ Gilded rims are usually separated by bands of color—black, puce, yellow, and green are typical of the neoclassical period. ❹ Cupid was a popular subject, shown standing on a plinth driving a chariot pulled by two animals. ❺ Finely painted detail can be seen on the faces of the figures and the snail's horns.

Piranesi-style Ornament

The engravings of Giovanni Piranesi were highly influential for disseminating the decorative motifs associated with the grandeur of ancient Rome. Artists and designers throughout Europe copied Roman emblems, using them as decorative ornament and blending ancient themes to create a distinctive style of austere splendor. **1** The mythical griffin—an animal with the head, wings, and claws of an eagle and the body of a lion—was a popular motif from antiquity. **2** The beast's traditional link with the god Apollo made it the perfect vehicle for sun- and fire-related themes, used frequently at this period to support torcheres, candelabra, perfume burners, and candlesticks, such as this Italian bronze piece. **3** Pedestals with urns featured prominently

in Piranesi's Roman etchings and engravings. **4** Modeled on Roman altars, urns were a popular motif in the highly ornamental designs of Robert Adam for all kinds of objects, including clocks, stools, and ice cupboards.

LEFT **A white marble and ormolu mantel clock by Matthew Boulton, *c*. 1776–77.**

RIGHT **One of a pair of Italian ormolu and patinated bronze candlesticks, attributed to Giuseppe Valadier, late eighteenth/early nineteenth century.**

ABOVE **Antico rosso Vienna vases, late eighteenth century.**

Vases

Discoveries at the buried city of Pompeii, Italy, fueled the fashion for ancient Roman designs. **1** In typical Roman style, the vases have a tubular shape, with handles set within the circumference of the main body, giving the appearance of unity and completeness. **2** The ground color is the red-brown monochrome favored by the Vienna factory. **3** This is offset by detail decoration, which is highlighted by combining white and black paint with gilding. **4** The figures are simple representations, but their flowing clothes, jewelry, and hair decorations give them a sense of movement. This is reinforced by the lively poses they strike as they dance around the bodies of the vessels.

Detail Directory

The archaeological discoveries at Pompeii and Herculaneum led to a renewed appreciation of the classical tradition. In France, a fevered reaction against the frivolous excesses of the rococo encouraged the rise of neoclassicism in the decorative arts. Architects adopted a style that leaned heavily upon distinctive classical designs, while the engravings of Piranesi disseminated this new taste for the antique. The Scottish architects, Robert and James Adam, concentrated on the shapes and motifs drawn from antique artifacts to cultivate their highly original style. From classical decorative motifs, they borrowed festoons, vases, urns, tripods, ribbonwork, rosettes,

Silver and Ceramics

Archaeological discoveries of marble and bronze provided the inspiration for handsome domestic objects. Vases, coffee urns, and soup tureens in antique shapes were decorated with beaded moldings, delicate festoons, and human figures scantily dressed in Roman attire. The wide range of motifs derived from classical antiquity include architectural ornament drawn from moldings, column capitals and entablatures, and decorative designs such as palmettes, anthemia, key patterns, and scrolling foliage.

Silver gilt coffee pot, by Paul Storr, 1797.

Design for Tèrm figures decorating plate warmer, by James "Athenian" Stuart, 1757.

Ormolu urn with bronze mounts, c. 1780.

Sèvres vase mounted with gilt bronze heads, c. 1781.

The Portland vase, made of cameo glass, late first century B.C., and imitated by Josiah Wedgewood.

Egg form lidded Sèvres vase, c. 1769.

Sèvres porcelain vase, 1781.

Furniture

Furniture designers took motifs and shapes from Roman architecture, including Vitruvian scrolls, fluting, columns, and palmettes. These were particularly suited to chairs and cabinets, where vertical elements could be exaggerated and embellished. Upholstery textiles were also designed in the Roman style, and became more and more stylized as the neoclassical revival moved into the nineteenth century. There was a natural crossover between the lighter details of rococo and the more fashionable features of Roman neoclassicism.

Detail of canopy bed.

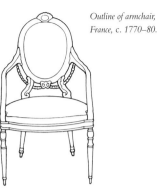

Outline of armchair, France, c. 1770–80.

Outline of giltwood armchair.

Giltwood armchair.

Detail of oval-shaped armchair back, France, c. 1770-80.

Chippendale sofa, c. 1765–70.

Detail of Adam design for sideboard ornament, 1762.

Detail of ceiling, designed by Robert Adam, 1762.

Paneling detail, by Robert Adam, 1760.

Panel ornament, designed by Robert Adam for Kedleston, 1760.

Design for girandole, by Robert Adam, 1767.

Surface Decoration

Roman representations of the human form gave designers a new approach to decoration. Men and women were portrayed with a new fluidity on ceramics, painted walls and ceilings, urns, and vases. Scenes from Roman mythology proved inspiring subjects, with the costume displaying the intricacies of flowing drapery, contrasting with smooth and volumetric anatomy.

Greek Style

Neoclassicism has a Greek as well as a Roman strand. It unraveled as Europeans and Americans ventured to Athens and other parts of Greece and saw Greek temples at first hand. In architecture, the Greek revival was expressed in purity of form. The style traveled slowly from England and France to America, and really made its mark only in the 1820s. The Bank of Pennsylvania in Philadelphia (1798) by B. H. Latrobe was the first building in America to use a classical Greek Order, the Ionic. In furniture and crafts, Grecian elements at first mingled with the Adam style before a stricter antiquarian approach prevailed.

ABOVE **The fireplace of Montpelier House, Maine, displays several popular classical Greek motifs, including swags, a vase, lyres, and white-painted columns** **supporting the frieze, giving a classical Hellenic geometric appearance.**

The phrase *goût Greque* (Greek taste) was coined by the French in the 1760s in an early wave of neoclassicism. It owed more to a Louis XIV revival than to Greek models. Boulle marquetry, *pietre dure* (hard or semi-precious stones worked onto decorative objects and tabletops) and figurative bronze mounts came back into fashion. *Goût Greque* was characterized by a brief surge of heavy furniture, dominantly decorated with urns, weighty festoons, Greek keys, and Vitruvian scroll patterns, designed for Lalive de Jully by Le Lorrain and others in 1756.

Lighter neoclassical forms superseded this singular form, but the Greek element remained as a theme alongside the Roman. By the time Louis XVI took the throne in 1774, the ornament of Greek temples, including palmettes, anthemia, and bucrania, was all the rage, even though the form of Greek furniture was not yet copied.

DIRECTOIRE STYLE IN FRANCE

French furniture-making and crafts came to a halt during the Revolution but picked up again in the 1790s. In the aftermath of the civil turmoil, an austere and simplified version of neoclassicism came into fashion, reaching its peak during the period of the Directoire, from 1795 to 1799. Without the money or inclination for costly materials and gold ornament, furniture from the period by

top-notch makers such as Jacob has little gilt enrichment and little or no inlay.

Republican symbols such as the cap of liberty appeared on wallpaper, fabrics, faience, and furniture. The Gobelins tapestry factory, Savonnerie carpets, and Sèvres porcelain all went back into production during the Directoire.

CLASSICAL GROUND OPENS UP

As the eighteenth century wore on, Greece became more accessible to the intrepid grand tourist. In London in 1732, gentlemen who had been on the grand tour founded the Society of Dilettanti (a word without pejorative overtones at that time). Members could at first propose only names of those they had met in Italy. In 1747, Avignon was admitted as a meeting ground and, in 1764, Greece. The toast of the Society was "to Grecian Taste and Roman Spirit," as Greek models gained acceptance among the group.

Members were artists and patrons and also sponsored the publication of books on classical architecture and antiques, providing the basis for neoclassical ornament. In 1762, architects James Stuart and Nicholas Revett published *The Antiquities of Athens*. This was the start of a steady flow of archaeologically accurate publications.

ABOVE **Sir John Soane's house in London, now a museum, displays a wealth of neoclassical detail. The architect collected antiquities and works of art.**

BELOW **The Greek influence can be seen in the style of the fireplace, with grouped columns to either side, in the parlor of the Nickels-Sortwell house, Maine.**

OPPOSITE PAGE **The arch
in the parlor of the
Tracy-Prince house at
Newbury port is
decorated in the newly
revived, neoclassical
Greek key design. The
Hellenic theme is
continued in the style of
the fireplace, with lyre
decoration and columns
to either side.**

BELOW **Neoclassical
styling is the most
prominent feature of
this Fredericksburg
drawing room. Note the
attention to detail in** **the fireplace frieze,in
the lozenge carving
above it and in the
cornicing around the
room.**

There was also a further stream of pattern books. Sheraton published his second, *The Cabinet Dictionary*, in 1803. It included elements taken from the Louis XVI style of French neoclassicism, such as colonnettes, feet like spinning tops, fluting, and ribbon borders. But there are also ornaments of the incipient Regency style: large scrolls and volutes, terminals in animal form such as aegricanes (ram or goat heads), dolphins, claw and paw feet, and lion masks.

THOMAS HOPE

Thomas Hope, a collector and patron of the arts, was a member of the Society of Dilettanti. In 1807 he published *Household Furniture and Interior Decoration*, which showed the classical rooms he had created at his homes in London and Surrey. Meticulously researched and reproduced furniture set the scene for his collections of ancient Greek and Roman objects. Like Adam, he believed in integrating furniture and interior architecture. But Hope was concerned with authenticity and never muddled his styles.

Hope did not intend his work to be a blueprint for people to copy, as this would be at two removes from the original. He wanted to convey the spirit of the antique. But a year after the publication of Hope's book, George Smith published *A Collection of Designs for Household Furniture and Interior Decoration*, which contained workable designs taken from Hope's ideas. This spread Hope's influence far and wide.

THE GREEK REVIVAL IN AMERICA

North Americans took to Greek architecture early in the nineteenth century. The Greek War of Independence from the Turks struck a chord with the American Revolution, adding zeal to the contemporary interest in classical architecture. The golden age of Greece was ideal for America.

The model for Greek revival architecture was the Greek temple, with its series of columns supporting a horizontal top, the entablature, and a triangular pediment at the top. On a Greek rectangular temple, the short sides have the pediment. This translated into the gabled front of the American home. The columns could be plain Doric with a fluted shaft; Ionic with an inverted double scroll capital (top); or Corinthian, with a capital formed of acanthus leaves. Columns could be giant Orders going up two stories at the front of the house, or normal size down the side or, most often, indicated by flat pilasters at the corners. The doorway was usually to one side, flanked by columns or pilasters with an entablature above. Houses were made of brick and stone. Any wood used was often covered with plaster and scored to look like stone. Detached city houses and farms in the Greek style are still widespread today.

Collector's Gallery

The taste for Greek-style domestic furniture and wares, developed along lines observed in Ionic ruins, at first merged with previous neoclassical styles. Eventually, purist trends led to the simple colors and bold shapes of Wedgwood jasperware and classic Waterford cut-glass crystal. It also gave birth to startling zoomorphic chairs, embellished with animal faces and paws, and bureau cabinets with painted iconic panels.

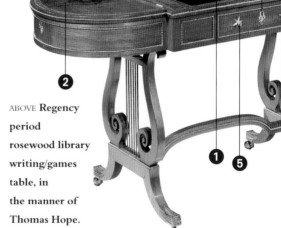

ABOVE **Regency period rosewood library writing/games table, in the manner of Thomas Hope.**

Gueridons

Gueridons, small circular tables designed to support candelabra, illustrate the understated and austere style current in France during the 1790s, the decade following the Revolution. Marquetry and other forms of decoration redolent of the wasteful luxury of the *ancien régime* were at odds with the political climate and disappeared from French furniture. **1** Unadorned mahogany was the preferred medium, but note how carefully the veneers and the timber have been selected for the beauty of their grain. **2** The top was often embellished with a border of subtle giltwood. **3** Ormolu mounts were pared down to a stark and striking simplicity, **4** and fillets inlaid into the carcass gave a strong vertical emphasis to the designs. **5** Forms were severely architectural and outlines composed of simple, unbroken lines.

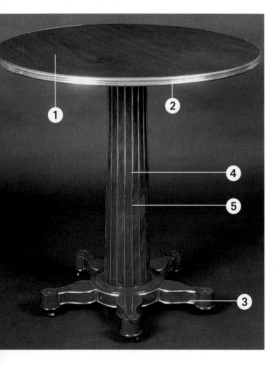

ABOVE **Pedestal table,** *c.* **1800.**

Gaming Tables

The tendency to informality continued during the early nineteenth century. Rosewoods imported from the Caribbean and the Atlantic coast of South America were the most highly prized medium for the realization of Regency furniture designs in Britain, as with this gaming table. Suitable for either a library or a drawing room, it combines two functions. **1** The central panel of the top slides out to reveal a backgammon board in the well, and can be reversed to reveal a plain leather writing surface. **2** The semicircular ends form two compartments suitable for storing gaming pieces or writing materials, enclosed by hinged flaps. **3** Trestle-end supports, shaped like classical lyres, are raised on splayed legs and united by arched stretchers. Distinctive and high quality brass and ormolu mounts were a hallmark of the Thomas Hope style; note the treatment of **4** the keyholes, **5** the star-shaped back plates to the handles, and **6** the castor caps with acanthus molding.

RIGHT **Suite of six mahogany armchairs, attributed to the Jacob brothers,** *c.* **1805.**

BELOW **Ebonized and gilt armchair in the manner of Thomas Hope, England,** *c.* **1810.**

Zoomorphic Armchairs

One of the most distinctive forms of French Empire furniture is that of the library armchair, its arms carved with lions' heads. This conceit, originally designed by the Jacob brothers, attained great popularity in Britain through the designs of Thomas Hope. ❶ The French originals were carved from mahogany. ❷ Typically, such chairs had tall backs and were raised on inwardly curving legs. English examples were more conspicuously extravagant, frequently made from exotic timbers or, as here, ❸ making extensive use of gilded decoration. ❹ Chairbacks were lower and panels of caning appeared both in the backs and forming the seats. ❺ Features of the style developed by Thomas Hope include the highly idiosyncratic carving of lions' heads (and other beasts), ❻ the boldly placed anthemion molding on the lions' chests, ❼ the dramatically hairy paw feet, and ❽ the lotus flower moldings visible on the rail in the chairback.

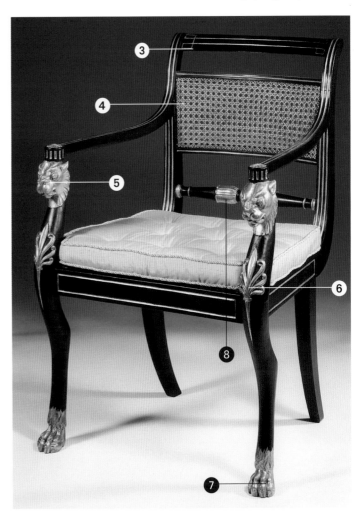

Dining Chairs

A striking change in fashion altered the appearance of
dining chairs in the early nineteenth century. Influenced
by the klismos chair of classical Greece, which had a
deep curving top rail held by a single central support
above the seat, the intricately carved and pierced vertical
splats to the chairbacks were replaced by emphatic top
rails, giving a strong horizontal emphasis to the design
of Regency dining chairs. **1** The proportions of dining
chairs changed, with seats
becoming smaller and narrower
and backs lower. **2** Front legs
were no longer square but
turned or shaped like sabers. In
Britain, stretchers between the legs
disappeared altogether.
3 Chairbacks were decorated with classical
motifs,
4 and reeded back
supports imitated
columns found in
classical Greek archi-
tecture.
Newly liberated
America was attempt-

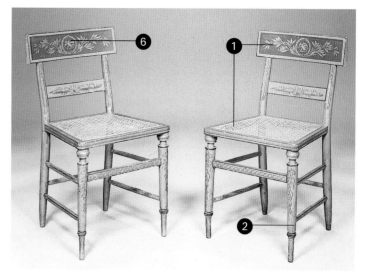

ABOVE **A pair of late Federal side chairs, attributed
to Hugh and John Findlay, Baltimore, *c*. 1815.**

LEFT **A Regency mahogany side chair,
England, *c*. 1815.**

ing to build a society modeled on the Athenian republic, **5**
and the eagle was adopted as its national symbol. **6** Costly
materials and extravagant decorative techniques were
eschewed, with classical details simply painted onto surfaces—on these chairs, red and yellow painted onto a yellow
ground.

Commodes

Outside Britain, the interpretation of the Greek style was
somewhat looser. In Italy the finest cabinet maker of the
period was Giuseppe Maggiolini, who is principally
renowned for his distinctive use of marquetry in the
classical idiom. **1** Fruitwoods and locally grown walnut
predominated; expensive exotic veneers such as kingwood
and tulipwood were used sparingly but to great dramatic
effect. **2** As with much Italian furniture of this period,
shapes and forms are decidedly conservative and
construction methods poor. Designers concentrated their
efforts on the decorative details of the surface. **3** Baroque-
style brassware sits rather incongruously next to a wealth of
classical ornamentation; **4** liberal use is made of palmettes
(in the uppermost drawer), stylized lotus flowers, and
general grotesqueries.

ABOVE **Walnut and marquetry commode, in
the manner of Giuseppe Maggiolini, Italy,
early nineteenth century.**

Secretaire Cabinets

Cabinet makers in northern Europe absorbed and adapted the Empire style to produce high quality, if somewhat heavy, pieces with an emphatically architectural style. **1** Marquetry designs using locally grown veneers were imposed on expensive imported mahogany carcasses. **2** Ormolu and brass mounts, such as the Corinthian capitals to the columns on the upper parts and the lion's head handles, are finely and crisply molded; **3** note the use of the Greek key pattern to the gallery atop the German cabinet.

On this Swedish secretaire, **4** the painted panels depicting classical scenes—delicately executed in muted colors—were influenced by the work of the decorator Angelica Kauffmann.

ABOVE **A mahogany and marquetry bureau cabinet, Germany, *c.* 1810.**

LEFT **Empire period mahogany secretaire cabinet, Sweden, *c.* 1810.**

Decanters

The Irish glass-making industry was transformed by the arrival in the second half of the eighteenth century of glass makers from England, fleeing the infamous glass excise act of 1745. Glass factories sprang up all over Ireland. Some proudly marked their product by the use of molds in which the factory name was imprinted. ❶ Distinct styles were developed by the various factories. Four of the decanters here are in the style of the Cork Glass Company, ❷ and the fifth is in the style of the Penrose Waterford factory. ❸ The Cork decanters are all club-shaped with minor variations and rather modest pouring lips. ❹ The Waterford example has a more generously rounded body and the pouring lip is noticeably wider. ❺ Cork decanters were frequently decorated with vesica (eye-shaped ovals) patterns, either cut or engraved around the center of the bottle. ❻ Typical of the Waterford style are the swags infilled with fine diamonds and interspersed with inverted fans. ❼ The two decanters lacking stoppers bear the imprinted factory marks of the "Cork Glass Company." The others can be attributed on account of their form and decoration.

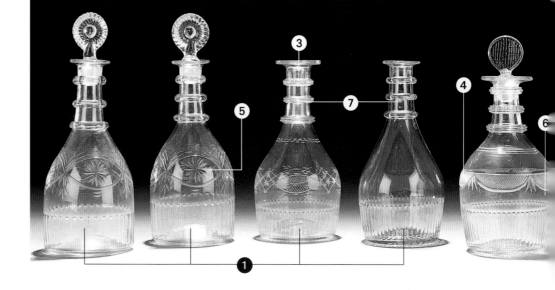

RIGHT **Group of George III period molded glass decanters, Ireland, left to right: pair of decanters, probably Cork,** *c.* **1810; club-shaped decanter imprinted "Cork Glass Company,"** *c.* **1790; plain club-shaped decanter imprinted "Cork Glass Company,"** *c.* **1790; cut and molded decanter, probably Penrose Waterford,** *c.* **1790.**

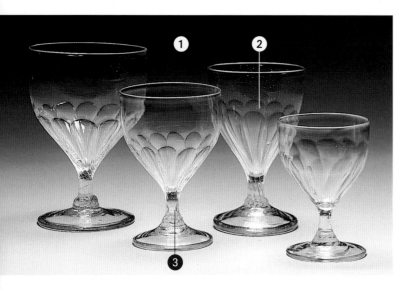

ABOVE **A group of molded glass rummers, England,** *c.* **1800.**

Rummers

The English rummer, a general all-purpose drinking glass, was developed in the second half of the eighteenth century and made in vast quantities in many shapes and sizes. Used for both formal and informal purposes, rummers could be decorated with sophistication, remain plain, or be anything between these extremes. The term rummer is a derivation of the German *roemer*, and has no connection with rum; indeed, the tipple of choice would have been gin. ❶ The glasses illustrated date to about 1800 and are redolent of the classical elegant shape so much in vogue at that time. ❷ The simple decoration, with wide molded flutes, emphasize and complement the limpid quality of the glass. ❸ Rather unusually, these glasses are made in two pieces: the stem is formed by pulling out the base of the bowl, therefore the molding continues visibly into the stem.

LEFT **A Regency period waterfall chandelier, England,** *c.* **1830.**

Glass Chandeliers

By the early nineteenth century, cut-glass chandeliers were highly prized for the refractive qualities of the highly polished glass. The form of the waterfall chandelier was developed, giving a dramatic effect to an elegant and simply shaped body with cascades of richly cut and carefully polished glass drops. ❶ The structure of such chandeliers is formed by a series of gilt-metal hoops, known as coronas, linked by gilt-metal chains. ❷ Typically, the uppermost corona is prominently decorated, in this example with a scrolling, stylized anthemion motif. ❸ Waterfall effects are achieved with swags of cut-glass button drops linking the top of the chandelier to the candle arms, and by the forest of icicle drops suspended from the concentric coronas at its base. ❹ The cutting of the nozzles, drip-pans, and the terminal orb with plain diamonds and prismatic steps are typical features for the period.

Silver Cups and Covers

The Greek genre in silver saw bold profiles, frequently enhanced by cast sculptural ornament derived from classical antiquity. During the Regency period in England, silver become ever more elaborate in keeping with the extravagant taste of the fashion-conscious Prince of Wales. **1** The simple shapes of silver items based on antique prototypes contrast with an increasing density of ornament at this time. **2** Sturdy cast sculptural decoration was frequently used for handles, supports, and finials, as with this racing cup. **3** The favored style for silver teapots was a squat, boat-shaped form that resembled a classical oil lamp. **4** Some examples contained bold fluting around the body of the pot.

RIGHT **A fine George III two-handled cup and cover (The Doncaster Race Cup), by Paul Storr, 1798.**

BELOW **Two Regency teapots by Paul Storr, England, 1813.**

Domestic Tableware

Although porcelain was extremely popular, especially among the wealthy, it did not supplant the cheaper earthenware. In the 1770s, Josiah Wedgwood invented jasperware, a dense, fine stoneware that was extremely versatile and could be turned on a lathe (engine-turned) and polished on a lapidary (gemstone) wheel. Later, he developed the "dip"

technique, applying a thin wash of one color over the ground of another, to save on the cost of cobalt coloring. ❶ The teapot reflects Wedgwood's concession to the prevailing fashion for romantic style, in which domestic scenes replaced what had come to be regarded as rather austere, neoclassical designs. The central body of the teapot is ornamented with figures engaged in activities representing daily life drawn from the scenes of domestic employment, modeled by Lady Templetown. ❷ The teapot is of cylindrical shape, and the base and lid have been engine-turned. ❸ The spout is fluted with acanthus leaf and shell terminals. ❹ The lid is decorated with leaves and ribbons in white relief, and the rim of the teapot is encircled by a white ribbon pattern. ❺ The base color is the characteristic Wedgwood pale blue, achieved by the dip method, and ornamented with white to give a pleasing contrast.

LEFT **Wedgwood blue and white jasper dip cylindrical teapot and cover, *c.* 1785.**

Naples Porcelain

In 1771, King Ferdinand IV established a porcelain factory at Naples. By the end of the eighteenth century and into the nineteenth, neoclassical designs had replaced the rococo and had come to dominate both porcelain and silver design, being equally suitable for both. The Naples factory flourished until 1806, using designs copied from antique marble and bronze artifacts. ❶ The sugar bowl and cover have an elegant and simple design showing the influence of neoclassical research. ❷ The bowl's graceful figure, with its simple drapery, is painted with clear lines on a white background in a central reserve bounded by gilded pillars. ❸ The rim of the bowl and its cover are decorated with concentric lines of gilt to enhance the figure, and the panels are joined by decorative gilded swags.

RIGHT **Naples (*Reale Fabrica Ferdinandea*) sugar bowl and cover, *c.* 1790.**

Detail Directory

Perhaps the most significant stylistic development at this time lay in the dramatic change in shape of decorative objects. The new taste for the antique led to the rejection of the lavish curves of the rococo in favor of pure classical forms. As the century progressed, the heaviness that had characterized the early phase of the goût Greque gradually evolved into a lighter and more delicate style.

Detail of giltwood sofa, by James Stuart, c. 1760.

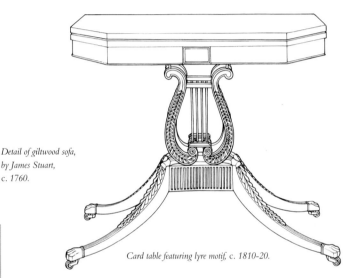

Card table featuring lyre motif, c. 1810-20.

Detail for chairback, by Thomas Sheraton, 1791–94.

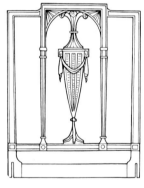

Chairback design from Sheraton's Drawing Book, 1791–94.

William IV dining chair.

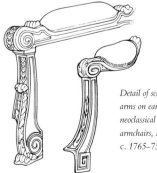

Detail of scrolling arms on early neoclassical armchairs, France, c. 1765–75.

Furniture

The casual, feminine curves of the rococo were abandoned in the neoclassical period in favor of more noble proportions and shapes derived from Greek and Roman architecture, frequently filtered through the grandeur of the Baroque tradition. In furniture this new style, pioneered by James "Athenian" Stuart in England and Louis-Joseph Le Lorrain in France, emerged in heavy rectilinear shapes ornamented with massive carved or gilt-bronze mounts inspired by ancient Greek architectural motifs. Motifs included weighty laurel wreaths, Vitruvian scrolls, Greek key patterns, lion masks, cornucopias, terms, and vases.

By the late 1760s a more restrained version of neoclassicism had developed, characterized by graceful and elegant proportions and fine sculptural detailing—paving the way for the austere, simplified Directoire style. Tables, chairs, and commodes of fine wood incorporated delicately rendered classical features such as tapering, fluted legs, shield or oval backs, fine gilt-bronze moldings, and sparely applied mounts featuring flower garlands, arabesques, and trophies.

Hepplewhite shield back armchair, c. 1780.

Porcelain, Silver, and Gilt Bronze

The neoclassical revival witnessed classical forms adopted for all kinds of decorative objects. The highly prized porcelain produced by the Sèvres factory imitated a wide variety of classical vase shapes for flower vases, potpourri vessels, teawares, and tablewares. The *goût Greque* favored boldly shaped vases painted with classical motifs, frequently embellished with gilding and sometimes mounted with gilt bronze. By the 1770s, the taste was for simple shapes, square-sided or conical cups with angular handles, and sleek and elegant egg-shaped vases with scrolling handles lavishly gilded to imitate gilt bronze.

Objects associated with classical antiquity, such as the lyre of Apollo or the tripod, captured the popular imagination in the form of clocks or lamps. Like porcelain, silver relied heavily on classical forms. Mass production of silver vessels was well suited to the fashionable new style, which was based on simple forms and an established vocabulary of endlessly repeated motifs. The transition from the rococo to neoclassicism was led in England by the Scottish architect Robert Adam, whose influential designs freely adapted and combined the classical vocabulary to invent a modern interpretation of antiquity.

Carved tripod, c. 1773.

Designs for candlesticks, c. 1765–68.

Profile of silver jug, c. 1776–77.

Detail of Sèvres vase, c. 1795–80.

Detail of Sèvres pot pourri vase with gilt bronze mounts, c. 1765–70.

Detail of gilt bronze and porcelain vase, c. 1767.

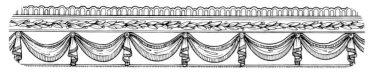

Gilt bronze scroll and foliage detail on commode, by Lelov, c. 1772.

Gilt bronze drapery frieze on secretaire, c. 1776–77.

Vitruvion scroll bronze mounts on writing table, by Le Lorrain, c. 1756–57.

Key and swag gilt bronze mounts on writing desk, by Dubois, c. 1760–65.

Gilt bronze key pattern and festoon detail of filing cabinet, c. 1756–57.

Two- and Three-Dimensional Ornament

Neoclassical designers drew extensively on the fertile classical vocabulary to ornament furniture, porcelain, and silver. The heavy architectural furniture of the *goût Greque* was typically embellished with massive draperies, festoons, urns, lion-paw feet, lion masks, Vitruvian scrolls, and Greek key patterns. As lighter neoclassical forms took hold, delicate motifs such as fluting, palmettes, and anthemia were incorporated into the repertoire of decorative ornament. The handles and covers of vases and urns were typically made in forms derived from the antique, including cherubs, ram, lion, or satyr masks, dolphins, volutes, and scrolling acanthus.

Profile of carved giltwood side table decorated with garlands, rams' heads, and acanthus leaves, Italy, c. 1760–70.

Broader Classical Interpretations

"There cannot be a king simple, he is only a king when dressed," wrote Napoleon, in power from 1804 to 1815. Like Louis XIV before him, he wanted the trappings of French art and interior design to reflect his ambitions and achievements as Emperor. His architect-designers, Charles Percier and Pierre-François Fontaine, created for him a luxurious style, both classical and exotic, that readily transferred to America. The French Empire style was picked up in America between 1810 and 1820, complemented by Regency in Britain. Biedermeier in Germany and Scandinavia produced more comfortable and accessible furniture and decorative objects than the grand Empire pieces.

The urge toward archaeological authenticity went for the form of furniture as much as its decoration in the late neoclassical period. Central to the Empire style in France and America was the Greek klismos chair. It had outcurved saber legs and a concave back and was often richly decorated with swags and trophies to emphasize Napoleon's status: the eagle from Imperial Rome; Apollo's mask like the Sun King; bows, arrows, and crossed swords to indicate his military prowess; swans for his wife Josephine; Egyptian gods such as Anubis; and sphinxes, caryatids, pharaoh heads, lotus leaves, and bulrushes, inspired by his Nile campaigns. Rich fabrics lined and swathed rooms, a reminder of the nomadic tented life on the march or, perhaps, a measure of the speed with which Charles Percier and Pierre-François Fontaine had to work to assuage their employer's impatience. Where fabric was not used to flank rooms, patterned wallpapers replaced wall paintings.

The best examples of the klismos chair in America are usually attributed to Duncan Phyfe (working 1768 to 1784), who had a New York shop employing one hundred staff. Both Phyfe and Charles-Honoré Lannuier (1779–1814) also produced spectacular examples of center-, sofa-, and pier-tables, often with three pillars connecting the base to the round top. Now that furniture was dotted around the room and people relaxed on upholstered sofas, these new types of table gained popularity. David's portrait of Madame Recamier reclining on

a sofa shows an archetypal French example of an Empire interior.

When Napoleon fell from grace the style changed little, although Napoleonic devices were avoided. The Restoration style of 1815 to 1830 often used bright and gaudy colors, with furniture in light woods such as maple inlaid with arabesques of dark wood.

REGENCY STYLE

Concurrent with French Empire was the British Regency, literally 1811–1820 when the Prince Regent ruled instead of his father George III, but in the arts taken to mean the late 1790s until the end of George IV's reign in 1830.

Regency drew heavily on the French style (without Napoleonic devices), including Greek and Egyptian motifs. It also had elements of the Gothick and of the Etruscan style, which were much used in Wedgwood vases designed for mantelpieces. Wedgwood based his vases exactly on the shapes and decoration of Greek vases (then confused with and called Etruscan—even his factory was called Etruria), but departed from the originals in color scheme. Largely red, black, and white, the Etruscan style used motifs similar to the Egyptian: lions, sphinxes, birds, and mythical harpies and griffins. Sheraton's last work, which was incomplete on his death but begun in 1804, *The Cabinet Maker, Upholsterer*

LEFT The drawing room of Deshon-Allyn House, Connecticut, is one of the finest examples of Empire/Regency styles. The English sofa (*c.* 1810) is painted in gold and black, the urns on the mantel are Wedgwood, while the chairs are in the style of Phyfe.

and General Artist's Encyclopedia, epitomized the style in forms such as X-shaped supports and animal motifs.

The Prince Regent himself was the most flamboyant patron of Regency art, seen at its most extreme in Brighton Pavilion by Henry Holland and John Nash. Its interiors were designed as a Mogul fantasy, with Indian, Chinese, and Egyptian themes predominating. The elegant town villas with bowed fronts and cast-iron railings were less exuberant.

BIEDERMEIER

The German-speaking countries and Scandinavia both reacted to and were influenced by neoclassicism, Empire, and Regency, fusing them into the style known as Biedermeier. After the Napoleonic Wars, money was scarce, but at the same time comfort and family life prevailed.

The shapes of furniture derived from the linear, almost two-dimensional neoclassical forms, with large uninterrupted veneered surfaces that avoided the ostentation of French Empire. Local fruitwoods, such as walnut and cherry, and birch, were favored. There was little ormolu or marquetry, just some inlay banding. Furniture was no longer pushed to the walls as it was during most of the eighteenth century, but instead chairs might be clustered around a window with indoor plants and caged birds linking sitting room to garden.

Munich and Vienna were particular centers of Biedermeier. The most important furniture maker and designer was the Austrian Danhauser. He produced a catalog in which shapes were sometimes radical semicircles. Other designs depended on Percier and Fontaine pattern books, with swan-neck sofas

ABOVE **Skolfield-Whittier House, Brunswick, Maine (restoration was finished in 1880) is filled with Eastlake-style** **furnishings and unique collectibles: bronzes, ivory figures, dinner services, clocks, china, paintings, and lamps.**

and chair arms, monopodia legs, swags, and lyres. Ceramics were made from simplified classical shapes, with thick gilding and sentimental enameled scenes. Biedermeier was at its best in the decorative arts from 1815 to 1830. After that hand-craftsmen tended to disappear in the mass production of the Industrial Revolution. The crisp clarity that was the hallmark of early Biedermeier gave way to the richness typical of the mid-nineteenth century.

LIGHTING AND COMFORT

Until around 1800, candles were the only form of indoor lighting. Increasingly, oil supplemented candlelight. Gas was used in large houses, but it was too expensive and foul-smelling for small houses. Developments in sanitation matched improvements in lighting. Efficient water closets were installed, sometimes neatly hidden in a cupboard. Water piped and pumped to the upper floors serviced the water closets and occasionally a bathroom, too, with a shower or tub.

In terms of comfort, the British were the envy of Europe around the 1820s and '30s. After refreshing himself in the bathroom, a fine gentleman could go and lie at the feet of a lady or stand in front of the mantelpiece, thumbs in waistcoat, and pontificate. Alternatively, he could recline in his dressing room on a springy upholstered sofa, while his wife did the same in her boudoir. Both could now read by the light of an oil lamp and ring the bell for a servant to bring an iced drink.

But such informality and luxury went out with the Victorian era, even while the technology that made comfort possible advanced by leaps and bounds.

BELOW **The dining room of Edgewater House (Barrytown, NY) offers a wealth of French Empire detail, in the dining table, the chairs by Duncan Phyfe, the ornate girandole over the mantel, the French Empire plates, and the bisque centerpiece.**

Collector's Gallery

Following the Napoleonic era in Europe, a plethora of classical styles were used in designs for multi-purpose gaming tables, sumptuous, upholstered daybeds and chairs, and playful ceramics and porcelain.

Regency Card Tables

About the time of the Battle of Waterloo, the card game écarté swept into fashion in the highest circles of British society; the Duke of Wellington himself is recorded as having been a keen devotee. Card tables, modeled on earlier tea tables, with the interior of their foldover tops covered with suede or baize, became an essential item of furniture for every fashionable salon. **1** Pedestal bases for such tables became popular. The form of this pedestal base, with its gun-barrel column and **2** swept, four-splay legs, is typical of the period. **3** The top of the table rotates so that the platform on which it sits provides a support when the table is folded open. **4** Rosewood remained the timber of choice. **5** George Bullock revived the fashion for decorating card tables with delicate, brass inlays of floral motifs, seen around the edges of the drawer, also at the clawed feet.

LEFT **Regency, rosewood and brass-inlaid card table, in the manner of George Bullock,** *c.* **1810.**

Occasional Tables

As the nineteenth century progressed, a certain heaviness manifested itself in British furniture design. This is the defining difference between Regency and William IV styles. **1** Moldings became boldly carved in high relief; note the edge of the tabletop and how it contrasts with the beaded moldings of the card table to the left. **2** Raised on paw feet, **3** pedestal bases with carved columns and tricorn platform bases were decorated with stylized acanthus leaves and scrolls, similar to those found in classical architecture.

4 Pieces like this imported Italian *pietra dura* tabletop were often brought back as a memento of a grand tour, and frequently tables were designed specifically to display them. A striking bird motif features in a central, octagonal panel, echoed by smaller panels on each side.

ABOVE AND BELOW

William IV rosewood occasional table with octagonal *pietra dura* top, *c.* **1830.**

Dining Furniture

In contrast to the opulence and formality of British furniture design at this period, the Biedermeier style—popular throughout the Austrian Empire, Germany, and the Baltic states—delighted in the use of locally grown fruitwoods. **1** Biedermeier chair makers reveled in the contrast of pale-colored timbers, ebonized features, and dramatic fabrics. **2** Decoration was minimal, with virtually no carving and only limited use of inlays. **3** Shapes were deliberately simple, chair legs of square tapering form had a slight concave curve.
4 Tables were raised on solid pedestals or solid legs and typically terminated in simple block feet. **5** It was the fashion to keep tables covered with cloths, so that only cursory attention was paid to tabletops—hence their plainness.

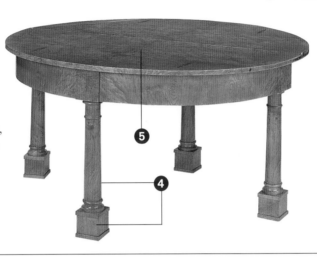

ABOVE **Set of Biedermeier fruitwood chairs with birch center table,** *c.* **1820.**

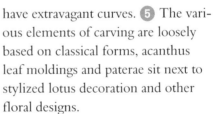

LEFT **Biedermeier ash breakfast table with foldover top,** *c.* **1830.**

Dining Chairs

Carving rosewood is an act of dedicated masochism. Rosewood is one of the densest and hardest timbers known, and when a solid block is chiseled, needle-sharp shards fracture off. For this reason, profusely carved rosewood dining chairs were manufactured only for a short period in the nineteenth century and are generally of the highest quality. **1** The overall design of these chairs, with carved horizontal rails across the backs, follows the Regency model. **2** The chairs are designed to take squab cushions to protect their caned seats; **3** note how the carving on the vertical rails supporting the back ceases just above the seat, at the boundary of the cushion. **4** The close grain of rosewood renders it structurally weak and a timber fundamentally unsuited to chair making. Therefore these front legs are somewhat chunky and

have extravagant curves. **5** The various elements of carving are loosely based on classical forms, acanthus leaf moldings and paterae sit next to stylized lotus decoration and other floral designs.

ABOVE **William IV dining chair with cane seat, early nineteenth century.**

LEFT **Birchwood Beidermeier chair; based on Empire style, Sweden,** *c.* **1830**

Upholstered Furniture

A luxury version of Biedermeier furniture existed alongside the more commonly seen, everyday productions. The architect Karl Friedrich Schinkel lived in Berlin and was commissioned on several occasions to design furniture for the Prussian royal family. **1** In keeping with the Biedermeier idiom, pale wood is a popular choice for chairs. This is, however, burr walnut, a timber cut across the root of the tree, highly prized, expensive, and much admired for its dramatic figuring. **2** Ebony line inlays in the Egyptian style, coupled with the solid scrolling arms and legs, look forward about 100 years to the art deco style of the 1920s. **3** Deep padding of the seats and backs emphasizes comfort as well as luxury,

and this—along with the use of vibrant upholstery fabrics, usually brightly colored and luxuriously patterned silks—is a hallmark of the Biedermeier style. **4** Playful zoomorphic elements were the height of fashion, with fearsome creatures, such as leopards, adorning arms. **5** Claw feet reappear for the first time in about 40 years, being more naturally carved than their eighteenth-century counterparts.

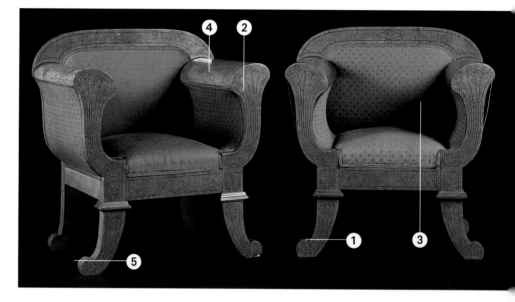

RIGHT **A pair of Biedermeier burr walnut bergères, after a design by Karl Friedrich Schinkel.**

Daybeds

Nineteenth-century literature is littered with references to young ladies and gentlemen in a state of semi-permanent collapse. The daybed, a form originally derived from the couches used by ancient Romans at their banquets, became a popular drawing room accessory on which pale and interesting-looking people could elegantly drape their limbs while indulging in the latest gossip. Daybeds of the later nineteenth century generally had the addition of padded armrests running half their length along the back. **1** One end of the daybed rises in a gentle S-shape, like the prow of a ship, **2** the other terminates in a built-in padded bolster.

3 The use of pale marquetry laid onto the contrasting dark mahogany imitates the British fashion for brass-inlaid rosewood.

4 The reeded urn-shaped legs are boldly molded and terminate in turned block feet.

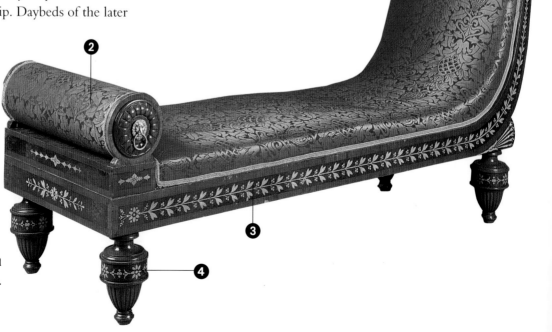

RIGHT **Biedermeier mahogany and marquetry daybed,** *c.* **1830.**

LEFT **Restoration period mahogany** *secretaire à abattant,* **France,** *c.* **1825.**

Gueridons

This magnificent table represents the last word in luxury, quality, and fashion of early nineteenth-century furniture design. A tiny amount of solid ormolu furniture was created in Paris during the Restoration period, and these pieces, inordinately expensive to manufacture, are seldom seen outside the great national and royal collections. ❶ Burnished and matte surfaces complement each other and are used here to emphasize the design. ❷ The decora-

RIGHT **Restoration period ormolu gueridon, with** *verre eglomise* **top.**

Secretaires

The form of the *secretaire à abattant*, with a vertical fall enclosing small drawers and pigeonholes above a series of long drawers, remained popular in continental Europe long after it had passed from fashion in Britain. French furniture design of the Restoration period is an almost seamless continuation of the Empire style. During the 1820s a slight heaviness of form became apparent. ❶ The French *secretaire* is remarkable for its pared-down elegance, the main decorative elements being the use of finely figured mahogany veneers. ❷ Drawers were opened by inserting a key, half turning it, and then pulling. ❸ The dark gray-veined marble top and the turned hemispherical feet are typical features.

In contrast, the German cherrywood *secretaire* is decorated with a profusion of classically inspired ornament; ❹ note the ebonized and gilt dolphins flanking the cylindrical cupboard above the fall, ❺ and the use of alabaster columns in the interior.

RIGHT *Secretaire à abattant,* **Germany,** *c.* **1825.**

tive details include quotations from the Roman style—in particular the treatment of the top; ❸ Grecian style—the winged busts supporting the top, and lion-paw feet at the base of the columns; and ❹ Egyptian style—the lotus moldings on the feet at the base of the table. The pinecone on which the stretchers uniting the feet are centered was an object of veneration as a fertility symbol for various ancient cultures. ❺ The decoration of the tabletop, with *verre eglomise*, is worthy of note. The rare painted glass top is resplendent with a rich decoration of silvered and gilt palmettes, flowerets, and foliated scrolls, on an antique-green background. ❻ Painted against this ground are six miniatures with musical themes: three represent cherubs or cupids playing tambourine, castanets, and handbells; the other three depict women, elegantly draped in classical gowns, strumming harps.

Viennese Biedermeier Glass

The Biedermeier period (1810-1850) saw the rise of a prosperous and educated middle class in Central Europe, and with it a new demand for less formal and extravagant applied arts. The two most famous artists working in this medium were Anton Kothgasser and Gottlob Mohn; they are renowned for the delicacy of their painting and their subtle use of color, and much of their work is signed. These beakers are examples of the simple elegance that became fashionable, being simultaneously both luxurious and understated. The glass by Mohn is dated 1813, and the glass by Kothgasser dates to about ten years later. **1** Then, as now, the Viennese were proud of their beautiful city, and richly painted

topographical scenes of buildings and monuments in Vienna, such as this view of the Schonbrun Palace on the glass by Anton Kothgasser (left), became immensely popular. **2** The glass decorated by Gottlob Mohn (right) features a romantic view of Heidelburg Castle above the Neckar river. **3** The simple shapes of these glasses made them ideal for this style of decoration. **4** The craftsman's signature, painted in gold, can be seen around the circumference of the base of the above glass.

LEFT AND ABOVE **Two Biedermeier period transparent, enameled beakers by Anton Kothgasser and Gottlob Mohn, Vienna,** *c.* **1820.**

Cut Glass

This group of glassware illustrates the changing fashion in glass cutting during the 1830s, with the emphasis of the decoration firmly placed on vertical planes. **1** The quality of cutting is of the highest order. The water jug is cut with highly polished plain flutes; **2** the claret jugs with rounded pillars, a style associated with the Waterford glasshouse in

the reign of William IV. **3** Necks and shoulders are cut with deeply incised prismatic steps to maximize the refractive quality of the glass. **4** Swan-neck handles are applied to the rims of these vessels, and the handles are drawn outward and downward to connect with the body. Note that the thickness of the handles is far greater at the rim than where they join the bodies.

LEFT **A pair of cut-glass claret jugs,** *c.* **1835, and a cut-glass water ewer,** *c.* **1830.**

RIGHT **Two Berlin ware plates,** *c.* **1835.**

Decorative Ware

Berlin porcelain also specialized in decorative ware—lavishly gilded and with fine artwork, giving the impression of framed oil paintings. By contrast, Vienna ware also developed the tradition of painted porcelain and the extensive use of gilding. ❶ Painted rim decoration gives the impression of a picture frame. ❷ Rim decoration exploits the graphic potential of leaf and flower motifs. ❸ Animals were favorite subjects. Horse racing was a much-loved sport and became

an increasingly popular subject for artists.
❹ Wild animals, such as the boar, reflected the hunting tradition. The wintry atmosphere is achieved by the restrained use of colors, limited to white, brown, and green.
❺ Topographical scenes, such as those painted on the Vienna saucers, reflect the increase in European travel by the wealthy classes and a desire to record the domestic fashions of the day, such as garden designs, architecture, or formal daywear.

LEFT **Three Vienna ware cabinet cups and saucers, left to right: 1825, 1819, and** *c.* **1830.**

Luxury Tableware

The Berlin factory is best known for its white porcelain with a slightly bluish tinge, skillfully painted landscapes, colors, and excellent gilding. **1** Berlin ware often copied designs from Meissen. Notable features include a crisply delineated edge, angular shape, and **2** domed lids surmounted by bulbous knobs. **3** Gilded edges are standard on bases, rims, covers, and handles. **4** Handles and knobs are decorated with moldings and painted in the typical puce, yellow, green, and iron-red colors. **5** Flower sprays often form the central decoration, delicately painted in exquisite detail using the same colors as on the moldings. Each spray is slightly different, but together the pieces form a coherent whole.

LEFT **Part of a Berlin dinner service, c. 1820.**

Ceramic Candlesticks

Wedgwood used black basalt stoneware both before and after he invented the defining jasperware finish. Rosso antico was a popular type of colored earthenware used to contrast with other materials. **1** Typical of late neoclassical design, these candlesticks are based on Roman architectural features. Formed in the shape of fish, the candlesticks sit on a plinth of black basalt decorated with shells of rosso antico. **2** A humorous touch shows the freedom designers were taking with neoclassical themes; human features are captured in the wide-open mouths and bulging eyes. The body area is broken up by incised scales and the overall effect is amusing and lively. **3** Elaborate modeling contrasts with the plainness of the basic material.

BELOW **Pair of Wedgwood black basalt and rosso antico candlesticks, c. 1820.**

Blackamoor Figures

African motifs had been used since classical times on sardonyx cameos, and in the late eighteenth century, the grand tour continued to foster the fashion for glamorous curiosities. Blackamoor figures were used to ornament a variety of objects, including candlestick and torchères, gueridons, furniture supports, and clock cases. ❶ Although they occasionally appear in native dress, ❷ blackamoor figures are often shown in servants' livery. ❸ This was sometimes enlivened by the addition of a turban encrusted with opulent jewels, reflecting the prevailing eighteenth-century fashion for exquisitely costumed black pages. ❹ The torch was a popular motif during the Empire period: its flaming incarnation was a symbol of Eros, the god of love, or the goddess Venus, who inspired the fire of love, rendering it an appropriate decorative ornament for candlesticks.

ABOVE **A pair of Empire bronze and ormolu twin-branch candelabra, late eighteenth century.**

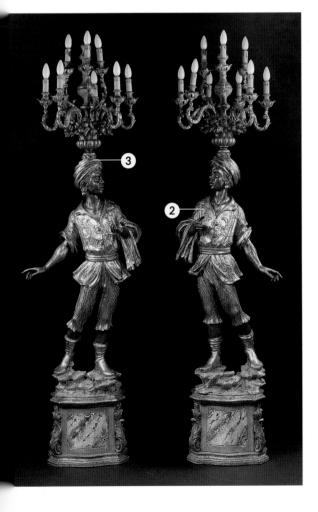

LEFT **A pair of painted and parcel gilt blackamoor nine-light candelabra, late eighteenth century.**

Detail Directory

At the beginning of the nineteenth century, Emperor Napoleon's travels in Egypt—together with his pretensions as the inheritor of the glories of ancient Rome—greatly influenced the new, luxurious Empire style. Duncan Phyfe pioneered the style in America, and in England, the Prince Regent's enthusiasm established the concurrent trend in fashionable circles.

Sofas and Chairs

Reflecting the demand for archaeological correctness, the form of furniture styles was as important as the decoration in Empire France. Finding favor in France as well as in England and America, the Greek klismos chair, with saber legs, a concave back, and curving supports, was typically ornamented with swags and trophies symbolizing the glorious military achievements of Napoleon. The varied vocabulary of decorative motifs included the eagle of Imperial Rome, the Sun King's emblem of the mask of Apollo, military symbols, and Egyptian themes reminiscent of the Nile campaigns. Other chair forms emulated the form of the Roman curule, with crossing double-curved legs.

The most popular shapes for sofas were also Greek adaptations; typical examples featured scrolled ends and lion-paw feet, or one low end with a short scrolled arm.

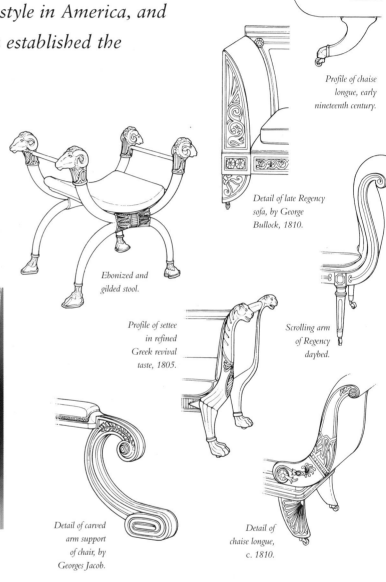

Profile of chaise longue, early nineteenth century.

Detail of late Regency sofa, by George Bullock, 1810.

Ebonized and gilded stool.

Scrolling arm of Regency daybed.

Profile of settee in refined Greek revival taste, 1805.

Detail of carved arm support of chair, by Georges Jacob.

Detail of chaise longue, c. 1810.

Detail of French Empire giltwood fauteuil, c. 1810.

George III pembroke table, c. 1790.

Regency table leg designs, from George Smith's Cabinet Maker and Upholstery Guide.

Tables

The Regency and Empire periods witnessed the introduction of a variety of new table styles in classical or Egyptian taste. Console tables or circular central tables, supported by a single pedestal, lion or griffin monopodia, lyres, full caryatids, or terms headed by Egyptian masks, superseded the thin tapering legs made fashionable by Thomas Sheraton. Writing tables rested on robust trestles reminiscent of the ends of Roman sarcophagi. Other new shapes included drum tables, sofa tables, and pedestal tables

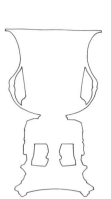

Silhouette of silver gilt vase on stand, by Paul Storr, 1811–12.

Profile of silver gilt coffee pot, c. 1810.

Outline of wine cooler, 1810.

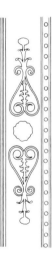

Sèvres porcelain vase, c. 1814.

Biedermeier mantel clock, Austria.

Empire bronze ormulu chandelier, c. 1810.

Two- and Three-Dimensional Ornament

As with furniture, the taste for the grandeur of antiquity manifested itself in designs for silver. Typically, Empire silver is dominated by bold profiles, embellished with a disciplined application of ornament and enhanced by cast sculptural elements. By the early nineteenth century, Egyptian motifs became increasingly more fashionable. The density of ornament was in marked contrast to the Biedermeier style in Austria, where popular French Empire shapes were stripped of elaborate decoration. Regency silver in England, championed by the workshops of Paul Storr and Rundell, Bridge, and Rundell also adopted antique prototypes, albeit heavier and more sculptural than its French Empire cousin. In ceramics, Empire vases were wider versions of Egyptian and Etruscan shapes. The ceramics produced in England by Josiah Wedgwood at his Etruria factory emulated decorative motifs seen on Greek vases, including lions, sphinxes, birds, mythical harpies, and griffins.

Detail of pedestal table with oak leaves and scrolls, c. 1817.

Decorative detail of pier table, by Thomas Hope, c. 1800.

Tented Style

Among the many celebrated innovations of designers Charles Percier and Pierre-François Fontaine was the lavish use of fabric draperies for interior decoration. Beds, and even entire rooms, were swathed in rich fabrics, mirroring the tented dwellings of military campaigns. Opulent rooms were created by looping silks and velvets in voluptuous sweeps over pelmets and on the framework of beds. Small rooms were made to resemble tents by draping fabrics on the walls and suspending them from the ceiling.

Drapery design for "Egyptian" bedhead, by Gillows, early nineteenth century.

Empire-style bed of Empress Josephine, c. 1810.

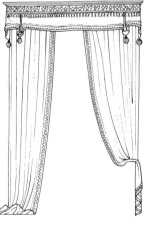

Drapery of bed, by George Bullock, England, 1816.

RIGHT **French patinated
and gilded bronze
and iron, 1870.**

FAR RIGHT **William IV
burr yew davenport.**

The Mid-1800s

By the second quarter of the nineteenth century there was an increased emphasis on comfort. There was a move away from the restraint of neoclassicism. Designers and architects began to look toward the rococo and further back to gothic styles for inspiration. However, in neither case were these pure revivals, but rather pragmatic adaptations of the original design genre.

Rococo and Gothic Revivals

As the applied arts began taking inspiration from a variety of decorative styles from different periods, the time for revivals was ripe. Yet, while artists were looking to the past, manufacturers were concentrating firmly on the future.

A wide diversity of influences was manifest in the applied arts by the second quarter of the nineteenth century; a common element among influences was that they were mostly historical. Prior to this period, only one style had held sway at any particular time. Differences between the prevalent styles of various countries were quickly becoming blurred, making it all the more difficult to identify the country of origin of a piece—from this and subsequent periods—from its stylistic details. For the next fifty years the decorative arts were dominated by revivals of different styles, albeit in a heavily modified form in many cases.

INSPIRED BY THE PAST

The rococo revival began as a reaction against the previously prevalent rectilinear, classical forms. In England, the revival began with the lavish designs and opulent forms apparent in the work of the silversmith Paul Storr, whose creations for the court were inspired by those pieces already in the royal collections; many of these were by the great silversmiths of the eighteenth century, including Paul de Lamerie. In France, the restoration of the monarchy led, initially, to prevalence of a less severe version of Empire style, particularly in furniture and metalwork, but by about 1835, designers were drawing inspiration from the rococo and also the Romantic movement, which was particularly influential through its sculptural forms.

The Gothic revival was a more conscious attempt by particular designers to create new styles in the decorative arts. As with neoclassicism, the Gothic revival involved drawing inspiration from the ornament, rather than forms, of an earlier era. In England and America, a broadly equivalent, but less academic, style was known as the Elizabethan revival, taking its inspiration from the ornament of the Renaissance and late medieval periods. The style is evidenced by repeated shallow relief carving on furniture, as well as the use of "bobbin" and other types of turning for ornamental purposes.

ABOVE **The epitome of a medieval fairy-tale castle, Eastnor Castle in Herefordshire, England, designed by Pugin, is one of the finest examples of the Gothic revival style in architecture.**

OPPOSITE **A variety of styles is displayed at Deshon-Allyn House, Connecticut, from the mahogany dining table with elaborately carved pedestal and legs (1840), to the veneered sideboard (1825), and fine girandole mirror (1815).**

BELOW **With its cathedral-like interior, intricately carved, extensive wood paneling and screens, and vast stained-glass windows, the House of Lords in Westminster, London, designed mainly by Pugin, is a striking example of the neo-Gothic style.**

LOOKING FORWARD TO THE FUTURE

Toward the middle of the nineteenth century, there were two main forces of development in the decorative arts: first, the introduction of new techniques and materials, and second, the evolution of international fairs, which provided a focus for manufacturers and designers and a rapid cross-fertilization of influence through the developed world.

Improved communication, massive exhibitions in London, New York, Paris, and other locations, together with factors such as the opening up of Japan, created a melting pot of different styles and influences. Furthermore, new innovation in the use and production of materials such as papier-mâché, in electrotype metal casting, and the widespread use of cast iron created a new range of opportunities for designers and manufacturers alike. It is easy to dismiss this era as lacking in originality in design with the emphasis on forms of historical revival, but the use, particularly of sculptural forms in furniture and other media, together with the development of new manufacturing techniques and materials, must only be regarded as innovative.

EXTRAVAGANCE AND DETAIL

A departure from previous forms led designers to create opulent yet practical and realistic furniture and interiors. In England, during the reign of William IV (1830–1837), there was a softening of form in many areas of the applied arts and a gradual movement away from rectilinear shapes and neoclassical motifs toward more naturalistic forms and details. Where legs on furniture had been either straight or saber-shaped, now cabriole legs, sturdier than before, began to reappear. During the early part of the nineteenth century, English porcelain factories produced services copying the form of eighteenth-century porcelain, but by 1830 the demand was for more extravagant neo-rococo forms, typified by extensive flower encrustation and a widespread use of gilding.

THE ROCOCO REVIVAL STYLE

In France, the epoch of King Louis Philippe (1830–1840) saw the widespread adoption of the rococo revival, with its asymmetrically arranged naturalistic forms, particularly scrolls and shells. In some cases designs closely replicated those of the original rococo, but more frequently they chose to draw only on the style for influence, and there is often a solidity of form about nineteenth-century pieces that is not seen in the almost "fantastic" rococo designs of the previous century.

As with the original rococo movement, there was an opulence about rococo revival interiors: carpets replaced marble or polished wood floors, and elaborate plaster moldings featured festoons of flowers rather than swagged drapes. Light fixtures in the form of chandeliers or wall appliqués were of gilt bronze and asymmetrical form. Many great houses built in Europe during the mid-1800s adopted this style of decoration, frequently to accommodate a mixture of genuine rococo and revival pieces. Portraits more often depicted sitters in contemporary rather than classical costume, and portrait busts in marble, which still remained popular, no longer portrayed their subject as a Roman emperor or goddess. By the late 1830s the French bronze foundries were producing sculpture and other ornaments, such as clock cases, with dramatized but

realistic portrayals of animals and historical and contemporary figures.

Although the rococo revival is considered to have been at its height between 1830 and 1860 in England and France, and slightly later in America, adaptations of the rococo style have been popular ever since. The Louis XV (and Louis XVI) style has frequently been chosen to give an impression of opulence, although the quality has varied from the precise replica furniture and ornaments made by Henry Dasson in the 1880s to the poorly made mass-produced pastiches available today.

THE GOTHIC REVIVAL STYLE

The influences extracted from the Gothic were purely decorative. Designers and architects took ornamental aspects of the original and fused them with elements of other earlier periods.

Unlike the rococo revival, which largely copied or adapted from existing pieces of an earlier period, the Gothic revival largely used the ornament of the period rather than specific artifacts as inspiration. The main practical reason for this was that the diversity of objects produced and the expected level of comfort in the homes of the better-off was dramatically greater than that of between 300 and 500 years earlier. Whereas in the Regency and Restoration periods furniture and furnishings often exhibited signs of Gothic influence, it was only in the 1840s that a more extensive repertoire of decoration evolved.

ABOVE **The great hall and chapel of Alton Towers, England, were designed and furnished by Pugin. He began the 15-year project in 1837, designing the altar,** **reredos, and the anterior screen. The chapel contains a huge stained glass window, a wooden arched ceiling, and a minstrels' gallery.**

AN ECLECTIC MIX OF STYLES

The rigorous design and ornament of the English designer and architect Augustus Pugin can be placed under the broad heading of Gothic revival, work which took particular inspiration from the forms of ecclesiastical buildings. In France, there were similar examples, notably the *Salon Gothique*, but also the evolvement of the quasi-historical style known as Henri-II. The equivalent of the latter in England and America was the Elizabethan or Renaissance revival, typified by heavily carved furniture in dark-stained oak and other dark woods, and including motifs such as lions or stylized and grotesque maskheads.

The use of wood paneling in interiors became fashionable between the 1850s and the early twentieth century. Concurrently, stained glass was used more widely for secular applications, and Gothic ornament on wallpapers, floors, and decorative tiles became widespread. The technical innovations in lighting during the century provided an ideal vehicle for elaborate forms—table, ceiling, and wall lights particularly lent themselves to historical motifs such as grotesques.

Collector's Gallery

The reaction against angular, classically influenced styles meant that furniture makers looked in two directions for inspiration—to the rococo and the Gothic. The solidity of the Empire and Regency styles stayed prominent and, once revived, the rococo style remained a popular source throughout the nineteenth century. The Gothic revival was initially fashionable in France and England, two countries with a strong tradition of this style of architecture.

Chairs and Benches

The rococo style was revived with a new emphasis on practical comfort and the addition of extravagant curves and scrolls. Gothic revival chairs and benches were more influenced by decoration than form. Indigenous woods such as oak and walnut, as well as mahogany, were used, and cast iron was used for outdoor furniture. **1** For the rococo revival, the emphasis was on comfort, with wood-framed upholstered backs becoming popular, even on dining chairs. Foliate carving was often used as a cresting to the chair back and also on the front seat rail. **2** Both easy chairs and more formal chairs developed curved backs, with oval shapes becoming commonplace. A wider range of drawing room furniture was becoming popular, including chaise longues and upholstered stools, from footstools to large ottoman stools. Buttoned leather was popular as a chair covering, particularly for library

LEFT **A walnut chair, signed and dated "Paris 1893", G. Fisseux, France.**

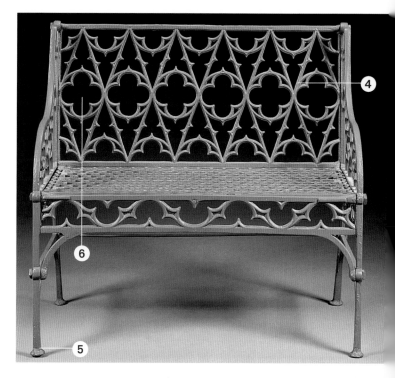

ABOVE **A Gothic green-painted, cast iron bench, United States or England, *c.* 1850.**

furniture. **3** Easy chairs tended to have short cabriole front legs, often with scroll carving toward the foot and splayed back legs. Dining and more formal chairs also had cabriole legs front and back, but of a more substantial form than was popular later in the century. **4** On Gothic revival chairs and benches, arched or pointed chairbacks were uniform, frequently with carved or molded details such as strawberry leaves. Solid seats were often used, making wooden chairs more appropriate as hall chairs rather than dining chairs. Iron benches were used in conservatories and gardens. **5** Chair legs were generally either of square form with carved Gothic details or of cluster column form, occasionally with more elaborate supports carved with maskheads and naturalistic details such as paw feet, influenced by Italian Renaissance furniture. **6** Details and motifs were often inspired by the architectural drawings of Viollet le Duc, published during the 1860s.

Tables and Desks

The style and ornament of rococo and Gothic revival tables could not have been more different, and drew on the contrasting values and tastes of the middle classes. Rococo-style dining tables and some smaller occasional tables still used the pedestal base that had become popular early in the nine-

ABOVE **Amboyna, walnut, and marquetry library table, Gillows,** *c.* **1870.**

ABOVE **Walnut center table, Crace,** *c.* **1860.**

teenth century. ❶ The overall impression of rococo revival tables was one of curves rather than straight lines. ❷ Tea tables, card tables, and library tables were often of serpentine form. ❸ Cabriole legs were once again fashionable. ❹ Gilt bronze mounts were widely used on legs, particularly on the "hip" of the leg and also the foot. ❺ Tabletops often had inlaid detail or marquetry. Elaborate carving was also reinstated. ❻ Rococo and neoclassical motifs were employed with restraint and subtlety. ❼ These

were often combined with turned crossbars, beading, and other non-rococo elements. ❽ Tables were designed for middle-class pastimes and, as a result, they incorporated new features, such as raised rims, drawers, castors, or dropleaves. ❾ Mahogany continued to be the fashionable wood of choice and its strong figure well-suited the rococo revival style. ❿ Gothic tables were usually of indigenous rather than imported woods. ⓫ Dining tables either had a massive central carved column, surmounted by a polygonal top, or

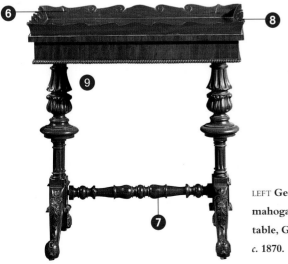

LEFT **George IV mahogany work table, Gillows,** *c.* **1870.**

ABOVE **Oak kneehole desk, Pugin,** *c.* **1875.**

were rectangular with substantial corner supports or central trestle end supports, again with substantial columns linked by a single stretcher. ⓬ The undertiers of tables often had elaborate tracery details together with carving to the stretchers. ⓭ Other pieces favored strong, unadorned profiles and medieval-style fittings, such as brass handles.

ABOVE **Rococo revival
harmonium cabinet,
Italy, *c.* 1860.**

Case Furniture

Within the rococo revival, there was a revival in the use of boulle-work (brass-inlaid tortoiseshell) for decoration on many smaller cabinet pieces and small tables. Tall, narrower chests (semainier or Wellington chests) became increasingly popular, as did large-scale wardrobes or armoires. Simpler rococo chests for bedroom use had changed little, but usually had rounded rather than angled corners, and were often on plinth bases, rather than bracket feet. Mahogany was the most widely favored wood, often with gilded finishes, and walnut and more exotic veneers were also used. Italian rococo revival pieces were far more elaborate than British or American designs. This is reflected in ❶ the quantity and quality of the marquetry, ❷ the elaborate nature of the carved embellishment, ❸ the use of exotic woods, such as ebony, ❹ and the curvaceous form of the overall design. ❺ The effect of the Gothic revival was so wide-ranging that ogee arched glazing bars were used on bookcases that had no other Gothic elements. ❻ Panels and solid doors sported arched moldings and other Gothic details, even though neoclassical or rococo motifs were often incorporated into the same piece. ❼ Plinth bases continued to be prevalent for larger items.

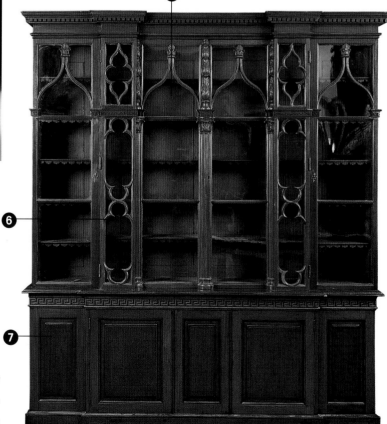

RIGHT **William IV
mahogany bookcase in
the Gothic style.**

Desks

The rococo-style bureau plat form spread from within France, on cabriole legs and often adorned with gilded bronze mounts. The upright, or secretaire-type, desk was still popular in Germany and other parts of Europe. The conventional bureau became less popular, to be replaced by a range of different types of desk, particularly of pedestal and kneehole form. These were often functional, but less angular than earlier in the nineteenth century. **1** German desks were less angular in form, including rounded corners and carved details. **2** Marquetry became increasingly popular, and strong contrasts were achieved with the use of ebony. **3** French polish was used to achieve the piano finish on wood furniture and highlight both the carved ornament and marquetry inlays.

LEFT **A carved walnut desk, known as a Schreibschrank, Germany, mid-nineteenth century.**

Upholstered Furniture

Upholstered items were generally influenced more by detail than form. **1** Quatrefoil motifs and miniature bosses in the fifteenth-century style were popular with Gothic revival designers. **2** These were often enhanced and highlighted by a gilt finish or red paint effects **3** Manufacturing innovations lead to an increased used of castors, coil-sprung upholstery, and deep buttoned seating.

RIGHT **Chaise longue with Gothic embellishment, Pugin,** *c.* 1830.

Glass Goblets and Tumblers

The Gothic revival style was the natural form of expression for the resurgent interest in spirituality and religion in the early nineteenth century. Religious scenes, which were very seldom seen on domestic glassware in the eighteenth century, made an appearance from about 1830. Design was also influenced by the Romantic movement. Novelists such as Sir Walter Scott, with their tales of medieval knights, inspired decorations, landscapes, and heraldic devices. **1** A tall bucket bowl raised on a rudimentary stem and lavishly cut foot is typically Bohemian. The proportions are rather heavy in comparison with British glass of the period. **2** Gothic elements within the engraving include the stylized elongation of bodies and limbs. In particular the body of Christ is distended and contorted away from the classical ideal. The medieval costumes and the seriousness of the scene are also Gothic elements. Dominik Biemann, perhaps the most talented glass engraver working in Bohemia at this period, was particularly famous for a series of portrait engravings. His work is always of a remarkable quality. **3** Romanticized decoration on glass typically focuses the attention on the landscape and castles, amid a townscape with mountains behind it. **4** The painted coat of arms looks back to the style of enameling popular in the seventeenth century.

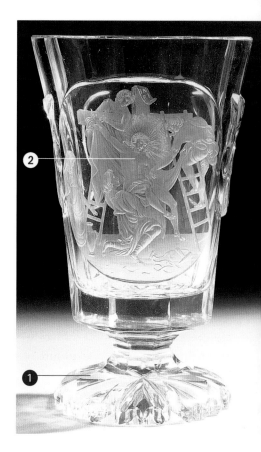

RIGHT **A cut-glass goblet, engraved with *The Descent from the Cross*, by Dominik Biemann, Bohemia,** *c.* **1835.**

5 Bohemian glass cutting of the 1830s is typified by a thickly blown and deeply cut shape, with particular emphasis paid to the petal-shaped foot. Also note the panels of hatched diamonds and the distinctive oval cysts flanking the enameled medallion.

FAR LEFT **Enameled armorial tumbler, Bohemia,** *c.* **1835;** LEFT **Enameled topographical tumbler, Bohemia,** *c.* **1820.**

Glass Vases

The rococo and classical revivals of the second half of the nineteenth century were more academically informed than the earlier revivals. Designers applied both modern and ancient techniques to imitate Greek and Roman styles. ❶ Vase shapes were often derived from the Portland Vase, with its tapering bottom often being replaced by a flat foot. ❷ The decoration of the Greek key pattern around the neck of the vase, and of Cupid within an oval, has been achieved by the ancient cameo technique: a bubble of clear, colorless glass is inflated within a thin layer of deep red glass, then this outer layer is cut away to reveal the clear glass interior. ❸ The glass surface was often rendered matte by etching, involving the exposure of the vessel to hydrofluoric acid. This process became widespread during the third quarter of the nineteenth century.

RIGHT **Flashed and etched vase, by Franz Zach, Bohemia,** *c.* **1860.**

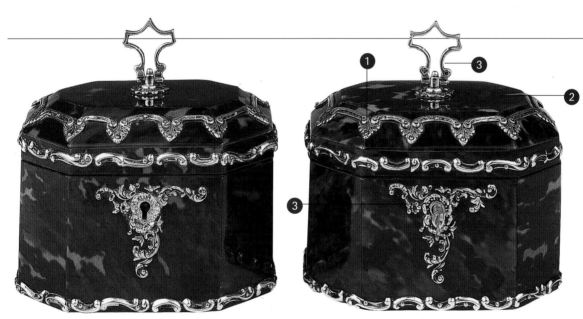

LEFT **A pair of tortoiseshell and silver mounted tea caddies,** *c.* **1865.**

Tea Caddies

In most cases, the Gothic influence on silver was limited to the type of decoration rather than the form of objects, and it was only later in the century that forms resembling those of the fifteenth and sixteenth centuries were replicated. Particular Gothic motifs were generally heraldic—with historical figures as finials—and set in arches around the base of large presentation caskets or centerpieces. ❶ Boxes and small objects in wood and other materials, such as tor-

toiseshell, were often mounted in silver. In the early nineteenth century, tortoiseshell boxes were sometimes molded with Gothic arches. ❷ The octagonal shape of these boxes is similar to neoclassical designs, but, unlike those, these have a domed rather than a flat lid. ❸ The pointed and waisted loop handle shown here is redolent of Gothic iconography, but the escutcheon is very rococo in its asymmetry and foliate scrolls.

Porcelain Vases

During the second quarter of the nineteenth century, the restrained ornament of neoclassicism was gradually superseded by a full-blown revival, and often embellishment, of the rococo style. This was manifest not only in the shapes that were popular but also in decoration.

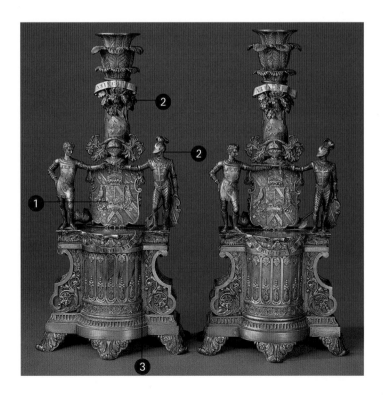

This style was prevalent in England but was often more restrained in America and France, where the heavy encrustation of flowers and leaves did not appear until later. **1** Garnitures of vases became very popular in the mid-nineteenth century. The largest, central vase did not necessarily resemble that of the side vases. **2** The most popular shape was the ogee, or drop bottom, but French factories such as Sèvres reintroduced the more neoclassical shapes with straight tapering sides. In England, Coalport used the classical campagna shape, but embellished it so that its classical origins were almost hidden. **3** The use of bronze mounts with porcelain was always commonplace in France but rare in England until later. **4** Neoclassical motifs were often combined with rococo details and dark blue backgrounds; purity of style was less important than overall effect.

LEFT **Suite of Sèvres gilt bronze mounted blue porcelain vases, France, *c.* 1860.**

Candlesticks

As in other media, the Gothic motifs used in ormolu were often combined on one object with motifs from other styles, such as rococo or a version of neoclassical. In some cases this information can help to reinforce identification of the date of the piece. Since gilded metal artifacts from this period are very rare, the decoration is influenced only by fashion, rather than any attempt to create an object that is accurately reminiscent of the Gothic period. **1** Heraldic shields were used in many media for decorative purposes, typically sparsely depicted rather than in great detail, although here they have a precise historical purpose. **2** Figures in armor, the helm, and oak leaf motifs can all be seen on Gothic revival pieces. **3** As with many Gothic revival pieces, the central column of the base of these candlesticks is architectural in form, with chased arches that are of Gothic inspiration. However, the whole form of these candlesticks is typical of the last stage of the dominant influence of classical decoration, with bold scrolls and acanthus leaves as seen in the Regency in England and the Restoration in France.

ABOVE **A pair of gilt bronze candlesticks of Gothic inspiration by Thomire, France, *c.* 1840.**

Decorative Plates

The widespread use of ceramic tiles as a decorative form saw the adoption of fourteenth- and fifteenth-century motifs such as the fleur-de-lis, heraldic beasts, and the quatrefoil. Pottery or earthenware was generally considered the most appropriate medium for Gothic designs, not least because porcelain had been produced in the West only for about the last 120 years. ❶ Although designed to have a function, the type of decoration on many dishes and plates indicated that they were actually intended to be displayed, often on the plate rack of a dresser. ❷ As with many decorated Gothic revival objects, the use of a homespun motto was an integral part of the decoration. ❸ The inlaid, or encaustic, design used for this plate closely resembles ceramic tile designs from about 1840, although the latter were not always decorated in the Gothic taste.

ABOVE **Minton earthenware bread plate designed by Pugin,** *c.* **1850.**

Ceramic Dinner Services

During the early part of the nineteenth century there was a rapid growth in the demand for ceramic dinner sets, particularly in England. By the 1830s the form of these, which had initially been inspired by the neoclassical styles of factories such as Sèvres, was becoming more elaborate and closer to rococo, with extravagant, often asymmetrical curves and naturalistic handles and borders. ❶ Plates were no longer of plain circular outline but tended to have wavy-edged borders. Likewise, serving plates were of rounded oblong form, again with wavy edges. The borders often featured raised scrolls to the edges. ❷ The carrying handles, such as those on the body and lid of a tureen, were often of elaborate scrolling form, although here they have been modified by the Chinese influence. ❸ The swelling bombé shape of all the tureens was sometimes replicated by the shape of the handles on the sauce tureens.

RIGHT **A Ridgway dinner service,** *c.* **1840.**

Detail Directory

Designers and artisans looked toward historical sources for inspiration, but modified them to suit the requirements of the day. The influence of the rococo revival saw a return to extravagant curves. Gothic revival designs were consistently inspired by architectural detail. During the flexible early period (1830–1850), some items that adopted a rococo shape had Gothic decoration.

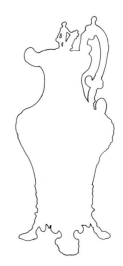

Profile of silver wine ewer, 1848–49.

Lighting

This area offers an interesting contrast between the two revival styles. Gothic ornament was used for Argand lamps in the 1820s and '30s, but as the Gothic style reached a more purist phase there was a return to some use of candles. Brass candlesticks of this style tended to architectural influence with pierced, crenellated drip pans, column stems, and quatrefoil or hexafoil bases.

Conversely, the rococo revival style was used for the more modern oil lamps, typically with curvaceous baluster stems, often glass or ceramic, with a glass reservoir and shade, terminating in a brass or other metal base for solidity and stability.

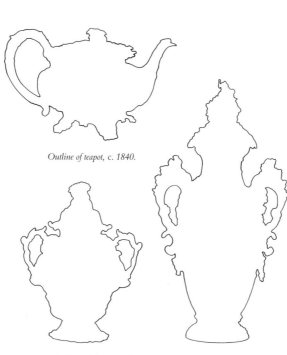

Outline of teapot, c. 1840.

"Coalbrookdale" vases, from the Coalport factory, 1830–35.

Coalport vase with leaf and scroll designs.

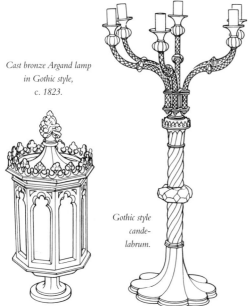

Cast bronze Argand lamp in Gothic style, c. 1823.

Gothic style candelabrum.

Three-dimensional Shapes and Decoration

For rococo designers, baluster and ogee shapes were once again popular, and virtually the whole surface was decorated, particularly with flowers on porcelain and embossed decoration on silver. Handles of vases, pots, and urns were curved and naturalistic.

The rococo revival also saw a widespread use of gilt bronze, partly due to fashion but also because new gilding techniques had made the process less expensive and less dangerous. It was often combined with patinated bronze to produce clock cases, lighting, fireplace equipment, and mounts for lamps and vases.

Industrial innovation now allowed England and the United States to produce cast and gilded mounts and handles for furniture. Putti were frequently used as ornament, usually cast in the round together with flowers, shells, and foliage.

As a part of the Gothic influence there was also an increased use of painted decoration, Gothic lettering, and flat motifs, particularly on furniture and ceramic tiles.

High Gothic-style chairback, North America, c. 1845.

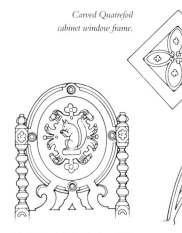

Carved Quatrefoil cabinet window frame.

Elizabethan-style chairback, c. 1835.

Carved trefoil chair undertier.

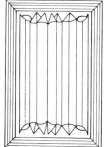

Linen-fold cabinet paneling.

Cabriole chair legs, England, c. 1835.

Chairs

For 20 to 30 years the Gothic revival influenced many chair designs. The two most obvious areas of influence were the back and the legs. In the 1830s and 1840s backs were usually solid, typically of pointed arch form and carved in relief with tracery. Subsequently, designs became more dramatic, often with open carving and naturalistic decoration. Early Gothic revival chairs often had conventional turned legs but later a wider range of more architectural supports were used and stylized paw feet were sometimes seen together with curved arch supports.

The "linenfold" panel was thought to be evocative of the Middle Ages, and its use was revived, particularly for chairbacks and also cupboard doors.

The rococo revival influence led to the prevalence of curved frame chairbacks either upholstered or with open leading, and the "balloon back," which was very popular in the second half of the century. Such chairs almost universally stood on cabriole legs.

Rococo-revival chairback, North America, c. 1845.

Rococo-revival chairback, England, c. 1835.

William IV giltwood open armchair, attributed to Gillows of Leicester.

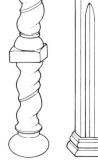

Gothic-style table leg, France, c. 1840.

Gothic-style table leg, France, c. 1835.

Gothic-style table base, attributed to George Bullock, c. 1835.

Tables

The taste for rococo revival furniture meant a return to the use of the cabriole leg, often of a particularly slender and elongated form for smaller pieces of furniture such as card tables. The legs usually terminated in brass cappings or "sabots."

Later Gothic revival tables often rested on relatively simple architectural legs, in some cases linked by architectural supports. Cluster and other columns became more popular for legs and stems.

Architectural Ornament

All pieces using Gothic and rococo styles as their inspiration adopted architectural details in their design. Small items might only have detail decoration, whereas larger pieces, particularly furniture, had boldly carved details, often in relief. Arches, trefoil, and quatrefoil motifs frequently occurred, often of pierced form but also as painted or relief decoration. Items as diverse as pressed-glass butter dishes, brass candlesticks, cast-iron firebacks, and wardrobes were made with Gothic relief decoration particularly on brass lamps and other metalware, while projecting tracery and simple leaf designs adorned furniture and metalwork.

Gothic-style settee back, North America, c. 1835.

The Machine Age

Rapidly advancing technological developments were now proudly displayed by manufacturers from all over the world at various well-attended international exhibitions. A ramification of this meant that decorative, detailed furniture became affordable for many for the very first time. As gas became a readily available power source, this also began to make life more comfortable for a far greater proportion of the population.

ABOVE **The facade of St. Pancras Railroad Station in London was built on a truly lavish scale between 1868 and 1872. Its expensive and elaborate construction may be explained by its** original use as a station hotel. Its imposing and distinctive Gothic architecture—with its striking roofline of towers and pointed spires—places it firmly in the Exhibition Era.

During the latter part of the eighteenth century, and subsequently the nineteenth century, there was a continual voracious thirst for innovation in the applied arts, partly spurred on by ever advancing technical developments. Some of the most significant developments for designers and architects included a new technique for the large-scale production of papiermâché, which was developed by Henry Clay in 1772 and improved on from 1830; the invention of pressed glass in America in the early 1820s; and the invention of electrotype casting in the 1830s and of electroplating in the 1840s. Furthermore, new adaptations and applications of existing techniques meant that by the mid-century the range of products available had increased dramatically. In North America, for instance, John Belter developed an innovative technique for laminated furniture construction. This meant that he could achieve a greater degree of intricate detail that would not otherwise have been possible.

The result of these developments, both of new materials and adaptations of traditional techniques, was twofold. First, the lower costs of less skill-intensive production made decorative furnishings and ornaments affordable to an ever larger number of people—all eager to buy this new merchandise. The second development was that in many media, the sheer quantity of detailed decoration that could now be included also increased considerably.

TURNING TO GAS AND METAL

There had also been a revolution in power sources for domestic lighting. By the middle of the nineteenth century paraffin oil was beginning to replace colza or whale oil and candles, particularly in table lamps. At the same time in England many larger houses installed their own gas supply, including Windsor Castle in the 1850s. Gas was a popular power source for ceiling and wall lights that do not need to be moved, and many antique lamps that have since been converted to electricity still bear the blanked-off taps of their original pedigree.

Although cast iron had been used for hundreds of years for firebacks, grates, and irons, it was only in the second quarter of the century that it became more widely used for furniture and furnishings, both for indoor and exterior use, with France, Germany, England, and the United States as major centers of production. Iron was used for statuary, but the growth in demand for outdoor

ABOVE **The International Exhibition of 1851 displayed the grandeur of Victorian design and the new advances in industrial production. The illustration of the Minton majolica water fountain from an 1862 editon of** *The Illustrated London News* **shows one** such example of the Victorian aesthetic. Neoclassical motifs form the springboard for the resplendent design, but these are subject to the functional ambitions of the piece and the extravagant aesthetic of the era.

ABOVE **Bowes Museum, Durham, England, is a mid-nineteenth-century version of an eighteenth-century French château. It emphasizes that revivalism—particularly of the French "Louis" styles—which was prevalent in the applied arts, could also be seen in architecture, particularly in the grand houses built for wealthy merchants and industrialists.**

sculpture, fueled by a rise in public commissions, had to be met in a different way. Manufacturers turned to traditional materials such as stone and bronze, using increasingly sophisticated casting techniques as well as newly developed materials, including durable ceramic artificial stone and "reconstituted stone," which is, in effect, cement with a metal reinforcement or "armature."

THE INFLUENCE OF INTERNATIONAL EXHIBITIONS

A further impetus to technical innovation was provided by the opportunity for manufacturers to display their creations at international exhibitions throughout the world during the second half of the nineteenth century. Factories were inspired to produce ever more elaborate showpieces using adaptations of old technology, and the English ceramic factories such as Minton, Wedgwood, and Doulton were keen competitors, as were bronze and metalworking foundries such as Barbedienne in Paris. This was also a period of great innovation in the design of glassware, which had primarily been functional until this time. The development of new techniques in Bohemia, the United States, and England created an array of affordable ornamental pieces.

The Great Exhibition, which took place in London in 1851, is probably the best known of the international exhibitions. Not only was this a showcase for the most elaborate and advanced products from around the world, it also

RIGHT **Castle Museum, York, England, is a typical example of a somewhat cluttered Victorian interior. It illustrates well the scenario against which the designers of the Arts and Crafts, art nouveau, and other movements later reacted. While the result is both comfortable and homely, the overall effect is of an amalgam of different styles and materials.**

provided a much greater awareness of the diversity of more traditional items and techniques, such as carved ivory from India and the Far East, wood carvings from Germany and Austria, and ivory inlaid guns from France.

A NEW INTEREST IN ORNAMENTATION

The overwhelming theme at this and many of the subsequent exhibitions was ornamentation. In 1851, the two most prevalent styles were Gothic and naturalistic, with the rococo and classical styles also visible. By the 1862 London Exhibition it was clear that many designers were being influenced by the opening up of Japan and its styles and iconography. By 1872 a new mood of simpler forms with less decoration was beginning to have great impact. There were many Paris exhibitions in the mid-nineteenth century, notably one in 1889, a prelude to the as yet unnamed art nouveau style. The Centennial Exhibition in Philadelphia, Pennsylvania, in 1876 had emphasized the continuing popularity of the revival styles, most notably the neo-Renaissance.

It should be stressed, however, that many of the exhibits were created purely for exhibition, and that in most homes the furniture and decorations would have featured elements of particular styles, but not to the same overemphasized degree or exaggerated scale.

BELOW **Long galleries lined with pictures and sculptures were a feature of many grand houses from the eighteenth century onward. Here at Cragside Hall, England, built in the second half** of the nineteenth century, the effect is softened by the use of carpet and a semi-vaulted skylit roof. The sculpture is, in some cases, less severe than that prevalent in the neoclassical era.

Collector's Gallery

By the mid-1850s, a melting pot of stylistic features was influencing furniture design. This was further complicated by the development of a new range of manufacturing techniques and materials such as the elaborate, laminated wooden forms of John Henry Belter in the United States, the bentwood furniture of Michael Thonet in Germany, along with papier mâché, carved wood, and cast iron. During the next 50 or so years, and with the exception of certain movements described below, furniture was generally elaborate with a high degree of ornamentation, and many of the styles produced were adaptations of earlier forms.

Bentwood Furniture

Thonet's bentwood chairs heralded a style that was still considered modern more than a hundred years later. As manufacturing processes increased in capacity, bentwood furniture became a relatively economical and versatile form of domestic furniture.

1 Chairs, such as the one pictured below, were curved through almost every plane and were very simple in form. **2** Despite the light appearance, the heat treatment used to bend and set the wood made it extremely strong at points of stress. **3** Traditionally, pale woods such as birch were used to make bentwood furniture, providing a light contrast to traditional nineteenth-century oak and mahogany furniture. **4** Cane or laminated wood was used for seating.

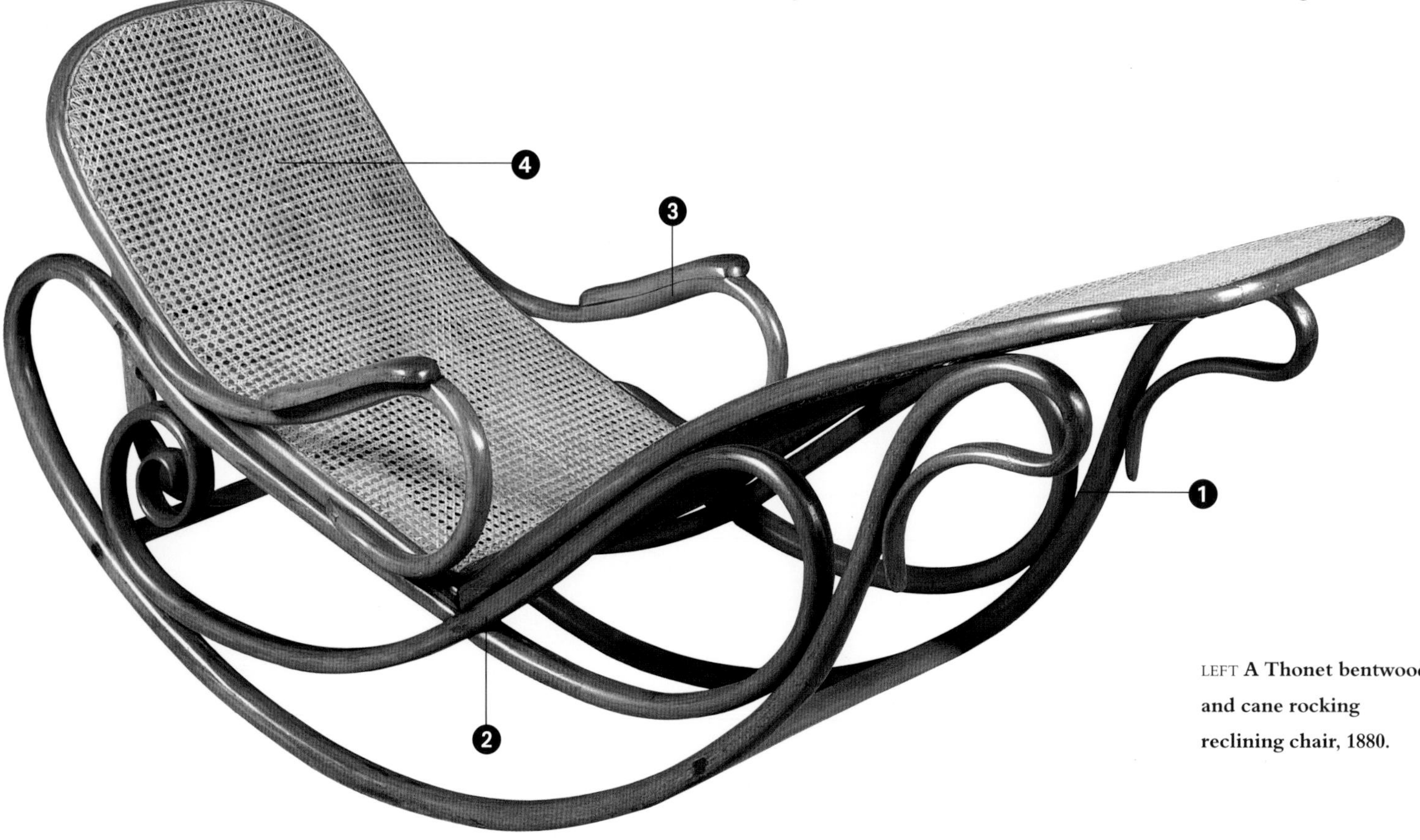

LEFT **A Thonet bentwood and cane rocking reclining chair, 1880.**

Belter Furniture

French rococo styles continued to be influential on post-1850 furniture, particularly in the area of seat furniture. Belter's designs for seat furniture, beds, and tables were executed in a naturalistic version of the rococo style.
❶ He specialized in carved and laminated decoration, using elaborate curves ❷ and foliate ornamentation.
❸ Improved springing techniques made seat furniture more comfortable and cheaper to produce. Manufactured metal springs were used to create a deeper, more comfortable seating area, increasing the luxurious feel that suited the rococo styling that permeated the nineteenth century.

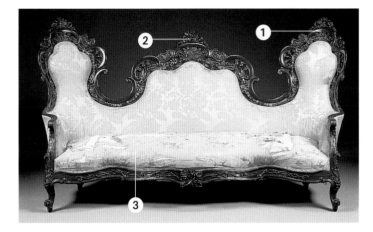

ABOVE **Carved rosewood sofa, by John Henry Belter, New York,** *c.* **1855.**

LEFT **Mahogany patent desk, by Wooton Desk Co., Indianapolis,** *c.* **1875.**

RIGHT **Edwardian satinwood and rosewood Carlton House desk.**

Davenport desk reflected the increasingly complex nature of middle class life. The Wooton desk was a combination of practical innovation with ornate decoration typical of this period. ❶ The curved front sections are hinged to either side and extensively fitted with compartments and pigeon holes. A writing desk is concealed within. ❷ Mahogany, and to a lesser extent walnut, were the most prevalent woods, but it was common practice to stain inexpensive white woods to simulate them.
❸ Classical motifs were far more elaborate than the clean lines seen in the neoclassical period. A large proportion of furniture had a mahogany exterior with drawers veneered in paler woods. ❹ Mechanized techniques meant that marquetry panels and insets could now be used on less expensive furniture. ❺ Every panel and angle was decorated either with a carving, moldings, veneers, or marquetry. ❻ Legs and uprights were usually turned, carved, or fluted, or a combination of all three.

Desks

A plethora of technically interesting designs developed throughout the Machine Age, of a range previously only seen in the days of Hepplewhite and Sheraton. Unlike the earlier period, most of the designs were extensively decorated and involved elaborate mechanisms. The Davenport desk, although first designed in the early 1800s, became more popular in the second half of the century. Together with a wide range of small tables—such as whatnots, étagères, and games tables—and music cabinets, the

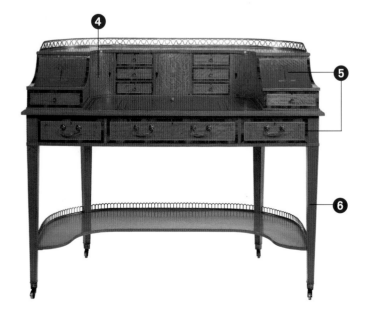

Display Furniture

Display furniture took three main forms: upright vitrines with glazed doors and sides; credenzas of waist height; and small glazed table cabinets. The glazed doors and panels of vitrines and credenzas were usually curved, either bowed or serpentine. **1** The shape of vitrines was generally influenced by the curves of the rococo period, **2** but with far more glass than originally used. **3** Vitrines were often veneered in kingwood or another exotic wood, and frequently decorated with lacquer scenes or porcelain panels in the Sèvres style. **4** Credenzas could be ebonized, often with boulle decoration, marquetry inlaid with walnut or more exotic veneers, or other combinations of French styles. **5** All forms of cabinet would invariably be finished with gilt bronze mounts.

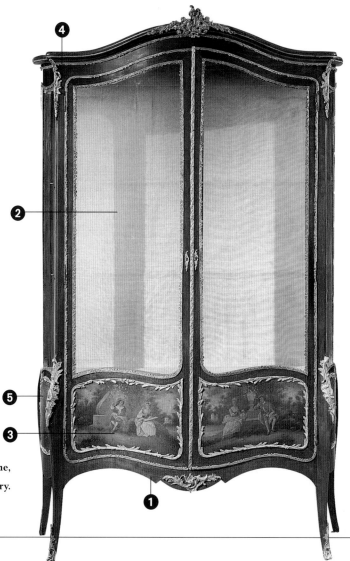

RIGHT **Vernis Martin vitrine, late nineteenth century.**

Papier Mâché Furniture

The papier-mâché furniture of Jennens and Bettridge is archetypal of the English drawing room in the mid-nineteenth century. The most extravagant pieces were commissioned by aristocratic clients, but more modest pieces, although ornate, were relatively inexpensive. **1** Typically, sofas featured elaborate gilt **2** and often mother-of-pearl decoration. **3** Another innovation of the industrial age, the properties of papier-mâché enabled the creation of elaborately curvaceous pieces, both in form **4** and decoration.

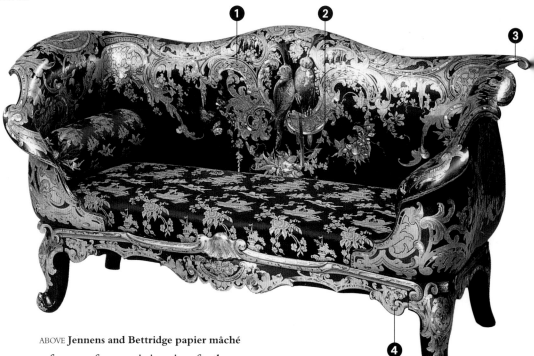

ABOVE **Jennens and Bettridge papier mâché sofa: copy of a commission piece for the Spanish Royal family,** *c.* **1860.**

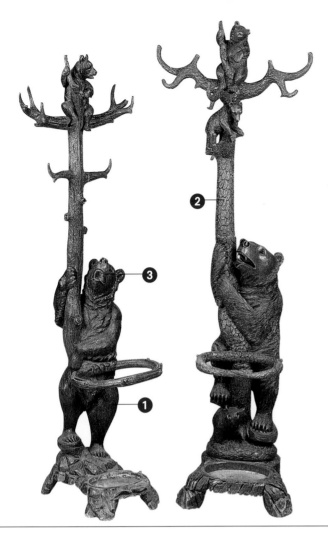

Animal-themed Furniture

Southern Germany and the Alpine countries were noted for elaborate wood carving. Some pieces of furniture took the form of animals, and these items were widely exported to North America. Although most pieces remained hand-carved, improved tooling methods increased the economic efficiency of producing elaborately carved furniture. **1** One variation was furniture based on the form of a carved bear. The animal would be incorporated into the structure of the item, such as a hallstand or a bench. Size was considered to emphasize the dramatic effect, and some carved bear pieces reach 4 feet (1.2 metres) high. **2** The bear would sometimes be shown holding a tree or grappling with another beast. **3** Often, the bear was represented with a grizzled expression, indicating the full power of its animal strength.

LEFT **Two carved and grained pine brown bear hallstands, Southern Germany.**

Vases and Ceramic Basketwork

One of the most notable features of ceramics made at this time was the emphasis on precise detail. This could be seen in a wide range of objects, from the almost photographic quality of the pictorial plaques made by the German K.P.M. factory, to the intricate and delicate basket work of the Belleek factory. **1** The hand-carved decoration of George Owen's work for the Royal Worcester factory was replicated in molded reticulated work from other English factories. The effect of this pierced decoration is reminiscent of Moorish architecture and was also used less precisely by the Hungarian Zsolnay factory. **2** By the 1880s, vase shapes were also becoming reminiscent of Moorish designs. Twin slender handles to the shoulder and long necks were distinctive features. **3** From 1880 to 1900, the emphasis switched from unrestrained and highly colored naturalistic styles, to paler, restrained decoration, often delicately heightened in gilt.

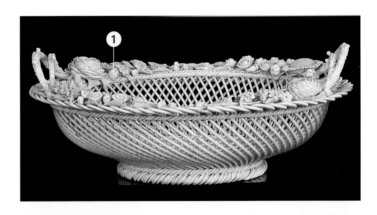

ABOVE RIGHT **Belleek pierced oval basket.**

RIGHT **Three reticulated Royal Worcester vases, by George Owen.**

Ornamental Ceramics

The impetus given to ceramic manufacture by the plethora of exhibitions from the 1850s onward, together with the benefits of technical progress, led to the creation of much larger objects than previously seen. Although some of these pieces were made purely for exhibition purposes, others were used in private homes as the fashion for interior decoration on a large scale took hold. Ceramic statues and urns designed for outside use, and usually unglazed, were made in England and France but were eventually superseded by bronze, iron, and lead, which were more durable, and reconstituted stone, which was less expensive.
1 Bronze mounted vases on a large scale in the neoclassical taste were an expansion of an existing form. Other ceramics were made using techniques particularly suited for large-scale applications. **2** Majolica glazed earthenwares, including seats for conservatory use, were particularly popular in the third quarter of the nineteenth century.

The most notable are the models of birds and animals that reflected the considerable interest in creating wildlife forms as realistically as possible in the decorative arts.
3 This elegant peacock is painted in shimmering blues and greens, with yellow and red detail.

LEFT **Minton majolica, life-size model of a peacock,** *c.* 1875.

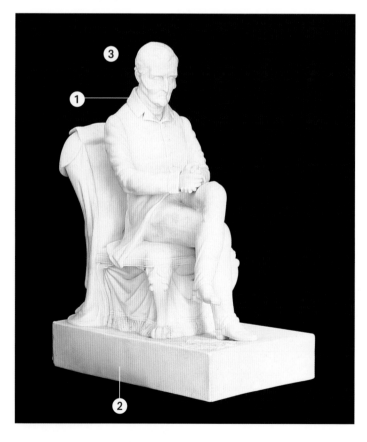

ABOVE **A Parian figure of the Duke of Wellington,** *c.* **1850.**

Historical Portrait Busts and Figures

Unglazed bisque porcelain busts and figures of contemporary and historical worthies were produced by Sèvres and other factories in the eighteenth century, but bisque wares became unfashionable in the first half of the nineteenth century when lavish decoration and colors held sway. Bisque busts had been popular partly because of their resemblance to marble—also one of the great attractions of Parian ware when it was invented in the 1840s. Although invented in England and first produced by the Copeland factory, Parian ware was also produced in many other countries, notably by Bennington in the United States.
1 Parian ware was used to create reduced-scale copies of ancient marble busts and statues, and was hugely popular for about 20 years. **2** Parian ware differed from bisque in having a slightly granular surface with a marblelike texture. **3** The range of subjects was initially primarily ancient, but was expanded to include other contemporary and historical figures such as the Duke of Wellington.

Porcelain Figurines

ABOVE **Meissen porcelain figurines in a selection of costumes.**

Although the porcelain figurines of the eighteenth century are the most distinctive and noteworthy, figurines were also produced in very large numbers in the second half of the nineteenth century. Porcelain figurines copying eighteenth-century designs are often crisply modeled, but should not be confused with the softer and less precise finish of soft paste porcelain. ❶ Many of the figures were highly derivative and often depicted in eighteenth-century costume. ❷ Meissen figures of the nineteenth century use less muted colors than those of the eighteenth century and are usually more precisely marked, with stamped rather than incised numbers. Generally, provided a figurine is of good quality, the less precise the mark the older it is, whereas printed marks and mention of countries or places of origin indicate a late date. ❸ Toward the end of the nineteenth century there was a revival of interest in porcelain figures and many of the major factories produced new models of more contemporary subjects, often very accurately modeled.

Sèvres Porcelain

For most of the second half of the nineteenth century, the neoclassical French style, based on Sèvres porcelain, in particular using a pale blue ground, was very popular. The differences between such pieces and those made in the eighteenth century were quite marked. The painted decoration was not of the same quality and had an individual character that is only seen in soft paste porcelain; the later Sèvres wares and that of its imitators were in hard paste. ❶ This style of decoration was mainly used for ornamental items rather than services. The main exceptions were cups and saucers, often sold singly, although they too were frequently meant for display rather than use. ❷ This type of porcelain was often used in conjunction with gilt metal mounts and as decorative embellishment to furniture and clock cases. Many mantel clock cases were made of this Sèvres-style porcelain. ❸ The most popular reserve (ground) color was a turquoise blue (bleu celeste), but dark blue (bleu de roi), dark pink, and green were also common. The typical themes of decoration were frolicking cherubs, historical portrait heads from the eighteenth century, and swags or trailing foliage with understated flowerheads.

LEFT **A Regency pendulum clock, designed by Andre-Charles Boulle.**

Paperweights

A completely new development in the manufacture of glass was the creation of millefiori paperweights in the mid-1840s. Although the technique is related to earlier Venetian glass, the innovative early designs were almost exclusively French and from three factories: Baccarat, St Louis, and Clichy. Subsequently, the paperweights have been produced in many countries, notably Bohemia, the United States, and England. The other distinctive type of paperweight produced by the French makers and later by others was the sulfure. These were simple but realistic representations of flowers, fruit, animals, or insects. The sulfures appealed for their close replication of nature rather than the intricacy of their detail. **①** Millefiori designs are produced by making patterned rods from colored canes of glass, then cutting slithers from different rods and arranging them to form the final pattern, as in these flowerheads. Some

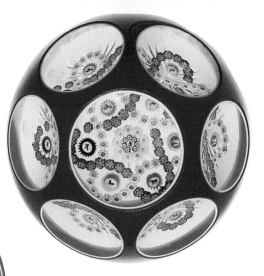

LEFT AND ABOVE **Baccarat cased-glass millefiori paperweights.**

paperweights can be identified by a maker's mark within the canes, but the majority are unmarked. Some of the most intricate paperweights have an outer case of glass which is cut away or "flashed" in the manner of Bohemian glass.

Cameo and Art Glass

Using a technique similar to that of pâte sur pâte decoration on porcelain produced at Sèvres and then at Minton, English glassmakers, notably Thomas Webb, produced a range of very fine cameo-like glass with details in opaque white on a colored ground. Cameo glass was imitated in similar, though less detailed, designs in molded glass. **①** The effect produced by overlaying a design on to colored glass was visually similar to that of cameo glass, in which a design is carved into a white outer layer of glass. **②** The designs were usually of finely detailed flowers and foliage on smaller pieces, and classical or mythological figures, such as this cupid, on larger pieces. **③** The major distinguishing feature between art and mass-produced glass was that each art piece was unique.

RIGHT **A Thomas Webb factory cameo, carved-glass vase by George Woodall**, *c.* 1890.

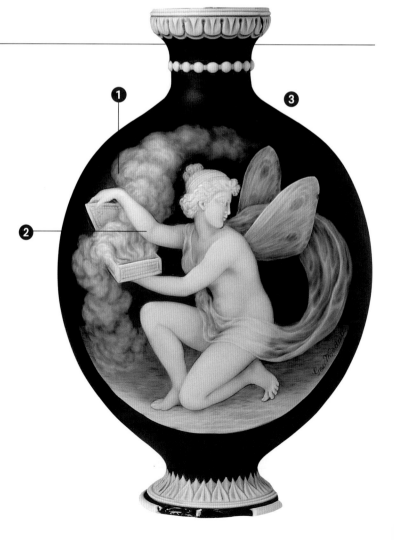

Bohemian Glassware

The Bohemian style of glassware refers to the range of heavy glass often "flashed" or cased in more than one color, and originally produced in that part of Central Europe. The style began in the second quarter of the nineteenth century and lasted throughout the century, although later items are often less elaborate and made of thinner glass. The style was gradually disseminated to other regions and countries, such as the United States. ❶ The range of objects produced was wide, with drinking vessels the most numerous: they included goblets in different sizes, beakers, and larger lidded cups. ❷ Bohemian glassware was predominantly ruby or cranberry in color, although amber was also relatively commonplace; blue was less common. The colors were sometimes combined or used with white flashing—the removal of part of a thin outer layer of glass to reveal a different colored or clear glass beneath, and occasionally heightened in gilt.

❸ Engraving was also used to decorate such pieces. Typical subjects might be religious or topographical, indicating that these glasses were often bought as souvenirs.

RIGHT **An engraved goblet, North Bohemia, *c.* 1880.**

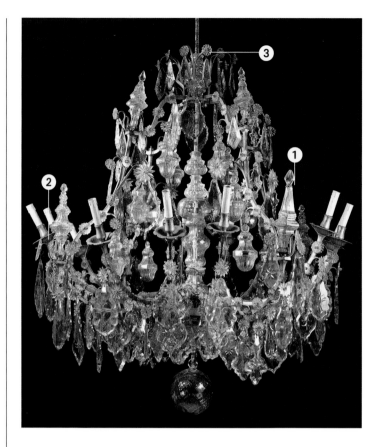

ABOVE **A gilt bronze and glass chandelier, France, *c.* 1840.**

Chandeliers

By the mid-nineteenth century, glass was once again becoming a popular material for ceiling lights, whereas gilt bronze, which required less maintenance and was more suitable for oil and gas lamps, had become fashionable in the previous 20 to 30 years. However, with the new possibilities offered by molded and colored glass, highly decorative and less expensive light fittings could be produced. ❶ The "storm shade" enabled candle and oil lights to burn more efficiently and provided an opportunity for decoration. ❷ There was an increasing use of mixed-media light fittings. A brass or gilt metal frame for strength and practicality, for example, could be combined with glass drops and applied details in clear or colored glass, particularly amethyst or ruby. ❸ Venice became a significant exporter of chandeliers and wall lights, and continued to be so into the twentieth century. Distinctive features are the use of additional decorative elements, such as projecting flowerheads and feathery leaves, frequently with shaded or colored details.

Naturalistic Silver

As with other media, during the second and third quarters of the nineteenth century, natural forms were a strong influence on the shape and decoration of silver. Examples ranged from chased figural scenes on tea services, to condiment sets modeled in the shape of owls. Plain or sparsely decorated silver was distinctly unfashionable and was largely restricted to reproductions of earlier designs.
❶ The chased or embossed decoration on hollowware was inspired by a wide range of themes, including classical mythology, the Far East (first China and later Japan), as well as the natural world. Cutlery handles were usually chased or engraved, often with flowers or foliage, and in some cases cast in the round with designs such as openwork trailing vine leaves, that were more decorative than practical. ❷ Sets of small spoons frequently had cast figural handles or finials. ❸ More elaborate and expensive silver items were almost sculptural in form and frequently cast, with the form of an object often considered as important as its function.

ABOVE **A Victorian silver and parcel-gilt dessert service, Elkington, London, 1890.**

Decorative Metalwork

In England, hallmarking regulations limited the extent to which other finishes could be used on silver items, but other countries did not have the same restrictions. In the United States, the firms of Gorham and Tiffany used colored metals and inlays to create decorative effects that can be compared with Japanese metalwares, and were generally more innovative than European factories at the same time. ❶ Russia has a tradition of silver decorated with niello and cloisonné, dating from the eighteenth century. Cloisonné work, including icon frames, small boxes, spoons, and tea-sets, was produced in Russia on a wide scale and to a high standard throughout the nineteenth century, until the Revolution in 1917. ❷ Like the champlevé enamel work utilized in France at the end of the nineteenth century, cloisonné was inspired by intricate Islamic metalwork. The most prevalent examples of this technique can be seen in clock cases and vases, shown in this example in vivid turquoise, blue, green, yellow, and black hues.

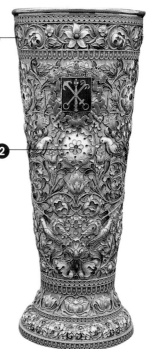

ABOVE **A Russian silver gilt and cloisonné enamel beaker by Ovchinnikov.**

Allegorical French Bronzes

Allegorical figures are typically young women, partially clad in quasi-classical costume, mirroring the representation of the female form in fine art at this time. The title of the subject is often inscribed on the base and the format was readily adapted to art nouveau themes at the end of the nineteenth century. Genre figures tended to represent artisans with attributes of their trade attached to the base and were frequently cast in Germany. ❶ The sculptor has used distinctive modeling and chasing to distinguish between the costume and the human figure. ❷ The bronze base is not made separately but is an integral part of the cast. ❸ The subject matter is a somewhat idealized genre figure typical of this period and in complete contrast to the classical and historical subjects that were popular earlier in the century.

RIGHT *"The Smiling Neapolitan Girl,"* **Jean-Baptiste Carpeaux,** *c. 1875*

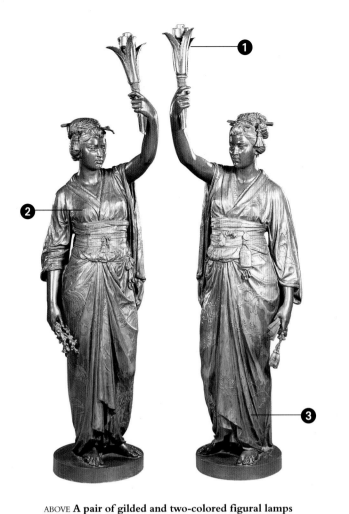

ABOVE **A pair of gilded and two-colored figural lamps
by Barbedienne, France.**

Barbedienne

In addition to bronzes designed purely for ornament, the French foundries, particularly Barbedienne, produced a wide range of bronzes that were functional as well as decorative. These would often be gilded completely or in part, instead of the traditional dark patination. Typical applications included figural lamps, inkstands, andirons, and other light fixtures . ❶ The pair of figural bronze lamps illustrated were cast by Barbedienne and are more than 4 feet (1.2 metres) high. The figures may originally have supported oil lamps, but have subsequently been converted to electricity. ❷ As with many objects produced in the second half of the nineteenth century, the subject matter illustrates the fascination with Japan as a source of ornament following the opening up of that country in the Meiji period. The figures are dressed in traditional Japanese peasant costume. ❸ The patination has at least three different finishes: it was often the case that the most desirable and expensive bronzes had a silver or gilt patination, or on occasion the two together.

Animal and Figural French Bronzes

Sophisticated casting techniques pioneered in France during the first half of the nineteenth century meant that good-quality bronze sculpture could be produced in large editions, and therefore became quite affordable. Developments in the "lost wax" casting technique, together with the technology to produce an accurate miniature version of a well-known statue—for example, the Marly Horses in Paris—increased the range and appeal of such statuettes. Figural subjects can be divided into three main categories: historical, mythological/ allegorical, and genre. Animal subjects can be the most dramatic. Their pioneer was A.L. Barye whose pieces, including animals locked in mortal combat, epitomized the Romantic era which also spawned the rococo revival. ❶ Horses, hounds, birds, and a

menagerie of other animal subjects were produced until at least the 1880s, with Barye, Mene, and Moigniez among the most popular sculptors. ❷ French bronzes are almost invariably signed by the sculptor. They usually bear a foundry mark, and often a seal referring to the casting technique used. With the exception of the impressionistic work of Dalou and Rodin, the treatment of the subject matter is usually realistic, as shown.

RIGHT **A group of cold-painted animals,
Vienna,** *c.* 1900.

Carriage Clocks

During the second quarter of the nineteenth century, a new type of accurate but portable clock was developed. Carriage clocks were usually encased in brass, and by the second half of the century, had become extremely popular. France was the main center of production, but they were also made in England and later in the United States. As with mantel clocks, many carriage clocks of French manufacture bear a retailer's name from another country on the dial. They would normally have been supplied with a protective leather carrying case with a glazed front panel, to tell the time without removing the clock. ❶ Non-striking timepieces can be distinguished

from clocks by the absence of a bell or coil gong behind the movement. ❷ The dial is normally of white enamel, ❸ but late (post-1900) examples often have a brass and simulated ivory dial. More decorative examples were made with painted porcelain or enamel side panels. ❹ The presence of a subsidiary small dial on the front of the clock indicates that the clock has an alarm. ❺ Earlier carriage clocks had cases cast in one piece, but later examples tend to have three-piece cases, as shown.

RIGHT **A champlevé enamel and brass carriage alarm clock/barometer, flanked by two other carriage clocks, France, late nineteenth century.**

Clock Garnitures

France was the dominant producer of decorative clocks during the nineteenth century, and in many cases the clock itself was flanked by a pair of candelabra or urns to form a garniture. The range of materials used varied, but would typically be a combination of porcelain or polished stone, mounted in gilt-metal. The latter would vary from gilt-bronze to gilt-spelter, or electro-plate for less expensive clocks. ❶ The mounts between the clock and the sidepieces should be very similar, although they were sometimes matched later. ❷ The form of the garniture was

often influenced by Louis XVI designs, with the use of pillar supports and urn forms. ❸ Each of the three parts of the garniture would often rest on a separate wooden stand, partly to protect polished surfaces beneath, and also to act as supports for the glass domes that were often used as protective covers to keep the decorative elements in pristine condition.

LEFT **A gilt-bronze and porcelain clock garniture, France, *c.* 1870.**

Mantel Clocks

As with carriage clocks, decorative mantel clocks, without side urns, were often made in France or had French movements, even though the name on the dial might be England or another country. The movements of these clocks are relatively simple, using a small pendulum. ❶ A typical combination of materials was gilt-bronze and painted porcelain panels on a blue ground, replicating the designs of the Sèvres factory, ❷ with figures or portraits bordered by flowers and swags. ❸ While the clock dial might often be porcelain, a more restrained form popular in England and Austria was a white enamel dial with clear Roman numerals. ❹ The milled disk or bun feet were almost universal on French mantel clocks at this time, beneath a projecting plinth with leaf-cast borders.

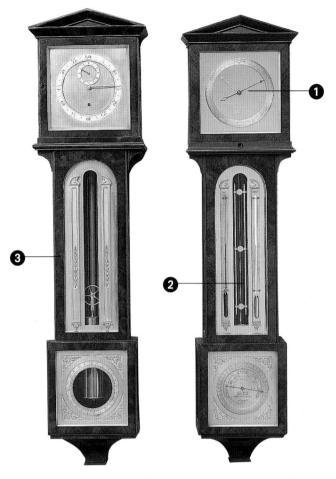

ABOVE **An unusual twin-dial barometer and thermometer in a mahogany case, *c.* 1880.**

BELOW **A gilt-bronze and blue porcelain mantel clock, France, *c.* 1880.**

Barometers

Early barometers measured atmospheric pressure using a glass tube containing mercury. By about 1800, the readings were indicated on a circular dial, rather than as formerly on a calibrated scale. In 1848, the aneroid barometer was invented. This measured pressure on a small metal box; although generally less accurate than a mercury barometer, aneroid barometers were much less expensive to produce. ❶ During the first half of the nineteenth century, most barometers were of "wheel" or "banjo" form, with the dial positioned about three-quarters of the way down the length of the case. ❷ Mercury barometers can be identified by an inspection cover on the reverse of the case, and usually the presence of a spirit-level gauge on the front, which was essential to keep the instrument upright to obtain an accurate reading. ❸ Although aneroid barometers initially had "banjo" cases, this was not technically necessary. Many have carved oak cases typical of the later nineteenth century and later examples were often circular in form, without a long case.

Detail Directory

During this period the range of influences on design and ornament was vast. This was a time when furnishings and ornaments were, without exception, extensively decorated, in many cases with a combination of different historical styles on the same item.

Influences on Decoration

The type of ornament ranged from rococo to "Japanesque" through neoclassical, Gothic, Renaissance, naturalistic, and Islamic. The Renaissance style made considerable use of mythological beasts and maskheads, combined with strapwork, paws and claws, and delicate scrolling foliage. The naturalistic style, as its name suggests, made extensive use of natural iconography, particularly fruit and foliage, and in its flowing shapes could be seen as a development of the rococo. There was little restraint in the use of natural ornament; virtually no part of an object remained undecorated.

Islamic style was particularly influential in the areas of glass and ceramics. Widespread use of tiles for decoration in the Middle East was replicated in the West at this time; bold, stylized flower and leaf designs inspired Western decorators and designers. Furthermore, there was a significant market for items such as clocks, watches, and glassware in Turkey, and many makers incorporated Islamic shapes such as stylized minarets into their exports. The influence of Islamic decoration was considerable during the second half of the nineteenth century. With the exception of handmade carpets, however, Islamic design had minimal impact in the West during the previous 300 years, nor indeed, has it made much impact since.

Rococo-style painted wall panel, France, mid-nineteenth century.

Japanese and Zoomorphic Forms

The Japanesque style was significant in that it often was used to decorate and furnish entire rooms. The timing of the start of the Meiji period and the opening up of Japan meant that the style of that country captured the imagination of designers in Europe and the United States for two reasons: first, it introduced what could be seen as a new range of ornament, giving it the attraction of the exotic; and second, the inherent restraint of Japanese applied arts was very appealing to those who sought an escape from the excesses of ornament that had previously evolved. It was interpreted in different ways, notably by the bold use of mythical bird and animal motifs, often on a strong turquoise or deep red ground simulating lacquer, but also in a more restrained form using images such as swallows and blossoming branches in a sparse and asymmetric manner. It was arguably the most influential style between the 1870s and 1890s until the emergence of the Arts and Crafts Movement and art nouveau.

Another noticeable feature at this time was the widespread use of human and animal forms, particularly as sculpture in the round or in high relief. Prevalent in metalwork and furniture mounts, these forms appeared not only on the most expensive pieces but, because of advances in metal casting techniques, also on more mundane base metal items, such as candlesticks and paper knives.

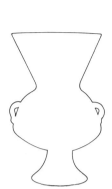

Outline of Islamic-style vase, France, 1867.

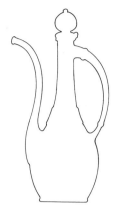

Outline of Islamic-style coffee pot, 1882.

Islamic-style porcelain vase, France.

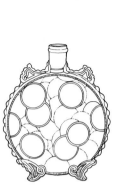

Japanese-style moon vase, by Royal Worcester, 1872.

Silhouette of parcel gilt jug, by Elkington, 1882–83.

Japanese-style jug, by Tiffany & Co., 1874.

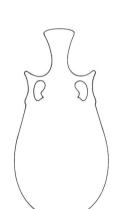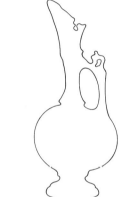

Profiles of porcelain vase shapes, England, c. 1870.

Foliage-themed porcelain decoration.

Islamic-style vase, Bohemia, c. 1870.

Ceramics, Glass, and Metalware

Designs were influenced by the East, near and far.
New shapes, hitherto not made in the West, included
the long-necked ewer inspired by Turkish coffee pots
and other vessels, the flattened circular "pilgrim
bottle" shape for vases, and the broad, conical neck
replica Islamic glass vessels produced in France.

When Japan reopened links with the West in the
1860s, Japanesque shapes, particularly in ceramics
and metalware, became popular. In many cases only
certain elements, such as naturalistic dragon or
"bamboo" handles and simulated bronze mounts
were used. This provided an interesting contrast with
the simplicity of traditional Japanese forms. By the
latter part of this period, vase shapes, typically ovoid,
became more elongated, with slender, often angular
handles, high-domed covers, and pale, defined, or
sparse decoration.

Profile of Sèvres-style urn, c. 1870.

Animal-themed porcelain decoration.

Marble bust of Proserpine, by Hiram Powers, c. 1850.

Louis XV-style grand piano, by Steinway and Sons, New York, c. 1882.

Rococo-influenced lady's bureau, walnut with bronze mounts, France, 1860.

Furniture

French rococo and neoclassical forms remained popular, particularly for furniture. French rococo also influenced the widespread popularity of soft, curvaceous shapes for furniture in other countries such as Britain and America.

In the 1870s and '80s there was a reaction against the over-ornate and heavy looking forms that had been commonplace. This was not a radical departure; highly decorative styles were still popular, but more slender and less solid designs began to evolve. This "slimming" trend could also be observed in furniture, where lighter woods with discreet inlays and pierced galleries and friezes created a less weighty impression.

The solidity and large scale of much furniture in the second half of the nineteenth century was emphasized by the use of plinth bases rather than feet and legs, often compounded by substantial superstructures and pediments. Design on a large scale was not limited to furniture and was particularly evident in the manufacture of floor-standing vases and bronze sculpture.

The cabriole leg, much in evidence throughout this period, was often extensively carved when used to support armchairs and more substantial tables, where a pair was often linked by a carved stretcher. Toward the end of the century the legs became more delicate. They were uncarved and usually used only on dining and salon chairs and the smallest of occasional tables. Slender tapering or fluted neoclassical legs then became more popular and of necessity were often linked by stretchers or an undertier for rigidity. Chairbacks became more delicate and were often not upholstered. Increasingly, larger items of furniture were raised on legs. Painted finishes became more popular, and inlay was used to break up the monotony of large areas of dark mahogany.

Handles from vases to chests of drawers became simpler; widespread use was made of more slender, angular forms. Throughout the applied arts the pendulum was swinging from solidity and profuse ornament to lighter but still highly decorative forms.

Cabriole legs on base of carved firescreen, c. 1860.

Rococo-style dressing table, walnut with bronze mounts, France, c. 1860.

Cabriole leg on baloon-back chair, c. 1835.

Mirrors

One of the notable features of interiors during the second half of the nineteenth century was the popularity of mirrors. Large "overmantel" mirrors were almost commonplace, and usually had gilded or, less often, painted surrounds. The plates were normally made of beveled glass; the frames ranged from plain molded with rounded corners to those with a shaped "cresting" or other more elaborate embellishment. The detail of the latter was usually molded in gesso (plaster) rather than carved, as earlier frames had been. Equally popular were Venetian mirrors with applied mirrored borders, often with etched decoration. The girandole mirror with candle arms, which had been made in limited numbers in the eighteenth century, became very fashionable. The girandole was made in brass and cast iron with hinged arms as well as the more traditional giltwood and gesso.

Many of the large pieces of wall furniture, particularly chiffoniers and sideboards, made extensive use of mirrors to enhance the decoration of a room and to heighten the impact of the array of clocks and ornaments displayed in homes.

Venetian glass-framed mirror.

Oval girandole mirror.

Shelved overmantel mirror.

Crested overmantel mirror.

Lighting

By this time lamps and light fittings were becoming increasingly ornate. Many chandeliers used a combination of gilt metal frames and glass drops, frequently colored. Venetian chandeliers and free-standing candelabra were often made from colored glass with additional projecting leaves and, in some cases, with the candle nozzles protected by "storm shades." Toward the end of the nineteenth century gas was increasingly used as a power source for light fixtures. Despite having been converted for electricity, many examples still retain the original gas taps. Another way of distinguishing such fittings from those designed for candles is that the arms are generally straight, in order to facilitate the flow of gas.

The design of free-standing oil lamps, which initially had an orb- or drum-shaped reservoir above a column surmounted by a globular shade, evolved into smoother shapes. The reservoir was incorporated into the base, and the shade was domed, not dissimilar to shapes of electric lamps in the early part of the twentieth century.

Outline of cut glass lamp, North America, 1890.

Burmese glass oil lamp, North America, c. 1880.

William Morris carpet,
c. 1881.

RIGHT **Advertising poster
by Colin Paul.**

The Design Age

*By the turn of the twentieth century, there was a
reaction against what many considered the over
elaborate and incoherent styles of the Machine Age.
This reaction was expressed in two forms: the
philosophical mood of the Arts and Crafts movement and
the freer, thematic aesthetic of art nouveau. The impetus for
these styles came from designers working across different
media and continued with Art Deco and true modernist styles,
such as Bauhaus.*

The Arts and Crafts Movement

In the wake of changes wrought by the Industrial Revolution—both in society and subsequently in the applied arts—many artists and designers sought a return to traditional values. William Morris and his contemporaries reacted against the machine age, together pioneering a movement that saw a return to the tenets of craftsmanship that had their roots in the Middle Ages. Architects such as Frank Lloyd Wright continued the trend.

ABOVE **Built from the timbers of two ships, the Liberty department store in London was built in the Tudor revival style in 1924 by Edwin Hall and his son. Many of the designers used by the store were key figures in the Arts and Crafts and art nouveau movements.**

Inspired by Morris, the Arts and Crafts Movement grew in England, and thereafter America, with the emphasis on individual craftsmanship and traditional techniques using native materials. However, in contrast to the revival movements, Arts and Crafts was typified by originality rather than a pastiche of earlier styles.

Arts and Crafts designers produced a great diversity of styles, which means that there is not always a clear boundary between this and other movements, particularly art nouveau. The fine metalwork designs of Christopher Dresser bear comparison with some of the designs of the Bauhaus design school thirty years later, whereas Dresser's designs for glass were of a sinuous form more akin to art nouveau.

THE ARTS AND CRAFTS STYLE

Arts and Crafts designers followed a philosophy based on the importance of hand manufacture, rather than the impersonality of mass production. Therefore, while particular style details can be detected, the Movement's influence is apparent in a wide variety of designers' work.

William Morris was the "father" of the Movement, but the foundations had already been laid by Augustus Pugin, who considered good design to be of utmost importance. Parallels can be drawn between Arts and Crafts designers and the materials and range of ornament used by Pugin—his later designs for furniture employing indigenous woods such as oak, his designs for wallpaper, and his enthusiasm for stained glass. However, unlike Morris, Pugin did not oppose modern manufacturing. He was closely involved in the manufacturing process and believed that the techniques involved in producing wallpapers,

ABOVE **Medieval-looking Cardiff Castle in Wales was "improved" in the late 1800s by architect William Burges. Both he and the castle's owner, the Marquess of Bute, shared a passion for pre-Raphaelite decorative art, considered somewhat "fanciful" by some.**

LEFT **In 1893 Frank Lloyd Wright revived the stained glass window in his Winslow House (Illinois). Wright was a firm believer in the principles of the Arts and Crafts movement, but he was more radical, and keen to experiment with mechanization in his work.**

LEFT **The Ames Gate
Lodge in Massachusetts
was built in 1882 and
designed by Henry
Hobson Richardson.
Dominated by rustic
stonework, the building
exploits a range of
influences, including
early Christian arches
and French medieval
farm buildings.**

fabrics, and furniture were of utmost importance.
This concern for handcrafting was a philosophy
shared by others involved in the Movement, and
meant that a proportion of the objects produced
had an identifiable ancestry. Furthermore, Morris
worked closely with other artists and artisans to
produce integrated interior designs incorporating
medieval, Eastern, and vernacular English themes,
together with plant and animal forms.

Unlike other eras in design, Arts and Crafts does
not have a consistent style. Influences are
widespread—the Far and Middle East, the
Renaissance and Gothic periods—with the constant factor being that the majority of elements
were handmade. The English architect Philip
Webb was a leading Arts and Crafts designer who
spent many years working with Morris, and he
designed complete interiors. His furniture, which was generally plain and substantial, influenced the work of later designers.

By the 1870s, there was a revival of interest in pottery, for ornamental as well
as functional purposes, signaled by the "studio potters," and confirming that
there was a burgeoning market for handmade products. Such an interest can
also be seen in metalwork where the Guild of Handicraft in England began to
produce finely worked silverware. Likewise in America, the Roycroft
Workshops in New York State specialized in copperware, pottery, and furniture.

ABOVE **The interior of
the Ames Gate Lodge
reveals muted colors,
traditional wood panels,
and a committed use of
heavy stonework.**

THE INFLUENCE OF ARTS AND CRAFTS

Some designers who predated the Movement produced designs that shared
some of its characteristics. Christopher Dresser's uncomplicated designs for
pottery drew heavily on two main sources: first, his own detailed botanical

studies, and second, forms of simple glazed wares from other cultures. He was not, however, involved in the manufacture of his own designs, many of which were intended for large-scale industrial production. The work of the architect and designer Charles Voysey is closely associated with Arts and Crafts, yet his furniture and designs for wallpapers, tiles, and fabrics have a delicacy that invites comparison with art nouveau examples.

By the early twentieth century in England, craftspeople still following the Arts and Crafts ethos were mainly producing simple, often rectilinear designs, having established a tradition that still survives today. In America, much of the impetus came from architects, notably Frank Lloyd Wright. In his Prairie House and other buildings, the furniture, internal fittings, and even furnishings were closely integrated so that his trademark open, geometric theme could be recognized throughout. He used both metal and wood for his furniture, in which practicality and consistency of design were of equal importance. Because Arts and Crafts was a philosophy, rather than just a fashion, elements can be recognized in the later styles of Mackintosh and Hoffman. Many craftsmen continued to work in this manner into the 1930s and beyond.

BELOW **The great parlor at Wightwick Manor, England, reveals the favorite Arts and Crafts motifs of medieval-style wall panels and simple vernacular furniture.**

Collector's Gallery

Arts and Crafts furniture was mainly influenced by vernacular styles. One constant aspect was the use of indigenous materials, but many furniture designers also used painted finishes, often with pre-Renaissance decoration. There was often a blurring between Arts and Crafts and art nouveau, particularly with designers such as Arthur Mackmurdo. In the United States, the philosophy developed along similar lines, but by the early 1900s, through the work of Gustav Stickley and Frank Lloyd Wright, it was more forward looking than in Britain.

Tables

In an age of increasing industrialization and design flexibility, the interpretation of form, rather than the form itself, became an increasingly significant factor in the design of tables. ❶ Some designs were a heavy but simple evolvement of Gothic, with angular tops and trestle end supports on larger tables, and angular, often simply carved legs on smaller tables, usually of oak or walnut in its natural color.

Other designs featured dark-stained or ebonized wood in the Aesthetic movement taste, of relatively light construction, often with turned supports and spindle galleries. Because of the lightness of construction this style was primarily used for side and occasional tables. Later Arts and Crafts tables tended to be of simpler form, usually of oak and sometimes walnut, with rectangular supports, often paired lengthwise or linked by stretchers on larger dining tables.

ABOVE **Arts and Crafts, Gothic-influenced, walnut writing table, England,** *c.* **1870**

Sideboards

As later Arts and Crafts designers continued
to reject the notion of ornament, key
pieces of household furniture, such as
the domestic sideboard, reflected this
tendency. **1** Essential elements, such as
door and drawer handles, were
fashioned in traditional brass and
followed vernacular styles. **2** The
figure of the wood was the main
attraction. **3** The stark angularity of
many designs was broken only by the
occasional curve along the top or bottom
edges.

RIGHT **Oak side-
board, Gustav
Stickley,** *c.* **1902.**

Informal Furniture

The austere minimalism of the Arts and Crafts movement is
also evident in larger pieces of seating furniture. Arts and
Crafts designs became increasingly restrained as they
entered the twentieth century, ironically showing similarities
with the more modernistic designs of the industrial-inspired
Bauhaus. **1** The desire for utilitarianism often resulted in
less-than-comfortable furniture—upholstery was confined
to the essential seating area. **2** Fabric for upholstered areas
was plain or followed the subtle, muted patterns of the day.
3 Ornament was kept to a minimum or absent altogether.
Profiles were straight, rather than curved, and were combined with spindles or slats.

LEFT **Oak settee, Gustav Stickley** *c.* **1908.**

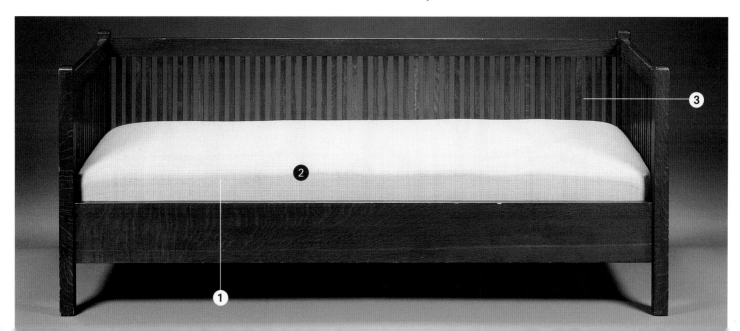

Chairs

There was no place for the well-upholstered Victorian easy chair within this style. Many of the Arts and Crafts styles were influenced by vernacular furniture, with local woods; oak or stained beech were used, rather than imported woods. **1** Immediately prior to the Arts and Crafts Movement, the Aesthetic Movement encouraged a taste for ebonized wood, often delicately turned and frequently featuring gilt or painted decoration. **2** Seats tended to be solid or simply upholstered, but rush, cane, and leather seats were also used. **3** Turned spindles on legs or chairbacks offer a sense of the vernacular. **4** Chairbacks were often rectilinear in form, with arms, where used, being flat in section. **5** The more vernacular styles might have horizontal rails,

ABOVE **Walnut armchairs with upholstered seats, Ernest Gimson,** *c.* **1905.**

RIGHT **Pair of ebonized armchairs, designed by Ford Maddox Brown for Morris & Co.,** *c.* **1875.**

known as ladderbacks. **6** Legs and stretchers were either of simple square or rectangular section or turned, but with an absence of carved detail, historical ornament or embellishment. **7** Traditional hardwoods, such as walnut and oak, were favored, as these represented the anti-industrial ethic of the Arts and Crafts movement. The weight and simplicity of the designs was used to exploit the natural figure and character of these woods. **8** Hand-construction methods are a key element of Arts and Crafts furniture, and these are most obvious on chair joints. **9** Slim spindle slats were a favorite device of designer Gustave Stickley, and achieved the simultaneous effect of solidity and elegance.

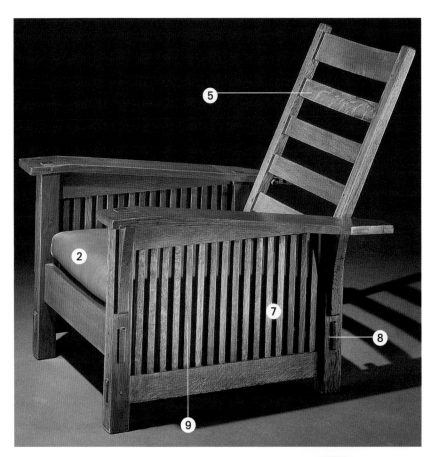

LEFT **Oak drop arm spindle chair, Gustave Stickley** *c.* 1908.

LEFT AND RIGHT **Walnut armchairs with upholstered and cane seats, Ernest Gimson,** *c.* 1905.

Case Furniture and Cabinets

The wall cabinet shows the furniture of the Aesthetic, Gothic-influenced, and Arts and Crafts movements at their most interesting and inventive. Cabinets were often more elaborate than other furniture of this movement, with the emphasis on high-quality workmanship. Plain oak was decorated with the most restrained inlaid motifs and stringing. **1** The Aesthetic Movement cabinet by Talbert is of relatively small size—less than 4 feet (1.2 meters) wide—and extensively decorated, but in a restrained manner. **2** It is veneered in walnut and amboyna in an orderly framework of ebonized moldings, almost producing the effect of looking through a window, thereby creating an impression of

ABOVE **Aesthetic inlaid cabinet, by Bruce Talbert, 1875.**

lightness. **3** The Smith wall cabinet has similarly shaped glazing bars, and although the decoration is more extensive, it is restrained within defined borders. **4** The turned spindle gallery, combined with the fact that the standing cabinet is raised on bobbin-turned legs and stretchers, diminishes the impression of solidity often given by wall pieces of this period. The latter feature harks back to European furniture of the seventeenth century. **5** Wall cabinets retained a strong architectural element with pointed Gothic pediments. **6** The simplicity of the vase of flowers and foliate

LEFT **Wall cabinet with ebonized, painted, and gilt decoration, by Moir Smith,** *c.* **1875**

inlay on the Talbert cabinet is in contrast to the profuse decoration of many nineteenth-century pieces, and may be indirectly influenced by the restraint of traditional Japanese applied art. **7** The Moir Smith cabinet is more extensively decorated, and the bird side panels on a gilt ground are of Japanese inspiration. **8** Proportions on vernacular-style Arts and Crafts cabinets were modest, and cabinets were often raised on simple bases. **9** The Spooner cabinet's coromandel veneer on the exterior, with a satinwood veneer

inside, is typical of the period, although a little more decorative than other Arts and Crafts furniture. **10** Characteristic ebony tracery on panel doors is subtle and restrained. **11** The drop handles on the drawers, the straight molded legs, the flattened cross stretcher, and the bun feet are all reminiscent of furniture from 1700, but in a pared down form, retaining the essence of these features but in a simpler manifestation.

LEFT **Coromandel, ebony and satinwood cabinet, by Charles Spooner,** *c.* **1910.**

Life Form Ceramics

In the 1860s, the Doulton factory revived the production of a hard pottery known as stoneware. It was this medium that was used by the Martin Brothers for their distinctive work of medieval inspiration. **①** The Martin Brothers are best known for their stylized models of birds with incised sgraffito decoration and grotesque, leering head jugs. **②** Each vessel produced by the workshop was unique. This is also the case with many other potters working at the time. **③** Glazes were generally thickly applied in restrained natural colors.

ABOVE **A group of pottery, Martin Brothers, *c.* 1900.**

LEFT **A stoneware tobacco jar and cover, Martin Brothers.**

Glassware

Whereas the preceding period had been noted for highly decorative and ornamental glassware, those designers working with glass in the Arts and Crafts Movement tended to produce simpler, more functional designs. **①** Colored glass was sparingly used, apart from the type of understated greens and ambers used in Dutch and German drinking glasses in the seventeenth century. **②** Like most Arts and Crafts objects, the glassware was handmade (blown), and the forms had little decoration, apart from subtle molding and delicately applied prunts. Most glassware drew on aspects from earlier periods, with baluster stems and discreet colored decoration.

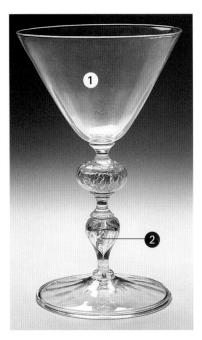

RIGHT **A goblet designed by James Powell, England, *c.* 1905.**

Moorish Ceramics

The designer William De Morgan was influential both in his use of luster glazes and in the iconography of his designs. These features, in turn, were influenced by Moorish and Persian pottery, although the type of decoration was highly individual. **①** Luster glazes were subsequently used by a number of other Arts and Crafts potteries, including Doulton, often in conjunction with Moorish or Chinese-shaped vessels. **②** De Morgan and other workshops also produced tiles in a blue and green Islamic palette, the iconography of which was largely based on stylized plant and leaf forms, as is the red ground on this dish. **③** De Morgan's red luster wares often depicted animal forms, such as this mythical dragon, and can be compared to early Italian majolicas.

ABOVE **A red luster dish, William De Morgan, *c.* 1880.**

Table Lighting

The most notable designers and makers of Arts and Crafts items in the United States were the Roycrofters, a community based in East Aurora, New York, who produced a range of pottery, metalwork, and simple furniture. **1** The Roycroft metalworkers were noted for their work in copper, which was typically hand-hammered. **2** There was no attempt to conceal construction techniques; projecting rivets on the bands toward the top and base of the lamp form part of the decoration. **3** Although produced by traditional techniques, Roycrofters pieces were often stylistically advanced; note the contemporary green and rose glass shade on this elegant lamp.

RIGHT **A Roycrofters hand-hammered copper lamp with leaded glass shade.**

RIGHT **Silverplated teapot, designed by Christopher Dresser,** *c.* **1880.**

Domestic Silver

One of the most influential designers of this period was Christopher Dresser. His work cannot strictly be described as Arts and Crafts, since it was specifically intended for industrial production, but certain features of his metalwork do bear a comparison. **1** Dresser's designs for metal vessels were very advanced, but certain features can also be seen in other metalwork of the period. **2** The slender angular handle was typical of Arts and Crafts metalwork, but it was more likely to have a caned rather than ebony insulator. **3** The simple spout was also a feature of Arts and Crafts, but a major difference was that rivet heads, and other details that are clearly evident on Arts and Crafts items, are not visible on Dresser pieces.

Enameled Silver

As with other media, the emphasis in silverware was on handworked forms; where there is applied decoration—typically in blue, green, or red enamel—this was also handworked. As with glassware, there are historical influences on the forms produced, many of which were made for presentation. **1** The twin-handled form of the bowl depicted is somewhat akin to a sixteenth-century example, although this is not a reproduction. The small figures in the handle show the liveliness of an updated version of a medieval object. **2** The surface of the metal was hand-hammered in order to emphasize the fact that it was not machine-made, at a time when there was an increasing premium on good craftsmanship. **3** Enamel decoration, when used, was generally limited to small plaques or motifs, contrasting with the all-over enamel decoration seen on pieces in other styles in the second half of the nineteenth century.

BELOW **Silver and enamel dishes and a bowl, by Omar Ramsden, England,** *c.* **1905.**

Detail Directory

The Arts and Crafts Movement narrowed the gap between designer and maker with a renewed emphasis on the artisans. Within this context, another loosely linked group of designers—the Aesthetic Movement— sought a departure from the prevalent heavy forms and ornament.

Hammersmith carpet, Jonathan Dearle for Morris & Co.

Peacock and Dragon design for drape, William Morris, 1878.

Textiles

An important feature of the Aesthetic and Arts and Crafts Movements was the revived impetus given to textile and wallpaper design, particularly through William Morris. The designs were printed as well as woven, often using one or two colors with repeated overall designs of natural forms. The great appeal of these designs was that, while visually interesting, they blended with, rather than overwhelmed, interior furnishings. They gave color and interest to what might otherwise have been somewhat stark interiors.

Silver finial, England, c. 1890.

Silver finial, England, c. 1890.

Steel andiron, Gimson, England, 1904.

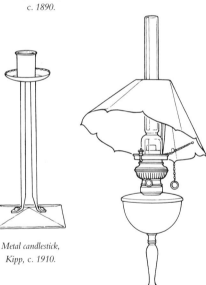

Metal candlestick, Kipp, c. 1910.

Brass oil lamp, by Benson, England, c. 1898.

Brass wall-mounted candle-holder, by Benson, England, c. 1887.

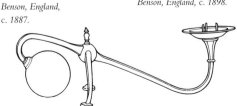

Glass, Ceramics, and Metalware

Three-dimensional forms varied from restrained with hand-finished detail to anthropomorphic pottery vessels and slender elongated metalwork designs. Many metalwork items were adorned with enamel plaques, usually distributed sparsely, that were either plain or decorated with medieval or Celtic scenes in a limited palette, particularly blues and greens. The plaques often carried simple mottoes or script. Other decoration on metalwork tended to be chased or embossed boldly but sparsely distributed, either as stylized natural forms or simple geometric motifs. Handles were wrought rather than cast.

Pottery usually had thick glazes, and restrained natural and solid colors were frequently used. Luster glazes were also used, particularly on tiles. The decoration was often molded in relief and tended to be of simple animal or plant forms.

There was no attempt to disguise the often slightly uneven nature of handworked materials, and in many cases a conscious attempt was made to emphasize this aspect. This is particularly apparent with metalwork, where items were obviously hand-hammered, and in earthenware ceramics, where the unevenness of the potting and the glazes focuses attention on the originality of each piece.

Christopher Dresser stands out for the unique quality of his work in this period, but he cannot be directly aligned with the Arts and Crafts Movement since his designs were intended for mass production.

Flowerhead motif for inlaid veneers.

Heart motif for enamel ware.

Leaf motif for chased silverware.

Flower motif for ceramic tile designs.

Flower motif for ceramic tile designs.

Shaker craftsmanship provided inspiration for the Arts and Crafts Movement. Detail of maple closet, Mount Lebanon, c. 1885.

Carved and Surface Decoration

The medieval period was the most prevalent source of inspiration. The Pre-Raphaelite painters evolved in parallel with some of the early practitioners of Arts and Crafts, although the latter became less elaborate into the twentieth century. Unlike previous styles from this century, Arts and Crafts designers did not seek actually to reproduce earlier designs, merely to use them as inspiration. Consequently, it is easy to identify an Arts and Crafts piece from the original items used as inspiration. Medieval-style inscriptions were in a particularly quaint style specific to this time, and unlike rococo revival furniture, Arts and Crafts designers usually left wood unstained.

Panel from inlaid mahogany vitrine, Morris & Co., c. 1890.

Stained glass firescreen with Pre-Raphaelite detail, England, c. 1885.

Narrow slat chairback.

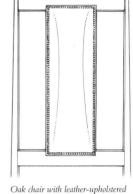

Oak chair with leather-upholstered single slat.

Carved chairback.

Furniture

With an absence of "designed" form, vernacular styles, such as American Shaker, provided a reference point for Arts and Crafts designers. For many, function once again became the primary factor. Arts and Crafts designers, such as Morris & Co., combined this craft ethic with medieval-style ornament and decoration.

Running parallel, the Aesthetic style was inspired by a desire to achieve a more adventurous scheme of decoration and furnishing, and consequently worked in a range of different media. The main inspirations were stylized Gothic and also Japanese motifs.

Chairs

Arts and Crafts chairs were designed as a protest against the excesses of Victorian manufactured products. There was a return to traditional techniques and materials, using vernacular styles as a starting point. Slat back chairs dominated, as did leather upholstery, turned feet, and rush seating. Carving was based on medieval or generic vernacular motifs. Morris & Co.'s "Sussex" chairs, known as the "Good Citizens'" furniture, were based on English country designs of the eighteenth century. Unlike most Arts and Crafts furniture, it was marketed towards those of more modest means.

Rocking chair with slat back.

Art Nouveau

Art nouveau crossed the boundaries between decorative, applied, and fine art, serving to blur the distinctions between disciplines. It provided a link between the craft and machine ethic, and allowed designers to embrace the twentieth century with confidence and vision. Few designers limited themselves to one medium or one particular marketplace.

The movement that is now generally referred to as art nouveau had its roots in many countries and took various forms. Although elements of the style were adapted for mass production, most early examples were individually made. This meant that many of the designs were almost impossibly curved, slender, or fragile and made more to be admired than used.

ART NOUVEAU THEMES

One of the first clearly definable examples of the style is the work of the Belgian architect and designer Victor Horta. In the 1890s in Brussels, Horta designed several buildings, including interiors, that display distinctive and original features. The buildings make extensive use of cast iron, both for functional and ornamental purposes, with sinuously curved balconies and railings. Windows are large and often curved, so that the overall impression is of lightness. The design of the furniture and fittings makes extensive use of curves, with glazed serpentine cabinet doors and slender cabriole legs. The use of cast iron in ornate tendril forms can also be seen in Hector Guimard's Paris Métro stations.

The work of French furniture designers such as Majorelle and Gallé is often asymmetrical, with a notable absence of straight lines, and is frequently inlaid with plant forms or, in some cases, more elaborate scenes. Asymmetry is also a distinguishing feature of the work of many of the French Art Glass makers, notably Gallé, Daum, and Tiffany, and is a recurring theme throughout

LEFT **The street furniture of the Paris Métro is a present-day reminder of the impact of art nouveau on several European cities at the turn of the twentieth century. In terms of art nouveau design and architecture, the combination of cast iron and glass in sinuous curves, together with the asymmetry of the street signs, are archetypal.**

RIGHT **As with the exotic furniture of Carlo Bugatti, the architecture of the Catalan Antoni Gaudi in Barcelona is unique. The unfinished church of the Sagrada Familia shares the obsession of the art nouveau with natural forms, in this case, reminiscent of rock formations or undersea creatures.**

mainstream art nouveau design. Rococo may be seen as the inspiration for art nouveau; while both styles share a lack of symmetry, art nouveau uses more extreme shapes and places a far greater emphasis on lightness of form.

The iconography of art nouveau places a particular emphasis on life, especially plant forms. In decoration, a common theme is the slender, long-stemmed plant with a single flower, often a tulip. Human forms are frequently almost ethereal, typically very slender young women with long, flowing hair and robes that often merge into plant or wave forms. As art nouveau reached a wider audience in the early 1900s, this type of ornament was often used on furniture and ceramics that were otherwise quite conventional in form.

A key feature of the style was a blurring between fine and applied art. The stylized figures and elongated plant forms of the drawings of Aubrey Beardsley are clearly related to the ornament used for interior decoration. Equally, the posters of Alfonse Mucha indicate a clear link between the two disciplines.

DEVELOPING THE STYLE

In Austria, a group of artists, architects, and designers formed a group known as the Secessionists, breaking away from the Vienna art establishment, the latter working in a style akin to art nouveau. Among the group was the designer Josef

LEFT **The facade of the Horniman Museum, London, is simpler than most public buildings erected at this time, and rendered in pale stone rather than the usual red brick. Note the subtle treatment of the polychrome and pillared friezes successfully incorporated into the art nouveau design. The supporting pillars are rounded to soften the overall impression.**

OPPOSITE PAGE **In contrast with the naturalistic forms of European art nouveau, Mackintosh's Glasgow School of Art, Scotland, is made of local stone with a fortresslike central facade. Although the windows are geometric, the outline is softened by the arched door pediment and the curved details to the front iron railings.**

BELOW **The Paris Universal Exhibition of 1900 provided a focus for many of the designers who had been developing the art nouveau style for the previous decade. The exhibition highlighted** **the growing gap between mass-market, nineteenth-century styles and the more forward-looking designs that were developing within the European art and design scene.**

LEFT **Designed by Hendrick Petrus Berlage, the Amsterdam Stock Exchange was built between 1897 and 1904. Berlage's architectural philosophy is illustrated by his minimal use of** **ornament, clear proportions, and concern with spatial relationships. This philosophy ran side-by-side with the commercial aesthetic of art nouveau.**

Hoffman, whose work was, at least in part, influenced by Charles Rennie Mackintosh. The work of both designers was something of a departure from the organic forms of the French and Belgian Schools. Both produced elongated, slender forms but in simpler materials than other art nouveau designers. Mackintosh tended to use painted or glass panel decoration, and designed complete interiors that were uncluttered. His work tends toward symmetry; however, the iconography of decoration is not dissimilar to other art nouveau designers, though more restrained. Hoffman's work, in fields ranging from furniture and interior design—often with the painter Gustav Klimt—to glassware, metalwork, and jewelry, tends to be restrained and elegantly slender, and provides a link between art nouveau and modernism.

Japanese art was an important influence on many art nouveau designers, evidenced both by the use of sparse and asymmetrical decoration and stylized rather than realistic flower and foliate ornament. The era as a whole was one of experimentation, which resulted in an extremely broad spectrum of design and ornament—from the exotic forms and materials of Carlo Bugatti to the geometric restraint of Josef Hoffman.

Collector's Gallery

The dominant feature of art nouveau is the slender nature of form and decoration. Forms were seen as genuinely new and moved away from the feel of the nineteenth century. The style evolved differently throughout Europe into two distinct forms: the naturalistic flowing forms of French designers, such as Gallé and Majorelle contrast with the more angular, less decorative work of designers such as Mackintosh and Hoffmann.

Cabinets

French art nouveau designers and manufacturers exploited the techniques used to make the rococo revival furniture of the second half of the nineteenth century. **1** Cabinet doors were veneered with kingwood, characteristic of high quality French furniture. **2** The traditional craft of marquetry was used to new artistic effect, such as in landscape scenes and naturalistic motifs. **3** Similarly, intricate carving was used to show off the furniture maker's skills; the naturalistic carving on the base of this cabinet is linked by a stem feature to the main body of the cabinet. This ornamental device is typical of the plant forms often seen in art nouveau furni-

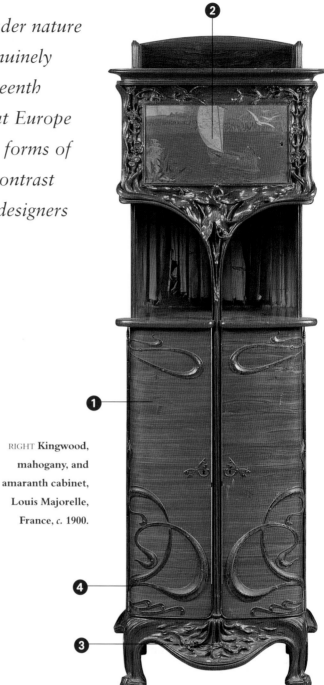

RIGHT **Kingwood, mahogany, and amaranth cabinet, Louis Majorelle, France,** *c.* **1900.**

LEFT **Two-part vitrine, by Hector Guimard, France,** *c.* **1900.**

ture. **4** Asymmetrical reliefs and corner mounts on doors show the new decorative relationship with the natural world. Other cabinets that concentrated less on the decoration and more on the form proved more significant. **5** Guimard cabinets favored open and curved superstructures aimed at lightening the effect of an otherwise solid piece of furniture. **6** The glazed sides and doors have curved edges to the glass in order to soften the linear form. **7** The moldings to the plinth, waist, and top have subtle foliate scrolls to the corners.

Tables

Many types of decorative furniture had evolved in the preceding fifty years, and these were often adapted in detail in order to conform to the art nouveau style. **1** Carving became flatter and bolder than before. **2** Asymmetrical marquetry reflected the influence of Japanese design at this time. **3** Supporting columns sported plant-like twists, emphasizing the preoccupation with living forms. Viennese and Scottish designers focused more on rectilinear forms, **4** with simple rectangular legs and square corners and edges. **5** The fashion for black materials is expressed here in the used black-stained oak.

ABOVE **Walnut and fruitwood marquetry étagère, by Emile Gallé.**

LEFT **Stained and limed oak table, by Josef Hoffmann.**

Pianos

The grand piano was the centerpiece in many homes at the turn of the twentieth century, and although its form could only be altered within certain parameters, the variety of forms provide an interesting comparison in styles. English pianos of this period adopted a more restrained version of the art nouveau style. **1** The legs and music-rest are open in order to lighten an otherwise heavy piece of furniture. **2** The use of pale satinwood and sycamore also make the instrument appear less solid. **3** Inlaid marquetry follows the art nouveau fashion, with single flowerheads and stylized flower sprays.

RIGHT **Bechstein piano, by J.S. Henry, *c.* 1904.**

Wardrobes

Bedroom furniture is often less distinctive and more functional than that in reception rooms. Wardrobes tend to conform to a solid, rectilinear shape. In many cases, the style indicators will be limited to small details. **1** Here, the shape is conventional, with the exception of the cornice, which reduces the solidity of the piece. **2** The arched profile above the door **3** and the similarly shaped inlay produce a softer impression. **4** This is further emphasized by the curved outline at the top of the doors. **5** The slender escutcheons **6** and curvaceous handles are a distinctive feature of art nouveau furniture. **7** The long-stemmed plant inlay adds a naturalistic element present in many examples of the style.

ABOVE **Inlaid mahogany wardrobe, by Wylie & Lochhead,** *c.* **1900.**

Bureaus

This bureau is narrower than traditional writing desks. **1** A curved apron and cornice balance the geometric nature of the overall design. **2** The stained glass decoration is typical of art nouveau pieces. **3** The stylized flowers are a favorite motif, and the use of the color pink breaks with previous convention. **4** The asymmetric handles are another typical feature.

LEFT **Black-stained oak bureau, designed by E.A. Taylor and made by Wylie & Lochhead,** *c.* **1903.**

Chairs

Charles Rennie Mackintosh and his followers developed significantly new chair designs, and broke with convention in their use of proportion. ❶ Mackintosh pieces have typically high backs. These emphasize the slender proportions and geometric form. ❷ Top rails were often curved, ❸ with a carved central section ❹ on top of two elongated splats. These were intended to resemble stylized flowerhead on slender stems. ❺ The arched apron linking the back legs is also a typical feature of Scottish art nouveau. The use of a dark green stain is typical of Mackintosh's enthusiasm for painted or stained wood.

In contrast, ❻ Josef Hoffmann's chairs often employed an adjustable sloping back ❼ and a hinged footrest. Although the basic form is angular, ❽ rounded corners ❾ and pierced "window" decoration softens the overall shape. ❿ The use of bentwood, first pioneered by Thonet fifty years earlier, is used for the arms.

ABOVE **Green stained oak chair, by Charles Rennie Mackintosh,** *c.* **1900.**

RIGHT **Stained beechwood reclining chair, by Josef Hoffmann,** *c.* **1905.**

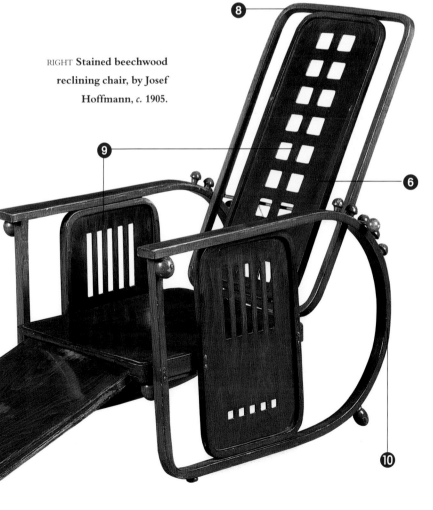

Domestic Ceramics

By their very nature, certain parameters restrict the design of table services, usually limited to decoration. The outlines of art nouveau earlier service are somewhat sleeker than conventional services, with oval rather than circular tureens and upswept handles with flattened edges. **1** The absence of molded detail on the edges of the plates and handles was typical of most nineteenth-century services. **2** The design is simple and understated, although technically advanced with a raised pâte-sur-pâte border. **3** The discreet border to the fish design means that attention is drawn to the motif, rather than distracted from it.

LEFT **A Rosenthal jugendstil fish service, *c.* 1910.**

Ceramic Vases

Art nouveau ceramic designers focused their attention both on shape and decoration, and those working in porcelain tended to emphasize the delicacy and smoothness of the material. This was particularly so with designers at some of the northern European factories, such as those at Copenhagen and Rozenburg. Designers working at this time experimented with shape, decorative iconography, and glazes. The result was often a merging of different colors, a lustrous or iridescent surface, and a concern with the overall effect rather than precise detail—

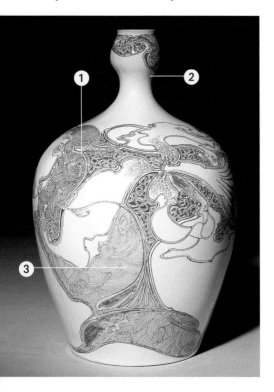

LEFT **Rozenburg eggshell porcelain vase, designed by R. Sterkin.**

ABOVE **A collection of Moorcroft pottery vases.**

akin to the mood sweeping through fine art at this time. **1** The finely drawn design emphasizes the delicacy of this eggshell-like porcelain vase. **2** The shape is a conventional ovoid, but the bud-form neck continues the plant metaphor popular with "new" designers. **3** Muted, natural-colored decoration is plantlike, but does not attempt to represent a particular plant form. **4** The range of shapes was wide, but a frequently occurring form is the plain ovoid vase of Japanese inspiration. **5** The squat, twin-handled vase is a typical art nouveau form, and here the handles are molded as if they are growing out of the main body. **6** The merging of shapes and colors, together with the depth of the glazes, creates the impression of an organic form.

Glass Vases

The iridescent glass produced by Louis Comfort Tiffany was known as favrile and was typically produced in gold or mauve and blue-green. The maker's name is usually engraved on the base and Tiffany versions of this design can be distinguished from those of other makers. The Bohemian Loetz factory produced a wide range of shapes for vases and bowls and were also influential on the designs of other factories, particularly in Austria. Unlike many other makers, Loetz glass is not usually signed. Certain glassmakers, particularly Tiffany and Gallé, produced work on a small scale that was technically difficult and therefore resulted only in very limited numbers of pieces, often used for exhibition purposes. **1** This is almost the archetypal art nouveau glass shape, and the mouth is formed as an exaggerated exotic flowerhead with undulating borders. **2** The long, slender

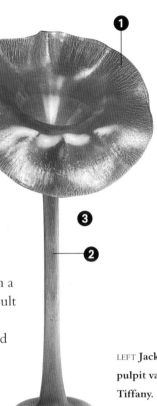

LEFT **Jack-in-the-pulpit vase, by Tiffany.**

stem is a typical feature of art nouveau representations of plant forms. **3** The representation of plant form is emphasized by the overall asymmetry of the piece. **4** Loetz pieces are often iridescent, with the exception of the central pink vase here. **5** Forms range from a relatively conventional baluster—but with a petal-like, wavy-edge rim—to a trumpet-shaped, three-handled vase influenced by Eastern forms. **6** Because of the slender, lightweight nature of the glass, most examples have a substantial base. **7** Most of the vases have swirling iridescent decoration, but in one case here, the design closely resembles the veins of a leaf. **8** Here, the broad trumpet neck and flattened orb body bear a passing resemblance to Japanese bronze forms. Like other Gallé vases, this is clearly signed with the maker's name. The body of this vase (right) is internally decorated, and **9** the relief petal and leaf decoration on the exterior have been carved on a wheel to produce a cameolike effect.

LEFT **A group of vases by Loetz and Austrian factories,** *c.* 1910.

RIGHT **Carved and acid-etched double overlay landscape vase, by Emile Gallé,** *c.* 1900.

Table Lighting

Table lamps are among the most sought after examples of art nouveau glass. Many pieces were decorated with carved landscape scenes and Tiffany, Daum, and Gallé were the most distinctive makers. Lamps made by Tiffany Studios were easily distinguished, with shades made of a mosaic of glass tiles, often forming exotic designs on the popular themes of flowers and insects. **1** The domed glass shade and the vase-shaped base are typical of earlier examples of art nouveau glass lamps. The painted flora and fauna blend seamlessly into a muted color ground, where shade and vase segments complement, but do not exactly match, each other. **2** The maker's mark, "Daum Nancy," is clearly visible on the lamp's shade. **3** The metal foot is for additional stability, as are the triple arms supporting the shade.

LEFT **A Daum landscape-design lamp and shade.**

Bronze Figural Lamps

The medium of sculpture was ideally suited to art nouveau ideas. Bronze casting enabled the most extravagant merging of the human form and costume into plant forms. Bronze sculpture was often used as a basis for lamps, typically as a figure, often in flowing costume, usually supporting a separate shade. At this time there was considerable experimentation with finishes on bronzes, including silvering, enamel details, and combining it with ivory. **1** The figure depicted is a dancer, a popular subject of early twentieth-century bronzes: the range of possible poses offered great scope to the sculptor. **2** The shade is formed as an integral part of the bronze, representing part of the dancer's costume. **3** The trailing hair and diaphanous dress appear to assume natural forms, the former plantlike, the latter wavelike. **4** The bronze finish has been gilded to create a more dramatic effect.

ABOVE **A gilt bronze lamp portraying the dancer Loie Fuller, by Raoul Larche.**

Floor Lighting

The standard lamp, originally designed for oil power, had become increasingly popular from about 1870 and was well suited to the slender metalwork forms of the Arts and Crafts and art nouveau movements. The advent of electricity introduced another dimension, since the new light source could be directional. **1** This standard lamp is particularly slender, the bronze base and stem providing rigidity. **2** The "Aladdin's lamp" at the top **3** and the stylized tripod paw feet are inspired by antiquity and would not have been used in European art nouveau. However,

the lamp is far more elongated than a classical example would have been. **4** The iridescent shade is set at an angle that would not be possible on a lamp converted from another power source.

LEFT **A bronze and favrile glass floor lamp, by Tiffany.**

Jewelry

The exquisite jewelry of René Lalique captures the essence of art nouveau in that medium. Unlike present-day pieces that place emphasis on precious stones, it is the form of his designs rather than the materials that capture the attention, with enamel techniques being extensively used. **1** Lalique pieces typically use insect forms for inspiration, in some cases combined with human figures. **2** The pale green and blue colors used in both pieces typify the almost ethereal quality of many art nouveau designs. **3** Many items of art nouveau jewelry were asymmetrical, like the "landscape" brooch above. **4** A notable feature of most jewelry in this style is its fragility and the delicacy of manufacture—especially in details such as the wings, in contrast to many pieces produced before and after.

ABOVE **An enamel, pearl, and gold brooch, by Aucoc.**

RIGHT **An enamel, aquamarine, diamond, and pearl pendant, by Lalique.**

Clocks and Silver Bowls

During the art nouveau period, metalwork was often made in asymmetrical forms, both in shape and decoration, and the individuality of a piece was considered a virtue. The early manifestations of art nouveau silver, as with other media, show two recurring themes: delicate forms and biomorphic, particularly plantlike, iconography. **1** The use of enamel with silver and other metalwares became quite prevalent, and the obviously handworked enamel dial represents a departure from the nineteenth-century perception of the clock as a precision instrument. **2** Pewter had largely been seen as a functional material until the late nineteenth century, but in the art nouveau period the slight softness of its surface, particularly when handworked, was considered to be appropriate for decorative use. **3** As a mechanical instrument, a clock would formerly have been enclosed in a symmetrical and typically angular case, but here the designer has ensured that all the lines are slightly curved in order to soften the profile. **4** This bowl is of a delicate, rounded form, almost reminiscent of a stylized flowerhead. **5** The embossed decoration, although detailed, is also bold, giving the effect of the branch of a tree wrapped around the bowl. **6** The use of hand-hammering contrasts with the texture of the decoration to make it appear more realistic. **7** The raising of the bowl on scroll feet reinforces the impression of lightness created by the design.

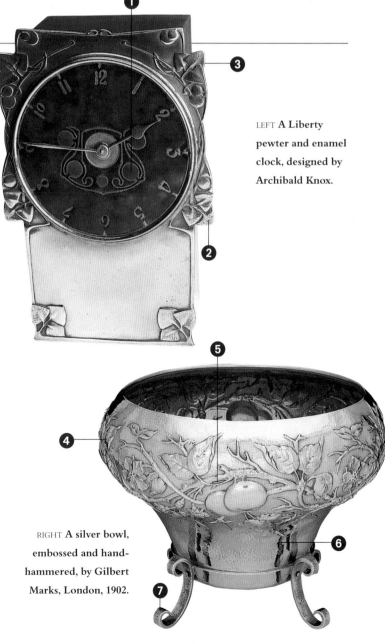

LEFT **A Liberty pewter and enamel clock, designed by Archibald Knox.**

RIGHT **A silver bowl, embossed and hand-hammered, by Gilbert Marks, London, 1902.**

Pewter

The decorative art nouveau style was widely used by makers of relatively inexpensive pewter and alloy objects, particularly W.M.F. and Kayserzinn in Germany. Such objects were often dramatically asymmetrical and incorporated stylized figural elements. They were usually clearly marked with the maker's stamp and often a pattern number. **1** When there is a sculptural element in the design of an object, usually an elegant female figure, the costume often merges into the design, particularly the base. **2** Where such items have carrying handles, they are often very slender because the metal is so strong. **3** As well as tending to asymmetry, most of these objects are extensively decorated with tendrils and other stylized foliage.

RIGHT **A group of pewter and other metalwork, mainly German,** *c.* **1900.**

Posters

During the art nouveau period, close links were forged between the applied arts and the burgeoning field of graphic art. This was partly driven by the increased demands of commerce through advertising. It was the time of the awakening of poster art, and the style of artists such as Alphonse Mucha and Henri de Toulouse-Lautrec incorporated in graphic form many of the elements seen in the applied arts. The inscriptions were usually brief and formed an integral part of the design. **1** Here, the central regal female figure does not appear to have a strong historical base, and the overall impression is one of fantasy. **2** The merging of the human form into a plantlike form, seen here in the headdress, is a recurring theme in art nouveau design. **3** The poster is asymmetrical, and the single border is decorated with stylized tendrils.

LEFT *"Au Quartier Latin"* poster, by **Alphonse Mucha, 1898.**

ABOVE **Invitation to the Glasgow Architectural Association, by C.R. Mackintosh, 1894.**

Art Nouveau Textiles

Surviving art nouveau textiles are far less prevalent than art deco examples. Certainly many interiors of this period used Middle Eastern rugs and carpets, but rugs and wall hangings were also produced by some of the major designers.
❶ The wall hanging below incorporates many of the themes prevalent in art nouveau style, such as the bird forms and stylized floral forms. The design is sparsely laid out in the Scottish style. ❷ Unlike the fantasy elements of the French School, the iconography is clearly recognizable.
❸ Like the designs of Mackintosh, the proportions are generally symmetrical, but the details are intentionally imprecise, indicating that the design is individually crafted.

Other Graphic Arts

Many of the foremost designers of this era, including Van de Velde, Bernhard Pankok, and Mackintosh, were commissioned to produce graphic designs, and the combination of fantasy and plant forms often recurs. ❶ The design of this invitation shows a more extravagant repertoire of images than Mackintosh's furniture or interior designs. It incorporates a combination of recognizable life forms, such as the doves, with extravagant fantasy foliage. ❷ The flowerheads are stylized and rest on impossibly slender stems, as is the case in much of the applied work of Mackintosh and other art nouveau designers. ❸ The letters of the inscription form an integral part of the design and are consistent in the absence of straight lines and symmetry.

RIGHT **An embroidered panel with Glasgow rose design, by Jessie Newbery, *c.* 1905.**

Detail Directory

As the name suggests, art nouveau was a conscious evolution of a new style, although with different manifestations in different countries. Perhaps unsurprisingly, art nouveau was, at least in part, influenced by earlier styles.

Drinking glass shapes, 1895–1908.

Hand-painted ceramics, England, c. 1900.

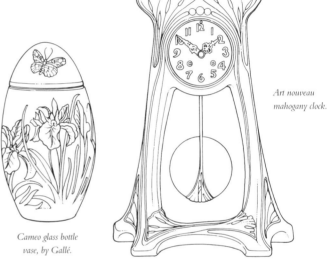

Cameo glass bottle vase, by Gallé.

Art nouveau mahogany clock.

Glass and Ceramics

Many of the forms could be described as ethereal, with a real departure from nineteenth-century solidity. This was most apparent in the area of glass. Glass and ceramics were frequently asymmetrical and often shaped as exotic plant forms.

Furniture

Much French and Belgian furniture can be viewed as a sleek version of the neo-rococo designs of the mid-nineteenth century, using similar materials but more extreme curves. This is particularly noticeable in chairbacks.

Detail of dressing table, by Plumet and Selmersheim.

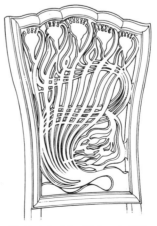

Chairback, by Arthur Mackmurdo, 1881.

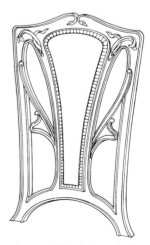

Continental chair splat decorated with art nouveau tendrils.

Graphic Art and Posters

The poster may be viewed as the archetypal art nouveau art form. Most feature a figure or group placed to the side or in a corner, but with elements trailing across or around the poster. The script has an almost organic quality with marked variation in scale according to the importance of that part of the message. The background is usually in muted and natural colors, particularly greens and browns, enabling the product or message to stand out clearly.

La Samaritaine *poster, by Alphonse Mucha, c. 1900.*

Wiener Werkstutte fork, by Hans Huttman, 1906; fork, by C. R. Mackintosh, 1902; fork, by H. Ven de Velde, 1902.

Metalware

Metal items also tended toward naturalistic asymmetry. This era gave a new impetus to jewelry design, with the exquisitely fragile insect and female forms designed by René Lalique leading the way. Most significantly, the emphasis was no longer on precious stones but on the creativity of the designer or maker, with glass and enamel prominently used.

During the early 1900s the work of Mackintosh and Hoffman signaled a move away from naturalistic forms toward elegant, elongated designs that in some cases were quite linear.

Silver pendant with scissors formations, c. 1900.

Surface Decoration

The decoration on art nouveau pieces is distinctive and not easily confused with that of any other style or period. Two themes predominate: the first, sinuous plant forms, often with a single, particularly tulip-shaped bloom; and second, ethereal female figures, either naked, often with long trailing hair, or dressed in flowing robes that frequently merge into trees or plants. The heart-shaped flower motif is also used on its own, as is the disembodied head of a wan young female, and virtually no art nouveau item is totally lacking in decoration. As with many of the shapes, the decoration is frequently asymmetrical and, typically, decoration and shape are closely merged.

The later art nouveau style tends to use decoration more sparingly, such as a few small flowers at the end of a knife handle or a single flower head on the top rail of a chair or the cornice of a cabinet.

Hand-hammered clock face, Wiener Werkstutte, c. 1905.

The Emergence of Modernism

Art deco design formed the basis of almost all domestic interiors in the late 1920s and 1930s, while technological advancements in mass production and materials gave the Bauhaus the impetus to produce practical designs for the modern world. Other modernist movements developed in Europe and North America, each with its own particular style.

By the second decade of the twentieth century, the work of designers such as Frank Lloyd Wright, Josef Hoffman, and Charles Rennie Mackintosh pointed toward a new direction for the applied arts. These designers produced completely integrated interiors and heralded a taste for uncluttered design. During the 1920s, designers began to use geometric forms, while ornament, when used, became stylized and uncomplicated. Increasingly, commissions were given for commercial applications such as hotels, as well as private homes. For private individuals, technological change was a great influence on their lifestyle, and innovation in design was often led by new products such as electric lighting, radio sets, and household appliances.

THE CASCADE EFFECT

Like art nouveau, art deco began with elaborate exhibition pieces, but it was not long before more everyday items were influenced. The Paris Exhibition of 1925 showed room settings with exotically veneered furniture in broadly rectilinear

RIGHT **The many motifs of transatlantic art deco design come together in this bathroom by Jacques Delamarre,** **from the Chanin Building in New York. Completed in 1929, it is a study in understated opulence.**

RIGHT **The striking curves of the Universita La Sapienza building in Rome illustrate the modernist tenet that simple, clean lines— with minimal ornamentation—create an elegant edifice.**

BELOW **The spacious library at the Boots factory in Nottingham, England, features subtle shelving units built into the walls. Plush reading seats surround imposing columns, with effective lighting overhead.**

shapes. Walls were generally plain or clad in veneers of wood, marble, or plain tiles, with geometrically patterned central rugs on otherwise uncarpeted floors. Windows were large with full-length drapes, and mirrors were extensively used. Ornaments and sculpture were displayed sparingly; ceramics designers concentrated mainly on functional items such as tableware and flower vases.

The overall impression was one of restrained luxury with comfort, when dining chairs had upholstered backs as well as seats. The materials used did not differ radically from those generally available thirty or forty years previously, with the exception of a limited use of chromed steel, mainly for fittings. It was the influence of this style that formed the basis of domestic interiors in the late 1920s and 1930s, although the individual components were mass- produced and the materials used often less exotic.

MODERN PRACTICAL
Alongside the mainstream deco style typified by the 1925 exhibition, there was growing recognition of a need for good design in mass-production. In Germany, this led to the founding of the Bauhaus movement by Walter Gropius, with two main aims: first, to unify architecture with the decorative arts, and second, to produce practical designs for mass production. Designers such as Morris, Dresser, and Michael Thonet had already worked with the former aim in mind, and Robert

BELOW **Considered an archetypal American art deco skyscraper, the Chrysler Building in New York became one of the most prominent features of the** **Manhattan skyline. Designed and built by the architect William van Alen in 1930, its striking tiers reflect the lines of the Chrysler automobile.**

Adam, Victor Horta, and Mackintosh, among others, had successfully achieved the latter. The Bauhaus was disbanded for political reasons, and many of its main exponents worked successfully in the United States. Many of their stylish industrial designs, particularly for domestic electrical items, were only produced in significant numbers after the Second World War. The distinctive nature of the designs was in their form; they generally lacked any ornamentation. Bauhaus and other designers in the 1920s began to work in a range of new materials, such as chromed and stainless steel, and plastics. Particularly innovative was their use of tubular steel and laminated wood in furniture designs, notably chairs.

The First "Chic" Industrial

By the 1930s, developments in transportation and architecture had influenced developments in the decorative arts, both directly and by providing an environment in which technological advance was considered desirable. The architecture of the skyscraper, such as the Chrysler Building, almost certainly inspired designers working on a smaller scale. The interiors of luxury liners and even airplanes provided designers with opportunities to

BELOW **The Hoover Building on Western Avenue in London, England, is a colorful example of art deco themes used in industry.** **The color scheme— with green, pink, and black detail against an off-white background— is typical of the style, from Miami to Europe.**

LEFT **The glassed-in balconies of the De La Warr Pavillion in Bexhill, East Sussex, England, echo the lines of a ship. This nautical theme is typical of art deco's love affair with transportation.**

work with modern styles, while the exterior design of aircraft and, more significantly, streamlined automobiles, influenced the appearance of domestic equipment such as radios and refrigerators, which were often encased in smoothly rounded curves, almost concealing their function.

PERSONAL LUXURIES

During the 1920s and 1930s, the introduction of a wide range of new and restyled personal accessories presented an opportunity for design innovation. Foremost among these were the wristwatch, cigarette lighter, powder compact, and fountain pen.

In each case the forms that evolved were a combination of function and modern style to an extent that did not receive widespread acceptance in the more traditional areas of the decorative arts until later on. Certainly the furniture designs of Mies van der Rohe, Marcel Breuer, Alvar Aalto, and Le Corbusier did not become popular until twenty or thirty years later.

BELOW **The bold rectilinear lines of the Rietveld Schroderhuis in Utrecht show a sparseness that heralded the new economy in modernistic design. Unlike Wright's organic approach—his structures were designed to blend with each particular environment—this building appears defiantly at odds with its setting.**

Collector's Gallery

More than ever before, the 1920s and 1930s saw designers integrating the furnishings of a building with its architecture. Walter Gropius, Marcel Breuer, and others began to use steel and other metals as a fundamental part of their furniture designs, enabling a radical change in the appearance of furniture. The Finnish architect Alvar Aalto experimented with laminated wood, which enabled him to produce extravagantly curved shapes.

Metal Furniture

A strong link between architecture and furniture can be seen in the work of Oscar Bach who, among other commissions, carried out work in New York for the Empire State Building, the Chrysler Building, and Radio City Music Hall. ❶ The overall shape of this planter is broadly geometric and typical of furniture from the second quarter of the twentieth century. ❷ The range of satyrs, birds, and other motifs on the frieze is traditional, but in their squat and rather two-dimensional treatment, could date only from the twentieth century. ❸ The elaborately turned legs and feet might date from any period, but there is a solidity about their appearance that is not usually seen in ironwork from the nineteenth century and earlier.

BELOW **Wrought iron and bronze planter/console, by Oscar Bach.**

ABOVE **An oak student desk by Ruhlmann,** *c.* **1930.**

The Art Deco Desk

Although many of the French art deco furniture designers used exotic materials, it is not these but the geometric shapes that are a constant element. Emile-Jacques Ruhlmann used both exotic veneers and lacquers, but also simpler materials, depending on the commission. ❶ This student desk is of a simple form, made from oak and lacking ornament. ❷ The desk has a plain frieze with a simple circular drawer pull, the latter in sharp contrast to almost any nineteenth-century cabinet work. ❸ The outsplayed legs are at an angle not usually seen in earlier furniture and are presumably held in place due to particularly well-secured joints.

Chairs

The architect Mies van der Rohe was one of the pioneers of the use of steel in chair design, both in tubular and strip form. He patented the design for a "springy" cantilever chair made of tubular steel and lacking back legs. He also produced designs for tables with tubular steel bases. **1** The design for this chair is relatively simple, with two intersecting curved steel supports producing a design that is strong, simple, and elegant. **2** As with many examples of furniture from the 1920s onward, chromed steel was used, in this case for the frame. **3** The use of leather strapping rather than conventional upholstery was an innovation adapted by other designers who used hammock seats and backrests. The strappings were normally covered by upholstered cushions, not shown here.

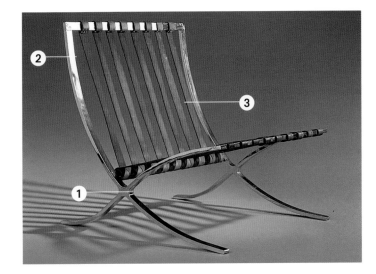

ABOVE **Chromed steel and leather "Barcelona" chair, designed by van der Rohe, *c.* 1930.**

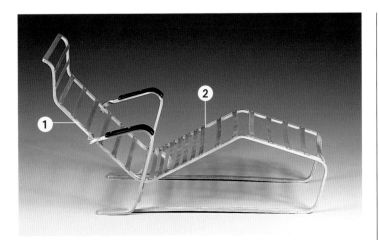

ABOVE **Aluminum frame lounger chair, by Marcel Breuer, *c.* 1935.**

Lounging Chairs

One of the most notable innovations of chair design in the 1920s was the development of loungers and semi-reclined chairs. Although they never achieved wide-scale popularity, such chairs made good use of the combination of strength and lightness of both tubular steel and laminated wood. **1** Marcel Breuer produced many innovative chair designs with frames of different materials, including aluminum. However, this did not prove to be a successful material for furniture manufacture, since, although light and strong, it was not particularly durable and was expensive to produce. **2** The contours of this chair, which would have been covered with cushions, closely follow those of the human body.

New Techniques with Wood

The Finnish architect Alvar Aalto produced designs for furniture appropriate for his buildings. He originally used tubular steel, but preferred to use wood, partly for the flexibility in its laminated form. **1** This chair encourages the user to adopt a semi-reclined posture, but unlike metal-framed chairs, where the seat is generally slung from the frame, this chair has a rigid seat. **2** The laminated plywood seat is shaped to allow the user a comfortable position. **3** The frame is made of laminated and bent birchwood, a material noted for its flexibility and widely used by Aalto, particularly for his trademark three-legged stools.

BELOW **A laminated plywood and birch chair, by Alvar Aalto, *c.* 1930.**

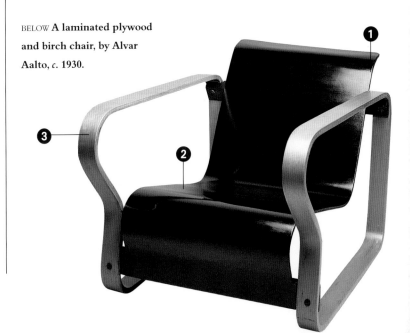

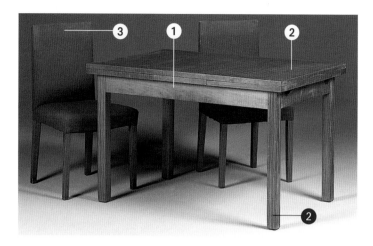

ABOVE **Mahogany dining chairs and table, by Gordon Russell, England, *c*. 1935.**

Everyday Furniture

Not all modern furniture produced in the 1920s and 1930s was as distinctive as the pieces shown left, but many of the influences and ideas filtered through to more affordable furniture, with simplicity and geometry being consistent themes. ❶ Dining tables during this era could often be extended by the use of integral drawer leaves concealed beneath the main tabletop, rather than external leaves, which had to be stored separately. ❷ The tabletop is severely geometric, and the legs are of plain square section. ❸ The chairs are simple in form, and like many chairs of this period, the backs are upholstered, thus concealing the structural framework.

The Dining Table

The geometric style was highly appropriate for dining tables and other large tables that, of necessity, have to be simple in form. Whereas small tables can be fairly decorative, any decoration applied to a larger table can be obtrusive. ❶ The veneer used here is a pale oak, which, together with other pale woods such as maple, birch, and bleached walnut, was very popular in the 1920s and 1930s. ❷ The table has a straight edge, without molding, to maintain a simplicity of form. ❸ The pedestal bears a strong resemblance to early nineteenth-century dining tables, with certain differences.

The central cylindrical column is completely plain in shape and decoration; the spreading cruciform legs are very deep but low to the floor, and the only decoration is a molded oval, giving a suggestion of a separate foot.

LEFT **An oak dining table, by Ruhlmann, France, *c*. 1924.**

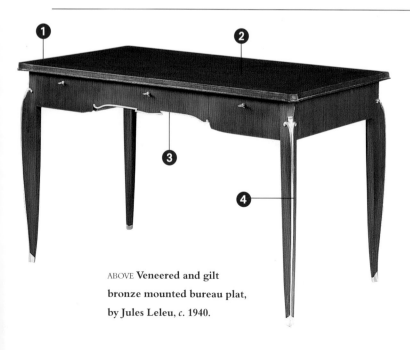

ABOVE **Veneered and gilt bronze mounted bureau plat, by Jules Leleu, *c*. 1940.**

The Second Revival

Reproduction furniture still held an attraction in the 1920s and 1930s, and many adaptations of earlier styles were made, in particular the Georgian designs in England and Louis XV and XVI styles in France. They were often streamlined and uncluttered compared with earlier examples. ❶ This bureau plat has the same basic shape as an eighteenth- or nineteenth-century piece, but the top has straight edges. ❷ It is veneered in one wood, not several, and is not inlaid. ❸ The plain frieze has a "kneehole" bordered in gilt bronze, and the drawer fronts form the entire frieze without borders. The drawer pulls are a simple one-piece form. ❹ The legs are a straightened version of cabriole with a gilt bronze line to emphasize their shape and simple angled sabots.

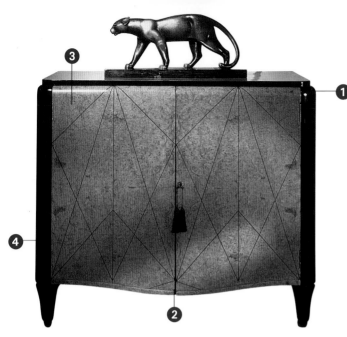

ABOVE **An ebonized and burl elm closet, France, c. 1925.**

Cabinets

The cabinet was often the focal point of an interior and many examples from this period have more detailed decoration than other furniture. **1** This cabinet is veneered in traditional woods, thuja and mahogany, **2** and inlaid with a landscape scene that owes a debt to eighteenth-century German cabinetwork. **3** The outline of the cabinet is distinctively twentieth century, with unframed panel doors and typical tapering cylindrical legs, slightly outsplayed and terminating in plain ivory sabots. **4** The architectural pedigree of the cabinet design can be seen in the simulated column pilasters with ivory inlaid capitals, albeit in a bold and somewhat simplified form.

RIGHT **Inlaid cabinet, by Company of Master Craftsmen, c. 1920.**

Closets

Many closets were less elaborate than their cabinet neighbors, although the themes of uncluttered outlines and generally simplified decoration, often geometric, consistently appear. **1** This cupboard has a rectilinear outline, somewhat softened by rounded corners and edges, **2** and a curved apron at the base of the doors. **3** Many examples of art deco furniture used pale veneers; here burl elm is used within ebonized borders. **4** The contrast between the ebonized and short tapering sides, and the elm doors gives the cupboard a low-slung, modern appearance.

ABOVE **Art deco cocktail trolley with glass panels, by Lalique.**

Cocktail Cabinets

The cocktail cabinet, with its mirrored and chromed interior, is almost symbolic of the era. More than ever, fashion was playing an important part in people's choice of furniture, and the popularity of cocktails in smart circles meant that a cocktail cabinet was an essential accessory. **1** This cabinet combines the functions of a bar and trolley and is made of a typical combination of plain veneers with chromed mounts. **2** The faceted figure eight shape does not draw on any historical precedent; generally, designs for cocktail cabinets were among the most radical for furniture at this time. **3** The top of the trolley has opalescent panels by Rene Lalique, the archetypal art deco glassmaker.

Glass Vases

Many of the designers of art nouveau glass began to produce simpler and more geometric designs in the art deco period, although mostly still using colored glass. By the 1930s, the transition to heavier, more solid and angular forms, and the use of clear and tinted glass, was almost complete. ① Glass vases sometimes had bronze mounts; the Daum vase shown is evocative of architecture of the period. ② The form of vases and other vessels produced in the art deco period tended to be simpler than those of the art nouveau period, frequently a simple cylindrical shape. ③ The decoration of this vase is very simple; the solid color and simple molding are the main elements, unlike the flower and leaf designs produced by the same factory earlier in the twentieth century.

ABOVE **A clear and frosted glass perfume bottle and stopper, by Lalique.**

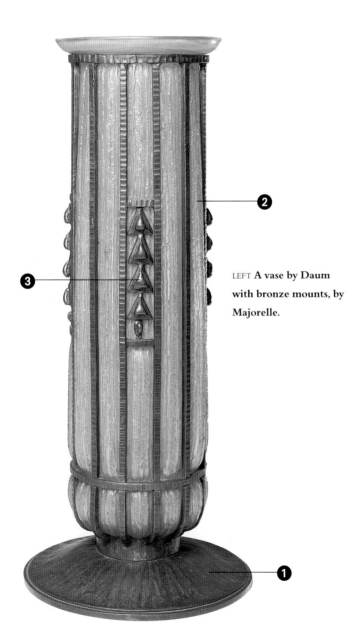

LEFT **A vase by Daum with bronze mounts, by Majorelle.**

Glass Scent Bottles

During the 1920s and 1930s, the perfume houses, particularly in France, began to commission specially designed perfume bottles and expensive packaging in order to enhance the exclusivity of their brands. Lalique was one of the most popular choices of designer for scent bottles. ① Perfume bottles were usually formed in clear glass, since the contents would provide an element of color, although some examples are in frosted or semi-opaque glass. ② Because perfume bottles were often kept in their original box, the shapes did not have to be practical. In some cases the stopper could be more substantial than the bottle itself. ③ The example illustrated shows the bold nature of decoration on art deco glassware by Lalique and others. The flowers and leaves are molded in relief and are boldly depicted rather than intricate, in contrast with much nineteenth- and early twentieth-century ornament. ④ The maker's name is clearly displayed with no attempt to merge it into the design, emphasizing how the brand name was beginning to assume greater significance.

Cocktail Shakers

As with the cocktail cabinet, the cocktail shaker was evocative of this era, in Europe from the 1920s and in the United States from the 1930s. Shakers were made in chrome and electroplate as well as silver, and were generally sleek and tapering. The Danish designer Georg Jensen, whose company's work had been high-ly regarded international-ly since the early years of the twentieth century, produced flatware with geometric deco handles, but also often retained naturalistic elements in form and decoration, such as flower petal or acorn motifs on cutlery handles. Jensen's hol-lowware was never entirely geometric, and vases and other vessels have clean flowing lines with restrained decora-tion.

1 Cocktail shakers were frequently supplied with sets of matching glasses, as were liqueur decanters in glass which were equally popular at this time. **2** This particular cocktail shaker, which is a late example, appears to have been influenced by aeronautic design with projecting side fins. **3** The polished metal finish of the shaker and glasses emphasizes the close link between contemporary industrial design and decorative items. **4** Jensen made use of matte finishes for some elements of his work, thereby producing interesting surface contrasts. **5** Although many of the basic forms were simple and geometric, Jensen used naturalistic details to create less severe shapes than the wares of many of his contemporaries. **6** Jensen silver tends to have simple handles, with single leaf or bud motifs, and the mounts often have naturalistic motifs, in a less complex form than those by designers of the art nouveau period.

LEFT **A cocktail shaker, by Georg Jensen.**

BELOW AND RIGHT **A silver-plated cocktail shaker and matching glasses.**

LEFT **Two three-piece silver and wood part services, by Puiforcat, *c.* 1930.**

Domestic Silver

The constituent parts of domestic services, whether silver or plated, were either of angular or plain rounded form, with bold contrasting handles in ebony or ivory, or Bakelite or other synthetic materials. These pieces were unobtrusive in a modern interior, blending particularly well with the chromed steel mounts in much furniture of the time.

1 The silver used for such services was no longer hand-hammered, as in the art nouveau and Jugendstil periods, but had a sleek, polished appearance. **2** The vessels were usually of a geometric and often squat shape, with little difference in basic form among all the parts of a service.

3 The handles, often the most distinctive feature, contrasted strongly both in material and shape with the metal part of each item.

ABOVE **A selection of bone china cups, saucers, and a coffeepot, by Shelley, *c.* 1930.**

Ceramic Tableware

English designers and factories, such as Shelley, also produced tablewares of geometric form with stylized decoration. They were far more popular as breakfast or tea services than for formal dining. The angular designs resemble those seen in other countries, although they were gradually replaced by simpler and more rounded forms.

1 In the mass-market, modern shapes were often used with traditional decoration, such as flower sprays, whereas the more exclusive designers tended to use minimal decoration. **2** The use of single bold colors for service wares, such as the vivid green of this cup and saucer, was an innovation of the early 1930s. **3** Although in keeping with the designs, angular teacup and coffeepot handles were highly impractical and contrast with the creations of the more functional design groups such as the Bauhaus.

Ceramic Accessories

Many of the most distinctive designs were for mass-market production, such as the designs of Clarice Cliff, whose pottery was readily available from High Street stores in London. Her work followed the constraints of practicality, but cup and other handles were often geometric and the decoration included bold blocks of vibrant colors. The most radical of her designs was for conical sugar shakers, designed in a shape of a rocket. **1** Jazz music was highly fashionable, and it was inevitable that such subjects would be featured in some of Clarice Cliff's work. **2** The form of this piece, particularly the pianist and the piano, are strongly geometric. **3** Clarice Cliff wares were affordable, and both the modeling and the decoration reflect this. The bold colors of her pieces partially disguise the fact that the paint is very simply applied.

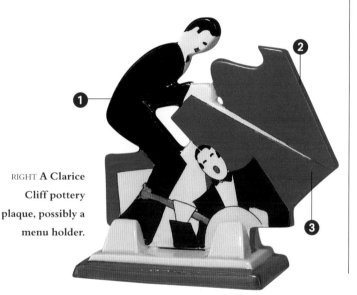

RIGHT **A Clarice Cliff pottery plaque, possibly a menu holder.**

ABOVE **A group of Wedgwood pottery vases, designed by Keith Murray,** *c.* **1935.**

Ceramic Vases

Unlike service wares, less functional items offered scope for experimentation with form. By the 1930s, there was a general shift to simple restrained forms, becoming less cluttered and consistent with interior decor. **1** Precisely manufactured pottery was well suited to the simplified designs of the 1930s, and the solidity of porcelain and pottery items contrasted with the delicacy of many pieces from the prewar period. **2** The use of solid decoration in pale and muted colors, including white, became fashionable in the 1930s. **3** When patterned decoration was used, it tended to be discreet; often the decoration was in the modeling, as with the horizontal banding shown here. **4** Handles were simplified for practical use.

Personal Accessories

During the 1920s, a new range of personal accessories evolved, partly because of a revolution in design for manufactured items and a wider range of individuals participating in conspicuous consumption. This was evident both in the types of items produced, such as cigarette lighters, powder compacts, and atomizers, and in the designs of more established possessions, such as cigarette cases and a wide range of jewelry. Cigarette cases evolved into slim objects featuring mainly geometric lines, with specific designs for women. Cases were often secured by a jeweled clasp—sapphires, in particular, were extremely popular in the art deco era. Sometimes the cases would be further personalized by a tasteful jeweled monogram. Silver or gold cigarette cases often had a discreet geometric border in black enamel, although in some cases **1** a more distinctive but simple design in colored enamels was used. Cigarette cases and compacts were frequently decorated with engine turning, although the example above has smooth sides.

ABOVE **White metal and enamel art deco cigarette case by F. Zwichl.**

Table Lighting

A distinctive feature of most art deco interiors was the table
lamp. Glass shades were popular, but unlike many art
nouveau designs, the base was likely to be made of metal.
By the 1930s, the glass shades were very plain, often
globular, whereas prior to this they were likely to have been
more decorative. **1** The glass shades tended to be simple in
shape, such as conical, in this case with geometric
reinforcement. **2** The decorative motifs, where used, were
often geometric. The Greek key design used here mirrors
the use in architecture of classical detail, which had once
again become popular. **3** The stem and base of such lamps
were usually of relatively simple form, typically a cylindrical
stem on a flat circular base. In the 1920s, these were often
formed in bronze with cast detail, whereas by the 1930s
chromed steel had become more prevalent.

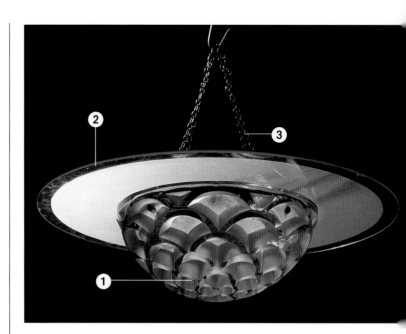

ABOVE **"Rinceaux", an amber glass ceiling
light, by Lalique.**

Ceiling Lighting

As the use of electric lighting became universal, designers
began to make use of the fact that it was omni-directional,
and fittings could be successfully merged into an interior
design. Both ceiling and wall lights were often flush fitting
and of opaque or smoky glass, frequently tinted, in order to
diffuse and soften the light. **1** Ceiling lights made
extensive use of thick glass, often tinted, with pale blue,
pink, and amber the most popular colors. **2** The overall
shape was usually geometric and uncluttered, lacking the
drops and pendants that were so prevalent in earlier periods.
3 The glass panels frequently bear a maker's mark; Lalique
light fixtures are almost invariably signed. They are usually
incorporated in a frame of chromed metal or bronze. **4**
Fan- and scallop-shaped forms were among the most
popular for wall lights, and these shapes can often be seen
in ceiling lights as well.

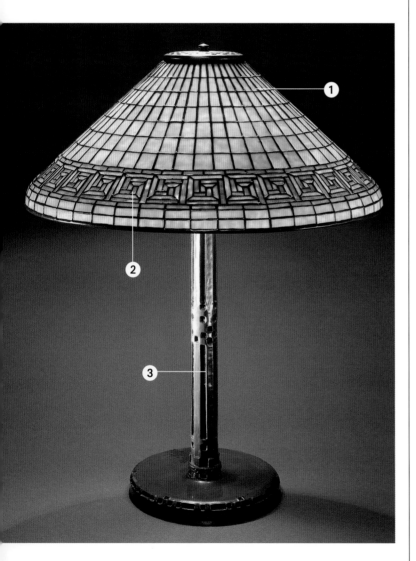

ABOVE **A mosaic glass and bronze lamp, by Tiffany,** *c.* **1920.**

Luggage

Many of the objects produced in this period reflect the changes in people's lifestyles. One development was the broadening of popular entertainment through cinema, radio, and recorded music. Another was the expansion of rapid and convenient personal travel by rail, ship, motor vehicle, and later airship and aircraft. All of these factors, together with technological advances, had a significant impact on the range of personal possessions. In the nineteenth and early twentieth centuries, luggage tended to be bulky and cumbersome, but as more people began to travel, a demand arose for luggage that was smart, easily portable, and functional.
1 Suitcases and other boxes were produced in lighter materials than leather, but with reinforced corners and edging to make them just as strong.
2 The range of luggage was large, from steamer trunks to handbags, which meant that it was less necessary to purchase a specific carrying case for a particular item. **3** Here is an early example of using a brand logo specifically and recognizably to distinguish a product.

ABOVE **A suite of luggage, by Louis Vuitton.**

BELOW **A Templeton's Axminster carpet, designed by Frank Brangwyn,** *c.* 1930.

Carpets

During this period, designs for carpets and rugs, as with furniture, tended to be simple and often geometric, with designers aiming to let them blend into the overall decor of an interior, rather than producing a dramatic effect.
1 Although some rugs had intricate rather than simple geometric designs, the impact was softened by a plain border in a neutral color. Unlike some earlier rugs and those produced in the Middle East, most rugs and carpets of this style were machinemade rather than handmade, consistent with the taste of the time. **2** Where more intricate designs were used, the color schemes were usually muted, and the design, as a whole, was normally understated.

BELOW **Gold rectangular wristwatches, dating from the late 1930s and 1940s.**

Wristwatches

Perhaps the most radical innovation in personal accessories was the wristwatch. It was in the 1920s that the wristwatch came of age—previous examples had resembled small fob watches on a strap. During the 1930s and 1940s thousands of wristwatches were produced, many of the finest examples by Swiss and American makers. ❶ In keeping with art nouveau and art deco design, geometric and rectangular shapes were the most popular for wristwatches, usually either in plain gold with a leather or metallic strap; other pieces were bejeweled for evening wear, often with diamonds mounted in platinum. Less expensive watches to be worn as a fashion accessory were decorated with rhinestone and paste.

Bronzes

During this period, theater, and particularly dance, had an increasing influence on forms in the applied arts, with references to sport also becoming widespread. One of the most dramatic examples of this influence can be seen on figurines, particularly in bronze. ❶ The combination of bronze and ivory was first employed in figurines in the late nineteenth century, but became widely used in the 1920s and 1930s. ❷ The bronze does not have a natural finish but is silvered and colored, the latter an innovation. ❸ The base is simple and geometric and partly made of green onyx, which was very fashionable at this time.

RIGHT **A bronze and ivory model of a skater, by Ferdinand Preiss.**

RIGHT **"Thence to Hyde Park,"** poster by Jean Dupas, 1930.

BELOW **Art deco airforce recruitment poster, "Pilote D'Avions,"** France.

1

RÉPUBLIQUE FRANÇAISE
MINISTÈRE DE L'AIR
AVIATION MILITAIRE

H.T

JEUNES FRANÇAIS
VOUS POUVEZ ACCOMPLIR VOTRE SERVICE MILITAIRE LÉGAL COMME
PILOTE D'AVIONS,
EN RECEVANT AU PRÉALABLE UNE INSTRUCTION AUX FRAIS DE
L'ÉTAT DANS UNE ÉCOLE CIVILE DE PILOTAGE.
LES CANDIDATS SONT ADMIS DEPUIS L'AGE DE 17 ANS ½
DEMANDEZ LES RENSEIGNEMENTS COMPLÉMENTAIRES AU MINISTÈRE DE L'AIR
DIRECTION GÉNÉRALE DES FORCES AÉRIENNES.SOUS-DIRECTION DU PERSONNEL.
35,RUE S.ᵗ DIDIER.PARIS
IMPRIMERIE.NATIONALE.-7-30

Posters

By the art deco period the power of advertising had been widely recognized and posters from this period quickly became sought-after collector's items. Highly stylized, the posters characteristically feature stark, angular images, elegant lettering and bold colors and occasionally dramatic use of black and white. **1** Some of the most memorable and exciting images from this period are found in travel posters and recruitment advertisements.

Toys

In the early twentieth century, the tinplate toy revolutionized the world of toymaking, as did several other innovations during the course of the century. By the 1920s, what had originally been a luxury product was becoming less expensive, and toys were produced throughout the industrial world, rather than exclusively in Germany where they began. **1** Early models had largely been accurate representations of actual vehicles, but this model demonstrates the increasing influence of fictional, and particularly cartoon, characters. **2** The

model is simply made using mass-production techniques, with a lack of accurate detail. The theme of personal, rather than public, transport had a far-reaching impact on design throughout the rest of the century.

1

3

2

RIGHT **A tinplate model with cartoon mice.**

Detail Directory

The availability of new materials and modern manufacturing techniques provided the driving force for forward-looking designs. Developments in architecture and transportation provided further impetus. Designs became uncluttered, with minimal ornament. The main emphasis was on function.

Glass decanter, by Adolf Loos, 1931.

Glass goblet, by Libbey, 1939.

Ceramics shapes and decoration, by Claris Cliff, c. 1930.

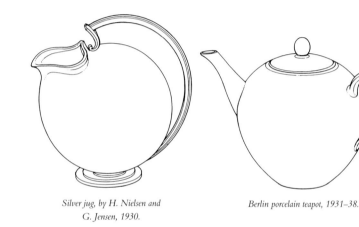

Silver jug, by H. Nielsen and G. Jensen, 1930.

Berlin porcelain teapot, 1931–38.

Fork, by Nielsen and Jensen, 1926.

Glass, Ceramics, and Metalware

Shapes inspired by the modern world and not previously used in the applied arts were now effective in decorative items. Prominent among these were the cone shapes used by Clarice Cliff and the "bullet"-shaped vases produced by a number of pewter makers.

Unlike furniture and larger items, which were rectilinear, ceramics were often made in simple rounded forms. Again the reason was not usually fashion but an endeavor to merge the requirements of form and function.

In the case of ceramics, understated lined borders and simple geometric designs were preferred. However, a wider range of bold, solid colors that had not been used previously began to appear. Interestingly, the more expensive pieces were often more subtly decorated than those pieces aimed at the mass market.

Jewelry

Geometric forms dominated the art deco and modernist styles. New materials and semi-precious stones were combined with more traditional precious gems, including onyx, marcasite, chrome, and acrylic. French designers were influenced by fine art trends, while North American styles showed the effects of modern architecture.

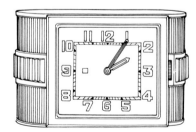

Watchface, by Cartier, 1935.

Diamond and sapphire ring.

Art deco diamond and sapphire ring.

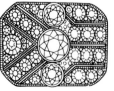

Art deco diamond ring.

Furniture and Lighting

Geometric and uncluttered forms held
sway. Radical changes in architecture meant
that interiors also changed radically,
particularly with furniture and lighting, and
in many cases there was no longer a
fireplace as the focal point in a room. The
boundaries between the fitted fixtures in a
room and the moveable contents became
blurred, with cabinets and other case furniture
supported on pedestals and plinths, rather than
legs. Ceiling and wall lights were often built-in,
rather than hanging or projecting. The more
expensive pieces of furniture were veneered in exotic woods, but
generally other decoration was limited to restrained parquetry. Of
course, within mainstream taste, many consumers still preferred
reproductions or pastiches of earlier
styles, and these were still produced in
vast quantities.

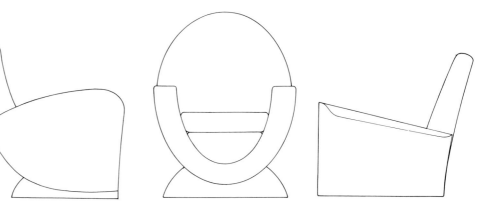

Armchair shapes, c. 1925.

Ceiling light, by Lalique.

Bauhaus steel table lamp, 1924.

*Macassar ebony and
silvered bronze desk,
Jacques-Emile
Ruhlmann, 1926.*

Steel and Bakelite

Two materials that had previously not been seen in
the decorative arts were used from the 1920s
onward: chromed steel and Bakelite. The former
came to be widely used for furniture legs or frames
and smaller pieces such as lamp bases and clock
cases. Apart from radios and electrical apparatus
Bakelite was used for handles, notably on silver and
plated items. Hardwoods, particularly ebony and
ebonized softwoods, were also used as contrasting
handles on furniture and metalwork. Handles in these
styles were quite distinctive in their simple and
usually functional forms, which could not be confused
with those of earlier periods. The curved form of
metalwork handles can also be seen in the arms and
seats of Le Corbusier designed armchairs.

Drawer handles, c. 1925.

Bauhaus pot handles, c. 1925.

Glossary

Acanthus: A Mediterranean plant with bold scallop-edged leaves, commonly used in a stylized form to decorate furniture.

Apron: The lower edge of a piece of furniture, usually curved or shaped, and frequently matching the cresting or cornice.

Arabesque: An intricate, interwoven design consisting of scrolling foliage and flowers.

Armorial: A term used to describe objects decorated with a coat of arms, such as plates or tankards.

Auricular: A style exemplified by curving asymmetrical forms, inspired by the shape of an ear or the interior of a shell. Seen mainly in silver forms and furniture ornament, auricular style was popular in the early and mid-seventeenth century, especially in Germany and the Netherlands.

Baluster: (1) A rounded shape that swells at the bottom, used for vases and furniture legs. (2) A slim pear shape used for finials, knife handles, and other silverware. (3) A type of glass stem resembling an architectural feature or furniture baluster.

Beading: An ornamental edging made from a series of half-spheres that are soldered into position.

Bombé: A term used for the outwardly curving shape of a piece of furniture. The form is often seen in French and Italian rococo case furniture, such as commodes.

Boulle: A type of marquetry that uses tortoiseshell and a metal (usually brass) inlay.

Bun foot: A round, turned foot used on furniture, common in the late seventeenth century.

Bureau plat: The French term for a flat-topped writing table, often covered in leather.

Cabriole: A double-curved and tapered furniture leg, often ending in a stylized paw. The design was inspired by animals' hind legs.

Campagna: An upturned bell shape used for vases.

Carcass: The main body or framework of a piece of furniture, over which veneer may be applied.

Castors: Small wheels placed under furniture feet to facilitate movement.

Chinoiserie: A style of decoration influenced by Chinese design. Occasionally fanciful, it was extremely popular in Europe during the eighteenth century.

Cloisonné: A type of enameling in which sections of a piece are separated by thin metal strips and filled with colored, powdered glass before firing.

Crackle: A ceramic glaze with deliberate hairline fractures.

Creamware: A white or cream earthenware with a transparent glaze, imitative of porcelain. It was developed in Britain around 1750 and later became popular in the United States.

Cresting: The carved uppermost decoration on a piece of furniture, particularly on a chairback or mirror frame.

Crizzled glass: The cracking and clouding of early glass, caused by too much alkali in the composition. This fault was largely eliminated by adding lead oxide, a process introduced by George Ravenscroft in 1676.

Ebonizing: The staining of wood to a black finish, used to mimic ebony. It is a common feature of nineteenth-century furniture.

Enameling: (1) The covering of a metal surface with a thin sheet of translucent colored glass. (2) A ceramic decoration in which the pigments are painted over the glaze.

Encaustic: A method of using heat to fix enamel colors to a tile or other ceramic item.

Engraving: (1) A type of illustration used in books. The design is incised as a negative image on the printing surface (wood, copper, or steel), then inked and stamped. (2) A decoration cut into the surface of metal pieces, such as silverware.

Faience: Earthenware that is decorated with opaque, colored tin glazes, produced in France, Germany, Switzerland, and Scandinavia.

Finial: (1) An ornamental knob on the handle of a bowl or spoon. (2) A projecting ornamental detail (e.g., small urn shape) at the highest point of any piece.

Firedog: An ornamental metal upright with projecting back supports, designed to hold burning logs in a fireplace. Also called an andiron.

Gadrooning: An edging decoration consisting of a series of projecting continuous semicircular ridges, sometimes set at an angle. Frequently, it is seen on sixteenth- and seventeenth-century Italian furniture, and eighteenth-century furniture and silver.

Garniture: A set used to decorate a mantel shelf or cabinet, consisting of three, five, or seven ornaments and often incorporating a central clock.

Guilloche: A frieze or border decoration made up of continuous circles or roundels that partially overlap.

Grotesque: A fantastic ornament or decoration composed of mythical creatures (satyrs, centaurs, etc.), outlandish vegetation, and bizarre faces.

Hard-paste porcelain:
Porcelain made from clay (kaolin) and feldspathic rock (petuntse). This is true porcelain as opposed to the soft-paste variety.

Hollowware: Silverware with a significant depth and volume, such as pots, cups, ewers, and jugs, as opposed to flatware (forks, spoons, and plates).

Inlay: A decoration in a contrasting color, material, or metal that is set into a wood or metal piece. It is most commonly used to decorate furniture.

Knop: A swelling detail in the stem of a vessel, or in an upright or stretcher of a piece of furniture. It is also used to describe a simple handle or terminal on the lid of a vessel.

Lambrequin: A drape or short curtain, typically in the form of a swag.

Lost wax: A technique for casting metal in which a clay-coated wax model is fired in a kiln. The heat causes the wax to melt, leaving a hollow clay mold into which the molten metal can be poured.

Lustre decoration: A shiny, metallic decoration used on glass, earthenware, and sometimes porcelain.

Majolica: Tin-glazed earthenware, usually of Italian origin. The style was adopted by nineteenth-century potters.

Marquetry: A decorative veneer applied to furniture in which shaped pieces of different types of wood (and sometimes brass, pewter, tortoiseshell, or bone) are used to create mosaics, floral patterns, or landscape scenes.

Molding: A length of shaped wood applied to the surface of a piece of furniture. Frequently, the shape is borrowed from architectural design.

Niello: A black inlay, consisting of a powdered metal alloy, used to decorate silver. The decorative technique was widely used in Russia in the nineteenth century.

Ogee: A continuous succession of two curves, one convex and the other concave, shaped like a shallow "S." The ogee was frequently used to decorate eighteenth-century silver and furniture; it is also known as "the line of beauty."

Ormolu: A term referring to gilded bronze or brass furniture mounts, derived from the French for ground gold.

Ottoman: A richly upholstered stool of varying size, sometimes with a hinged lid concealing a storage area.

Pad foot: A type of furniture foot that is rounded and rests on an integral disk.

Parquetry: A furniture veneer made from shaped pieces of wood (or other material) that interlock like a puzzle to form a regular geometric pattern.

Patera: An oval or circular motif, often incorporating a leaflike design, used to decorate furniture and silver.

Patina: (1) An oxidized finish on a bronze, which may be created naturally or artificially. (2) The surface finish on other antiques, especially furniture.

Paw foot: A type of foot on a furniture leg that is shaped like an animal's paw.

Pier cabinet: A cabinet with narrow proportions, often made in pairs to stand on the projecting vertical sections of a wall, usually flanking windows.

Pietra dura (dure, plural):
Decorative work using inlaid semiprecious stones to depict scenes, coats of arms, geometric patterns, etc.

Prunt: A chunk of colored glass used to decorate the body of a glass piece; it is sometimes shaped.

Rocaille: The stylized rock and shell decorative motifs often seen on rococo furniture.

Roemer: A Dutch or German goblet-shaped drinking vessel, originally made of green glass. The term was later anglicized as "rummer."

Schwartzlot: A linear style of ceramic decoration using shades of black.

Serpentine: A furniture decoration shaped like an undulating curve, bowed in the center and concave at the ends.

Sgraffito: A technique for decorating ceramics; the design is incised through the glaze or slip to reveal the color of the body beneath.

Soft-paste porcelain: A type of porcelain made from clay and powdered glass or frit. More gritty than hard-paste porcelain, it is usually thickly potted and holds less detail.

Stretcher: A strut connecting the legs of a piece of furniture.

Vitrine: A display cabinet with a glass front or lid.

Index

Page numbers in *italics* refer to illustrations

Credits

Quarto would like to thank and acknowledge the following for supplying pictures reproduced in this book.

(Key: l left, r right, c center, t top, b bottom)

Architectural Association: p28t (Miss Canon Parsons); p38 (Nabil Shghadi) ; p41 (David Stewart); p52t (Miss Canon Parsons), b (Woodmansterne) ; p53 (Miss Canon Parsons); p78 (Simon Rae-Scott); p79t (Simon Rae Scott); p90 (Miss Canon Parsons) ; p91 (Miss Canon Parsons); p93 (Simon Rae-Scott)

H. Blairman & Sons Ltd.: p138bl; p139tr; p178b

Boots Company Plc.: p201b

J. Allan Cash Ltd.: p39t; p51; p63; p64; p76; p77; p134; p137; p148; p186b; p202r

Christie' s Images: p1; p2; p10tr; p11tl; p15l,r&b; p16; p17t; p19t,bl&br; p20t; p21t&b; p22bl&br; p23t; p24; p25; p30t&b; p31t&b; p32t,c&b; p33t,c&b; p34t,c&b; p35tl&bl; p36bl,bc&tr; p37tl,cl&cr; p42tr&br; p43cr&br; p44tl,tr,bl&br; p45t,c&b; p46l&r; p47tl&br; p48bl; p49; p54cl&br; p55l,r&b; p56l,r&b; p57l,r&b; p58t&b; p59t,bl&br; p60bc; p61tl&tc; p66l&r; p67tr,bl&br; p68t&b; p69tr,cr&br; p70t,c&b; p71tl,tr,bl&br; p73tl&br; p75bl; p80br; p81t&b; p82t,c&b; p83tl&bl; p84tr&br; p85t,c&b; p87bl&br p95tr; p96tr&br; p97b; p98t&b; p99t,c&b; p100cr&bl; p101tr&bl; p110t,c&b; p111tr; p112t; p113; p114t&b; p115t&b; p116cl; p123tl,tr&br; p124t&b; p125tl; p126tl,tr&b; p127t&b; p128t&b; p129l&r; p131c; p133; p138tr; p139bl&br; p140br; p142t&b; p143t; p144t; p145t; p147cr; p152; p153tr&br; p155tl&cr; p156t&b; p157t; p158t; p159bl; p160tl,tr&br; p162t; p163t&b; p166tc&tr; p168; p169; p175t&b; p177t&b; p180tl; p181tl&br; p182tr; p183cl&tr; p188l&r; p189tl&tr; p191t&b; p192cr&br; p193tl&br; p194tr; p195t,c&b; p196t&b; p198; p199cl&br; p205t,c&b; p206t,c&b; p208tr; p209t&b; p210t&b; p211t,c&b; p213t&b; p214l&r; p215tl&tr; p217cr

Rupert Cavendish Antiques, London: p103tl&tr; p111bl; p123bl; p125bl; p207tl

De La Warr Pavilion, Bexhill: p203t (C. Parker)

Drouot Richelieu: p89; p109t; p117br; p157b

Farabolafoto, Milan, Italy: p201t

Hotspur Ltd.: p9tl; p12; p13br; p48tc; p83br; p94tr; p95cl

Kippa, Netherlands: p187t; p203b

Mallett: p8tr; p10tl; p11cr; p18; p20b; p23b; p35cr; p37br; p42bl; p47bl; p54bl; p60bl; p74tr; p80tr; p84bl; p86bl; p87bc; p88; p94bc; p95br; p96bl; p97t; p101tl; p102tr; p103cl; p116br; p122bl,tr&br; p143b; p174; p180bl; p182cr; p224

The Millinery Works Ltd.: p176t&b; p190t&b; p197t&b

Partridge Fine Arts plc: p8br; p9bl; p61br; p75tl; p112b; p130cl&bl; p131tl&tr

Pictures Colour Library: p171t; p202l

Ronald Phillips Ltd.: p11cl; p73bl; p86tr; p108tr; p109br

Courtesy of Phillips International Fine Art Auctioneers: p6; p132; p139tl; p140l; p141t&b; p144b; p145b; p153cl; p154t&b; p155br; p158b; p159tr; p161t&b; p162b; p164; p165cr&br; p166tl,bl&br; p178t; p179; p180tr; p181tr; p183cr; p189br; p194tl; p208bl; p212tr; p215br; p216cr

Courtesy of Phillips New York: p192tl; p193bl; p194bc; p204t&b; p207cr; p212bl

Paul Rocheleau; p26; p79b; p92b; p104; p105b; p106; p107; p118; p119; p120t&b; p121; p135; p171b; p172t&b

Ann Ronan Picture Library: p149

Maurice Segoura: p7; p43tl; p69tl; p74br; p75tr; p108bl; p125tr

Spectrum Colour Library: p27; p28t; p29; p40; p62; p136; p150; p170; p184; p185; p187b

Woodmansterne Limited Watford: p28b (courtesy of the Wellington Museum); p92t; p105t (The Trustees of Sir John Soane' s Museum); p151t&b; p173; p186t

All other photographs and illustrations are the copyright of Quarto Publishing plc. While every effort has been made to credit contributors, Quarto would like to apologize should there have been any omissions or errors.

LEFT **Queen Anne gilt gesso single chair, English, *c.* 1710.**